Mona Vale Library
Growth through Knowledge

Renewals:
9970 1600
www.pittlink.net

McPHEE GRIBBLE PUBLISHERS

NO PLACE FOR A NERVOUS LADY
Voices from the Australian Bush

Lucy Frost was born in 1943 and spent her childhood in Texas, her adolescence in Tennessee. She went north to a Pennsylvania women's college to study for her B.A. and then further north again to the University of Rochester in upstate New York, from which she took an M.A. and Ph.D. Her first teaching job was at the University of California at Los Angeles. She left the United States to take up a position in the English Department of La Trobe University, Melbourne, in 1970, where she is now a senior lecturer. She is the mother of two girls and lives in an inner Melbourne suburb, and is at present working on a book of Annie Baxter's writings.

NO PLACE FOR
A NERVOUS LADY

Voices from the Australian Bush

LUCY FROST

McPHEE GRIBBLE PUBLISHERS

McPhee Gribble Publishers, Melbourne
Copyright © Lucy Frost, 1984
First published 1984
Reprinted 1984, 1985, 1989

Typeset in Singapore by Richard Clay
Made and printed in Australia
by The Book Printer

National Library of Australia
Cataloguing-in-Publication data
Frost, Lucy, 1941-
No place for a nervous lady.
ISBN 0 86914 076 0
1. Women pioneers – Australia – Biography
2. Australia – History – 1788-1900. I. Title.
994.02'092'2

McPhee Gribble's creative writing programme is assisted by the Literature
Board of the Australia Council.

for Robert,
who found Annie Baxter for me,
and so much more

These look more like crofters' cottages in Scotland than settlers' huts in Australia. The snowcapped Tasmanian mountain – probably Mount Wellington – is a reminder that the bush could be cold and wet, as well as hot and arid. Date unknown.

CONTENTS

 A gully too rough to be cleared might later offer a cool retreat on summer days. Here, a woman reading her book is almost lost amidst giant ferns, remnants of a rainforest in the Gippsland region of Victoria. Photograph by N. J. Caire of Melbourne, in the 1880s.

FINDING THE WORDS FOR A BUSH LIFE

The high plains of north Texas where I spent my childhood is a land of harsh extremes. In the summer, a river marked on the map could turn into nothing more than a sun-cracked indentation crossing a prairie studded with cactus. Winter brought blizzards sweeping over the treeless land, and then my father would repeat the local saying, 'There's nothing between Amarillo and the North Pole except a barbed wire fence.' The land itself seemed to resist the European settlers who wanted to run cattle and grow wheat and build houses. The settlers came anyway, and as a girl I listened to old men tell stories of how they bought their land for fifty cents an acre and lived in homes which were nothing more than holes dug in the ground and topped with sod roofs. Occasionally I saw the ruined remains of these dug-outs. The frontier was not far away.

I was not thinking of Texas, or of any frontier, when I came to Melbourne thirteen years ago, but some time later I read the short stories of Barbara Baynton in *Bush Studies*, and my thoughts turned back to the women in those Texas dug-outs. They were Baynton's contemporaries on the opposite side of the globe, and I wondered how much their lives might have had in common with this Australian daughter of a carpenter and wife of a small selector, who had been born, raised, and married in the bush of New South Wales during the second half of the nineteenth century.

Baynton wrote her stories during the 1890s and published the collection called *Bush Studies* in 1902. The men and women in these stories are brutalized and brutalizing. Either they are victims or predators, and although they may suffer, their pain never seems to lead to anything positive. The bush itself is not made explicitly responsible for dehumanizing its inhabitants, but there is a very definite sense that to live in the bush is to partake of misery and callousness.

This grim picture of bush life is strikingly different from the invigorating stories Australian men were writing at the same time, stories about mateship's pleasures, the drover's stamina, the swagman's charm, the battler's admirable endurance, the bushranger's daring. I had heard very much the same sorts of stories in America, although the characters had been cowboys and ranchers and the gunmen whose graves I saw in the Boot Hill cemetery when we picnicked in the ghost town which was once Tascosa. Women played decidedly secondary roles in the stories I knew. They might dress in red and work the town's saloons. Otherwise, they were sure to be found on some isolated farm or ranch, stalwart companions to men whose roughness they civilized, whose loneliness they kept at bay.

These were far more attractive stories than Barbara Baynton's, but perhaps that should come as no surprise. After all, I realized when I had read *Bush Studies*, the popular stories of the American frontier and of the Australian bush do not encourage a reader to ask realistic questions about women. As a child growing up on the tales of old Texas, I did not know how the women in those dug-outs found their food, much less cooked it, although I was well-informed on the subject of chuckwagons and the problems men had feeding other men on the long cattle drives to market. And while the men were on the trail, how did the women feel about being left alone? No stories seemed to cover that, but then I had not asked whether life on the frontier might look somewhat different if women, rather than men, were placed at the centre of the telling. Would they have told stories like Baynton's? Was her vision peculiar?

It certainly seems odd when compared with what other Australian women were publishing at the time. For the most part, their work endorses popular taste in the Victorian Age. The bush in their fiction is coated with a sweet and sticky sentimentality. Apparently they can allow the bush to be exotic, but nothing about it must remain disturbing for very long – unlike the abidingly strange world of Barbara Baynton.

The women who published were not the only women who wrote, of course. What happened in those letters and diaries where the intention was not avowedly 'literary'? Did they ever share Baynton's harsh view? Or were they, too, cloyingly sentimental?

Certainly the diary of Elizabeth Tierney was not sentimental, although it quickly reminded me that women could write boring prose without relying on outmoded literary devices to send their readers to sleep. This complaint may be rather unfair to Mrs Tierney, however, because her diary was intended as a record of her farm rather than her inner life. She had moved to the farm near Mudgee, New South Wales, in the early 1890s after the death of her husband, who had been teaching at Eurunderee ever since the public school opened there in 1876. Henry Lawson had been one of his first pupils. John Tierney's death left his wife with six children, ranging in age from eight to twenty-one. The ledger she began in 1896 chronicles her determination to make a success of her family and of her farm. At first the entries do little more than record gallons of milk produced and expenses incurred. Gradually, information about the weather creeps in, and then about family activities:

> 22 July 1900. Sunday.   Cloudy like rain. Went to Mass. Retta, Katie & Leo & Rhonda White went down to Brother Johns to play Tennis, the girls stayed for tea. The boys came home with them. Spent a pleasant evening.

Even when Elizabeth Tierney relaxed, as she clearly did on this Sunday afternoon, she never abandoned entirely her stance as the woman who had everything under control, who was tough-minded though caring, who would find introspection a weakness and emotional outbursts a flaw.

This sense of remarkable strength and a determined focus on the daily life at the farm takes on a dramatic edge in the entries following that tranquil Sunday, for during the week three blacks – Jimmy and Joe Governor and Jacky Underwood – were on the run in the immediate vicinity of Mrs Tierney's farm. They were killing people Mrs Tierney knew, neighbours. Rumours were everywhere, the countryside was frightened. Mrs Tierney could at least have gone into town to stay with relatives for a few days: she remained at the farm, and kept on with her washing and her children's routine, although as the week progressed, her mind contracted with a fear she never expressed as private emotion.

> 23 Mon   Like rain did not wash Mr & Mrs McKay were murdered at Reedy Creek Gulgong by the Blackfellows, the same ones that killed the Newberry family on Friday night. The police & civilians & Trackers after them, they are traveling fast.
> 24 Tues   Fine day. We washed. Retta went for violin lessons. I paid Mr Walshe 11/- for 6 lessons. The Blacks murdered Mrs O'Brien & child & wounded one other woman at Ulan and Casselles on their way to Waller where they intend to kill more. They have killed eight altogether.
> 25 Wed   Terribly windy. Katie went down to Johnies in the morning One of the blacks, Jackie Underwood, was captured at Leadville all the police & Civilians after the other blacks. China War raging.
> 26 Thu   Cloudy like rain. Retta went down to Johnies to get our tea, 20 lbs at 1/6, from Griffiths Bros. I don't care for it. There are over 50 policemen & a lot of civilians & trackers after Jimmie & Joe Governor, the blackfellows & murderers. The Breelong murder which happened on the 20th

inst. was the cruelest & worst murder that was ever committed in Australasia, there was four killed with tommighawks & two not expected to live.

27 Fri   Fine day. We heard that Pat Tierney of Waller was shot but fancy it's only a rumour. Kernin Fitzpatrick of Waller was shot dead by the blacks.

28 Sat   Beautiful day. The Blackfellows were supposed to have been seen in the police paddock All the Volunteers after them & a lot of civilians also. Everyone is armed & prepared for them as they are about   Joe & Fred Muller came up they thought we were frightened.

Through the restrained prose of Elizabeth Tierney there emerges the familiar image of the mythical bush mother, courageous and in control, however desperate the circumstances. These are admirable features, but they make for a monotonous diary in which even the outside world is reduced to the sparest of details, while her inner world − over which silence reigns − may be glimpsed only by inference.

Most of the letters and diaries I read reveal much more. This is partly because even if they are not entirely private, they are usually unofficial. Few women were in the position of Elizabeth Tierney, who after all had begun writing because she was in charge of a farm and needed to keep records. The pounds of butter churned by other women, the number of eggs gathered, the market prices for their produce, were simply part of the total farm records kept − if any were kept. No one, needless to say, maintained ledgers to count meals prepared, floors scrubbed, clothes washed, or nappies changed.

Given the long hours these women usually worked, their bothering to write anything may seem strange, but personal motivations could be as strong as economic ones. Obviously most emigrant women wrote letters to the family left behind. Love and a sense of obligation impelled them to do so. These women wrote for their own sakes, too, I suspect. As a migrant myself, I understand something about the peculiar psychological effects of growing into adulthood on one side of the globe and then taking up life in what must by definition be a strange environment tens of thousands of miles away from 'home'. Once a life is sliced into two segments by such a move, it feels almost as though one were a fictional character who had got oneself into two different novels. A human desire for unity, for an integrated personality, may make a woman yearn to merge the two novels into a single continuous narrative. She cannot. At least by sending and receiving letters from characters in her first life, the emigrant could keep a sense that it was real, not just something dreamed out of moments of

Sometime during the 1850s, her face gentle and careworn, Mrs Okley posed for her
portrait. Perhaps a photographer travelling around Western Australia had talked
her into sending a likeness 'home'.

unhappiness. This was especially important to the women who found themselves taken at a much lower value by people around them in the colonies than they had been at home. If an emigrant woman could hold fast to the values and beliefs of her first life, then she had her own weapon against the blows she felt buffeting her. This survival tactic had its dangers, however. It could become an excuse for refusing to adapt to anything new.

Writing letters was also a way of keeping both 'novels' going. Chapters from the new life could be sent to keepers of the old, and eagerly awaited letters from the first life brought the latest episodes telling what was happening to familiar characters in chapters where the emigrant woman herself no longer appeared. It was all rather similar to the social phenomenon of people standing on the wharves in Melbourne and crying out to the arriving ships for news about what happened in the latest instalment of a serialized novel by Dickens. A lone woman could await news of an obscure family just as eagerly – and impatiently. Letters took a long, long time (thus reinforcing the sense that what once was her ordinary life had now become a story available to her only through words). From the time a woman in the bush wrote a letter asking a question of some European correspondent, until the moment when she got her answer, a year might pass. Even in the early 1860s the chances were almost three to one that a ship from Europe to Melbourne would take more than one hundred days, and then the mail must find its way to the bush. Perhaps the sheer difficulty of correspondence encouraged the emigrant women to make the best possible use of their opportunities for letting people know what their lives were like in a foreign land by offering them the detailed observations which make their letters of continuing interest to us.

In addition to writing letters, some women kept diaries. There was a convention of keeping diaries among women of the nineteenth century – among middle-class women, I should add. The accounts I have included from women who were not middle-class are either letters or reminiscences, and it goes without saying that the voices of many women who lived in the bush during the last century could not write, and their voices now are silent.

Not all of these women have faded from sight, just the same. Some remain visible in the pages of other women who populate their scenes with servants, neighbours, the chance acquaintance met on board a ship or on the road. The secondary characters might well have chosen to portray themselves differently. Maria might argue that her ways were less filthy than Annie Baxter claims. Mary might protest indignantly that she had as much right as Penelope Selby's sister to have a baby and she didn't want Mrs Selby referring to it as a 'piccaninny'. Maria and Mary might both have asked for their surnames to be included. They were grown women after all, not children. Louisa Lamb, on the other hand, might feel comforted to know that Louisa Clifton was sympathetic to the despair which almost cost her life. Whatever these secondary characters might think of their portraits, we as readers can appreciate their presences because they expand personal accounts into social vistas.

Some women wrote with a much keener eye to social detail than others, as one would expect. Even women who would not have seen themselves as particularly aware of the larger world, or interested in it, can offer insights into attitudes and values. The thirty-one-year-old Agnes Henty, for example, spent much of 1868 pencilling woeful complaints into a commercially produced diary which in itself was a comment on her social status, although she was too busy thinking about her personal plight to consider such abstract ramifications. She had married into what was to become a famous family in Victoria. Her husband was an ambitious squatter who claimed to be the first white child born in the Port Phillip District. It may have been appropriate to Richmond Henty's aristocratic aspirations that his wife should have exactly the same daily diary as any wife of a country squire in the Home Counties of southern England, but the effect is quite bizarre. Reminders of special occasions have been printed as headings for particular days, much as they are now when one buys a commercially printed diary. The occasions are presumably of relevance to the keeper of the diary, and yet Agnes Henty must have been at a loss on 22 February when she read: 'Cambridge Term divides at Midnight'. Understandably, she ignored this revelation. Miserable as she was at the time, she did not enjoy its comic incongruity.

For months her unhappiness preoccupied her mind. Stuck out on a station with no woman of her own class in the vicinity, her social contact limited to men who were coming and going on business, she often began her diary entry with some variant of 'Alone all day as usual.' She resented her husband's frequent absences. At some stage – probably later, since this handwriting is distinctly larger than the rest – she seems to have gone back through the entries and counted his absences so that under the entry for 19 October she could note: 'Richie away 183 days up to this date'. Complaints of loneliness apparently irritated her husband, who thought that being a mother should satisfy any need she might have. Three days after the birth of her most recent child, the entry reads:

> Richmond away all day at Hamilton – did not return until 9 oc – Dr W came – Richie called on the Franks & Judge Molesworth – Home by Tar-rington – I very weak – & low – Richie wondering why infant does not bless me and said he would not come in again –

To make matters worse, Mrs Henty's health was bad. At the top of her entry for 15 June she has written: 'Sick any 85 days out of 150.'

Mrs Henty hated living in the bush for reasons that had nothing to do with the location itself, the landscape. Of course the term 'bush' was used to cover a multitude of landscapes from the semi-arid districts of the Wimmera where some of the governesses were sent, to the cold moun-tain regions of Tasmania. Whatever the location, women in the bush are generally imagined as hard at work from dawn to dusk and often into the night. Agnes Henty does not fit this picture. As the wife of a wealthy man, her role was to do no work. Even her children were under the care of nurses. Whether these domestic arrangements were her idea or her husband's, the fact remains that the bush was every bit as lonely for her as for the wife of a poor cocky. Isolation knew no class boundaries. On 10 February the entry reads:

> Splitting head ache sent a long letter to Richie saying how unkind it was to leave me so much in this dull bush prison & asking him to let me go home if he could not afford to let me live in Melbourne.

Would Elizabeth Tierney have been sympathetic?

I doubt it. And that is part of the fascination. A sense of personality is coming through with a strength that raises questions like this and makes answers possible. As I read more and more letters and diaries, I found myself listening to the voices of women who often spoke so frankly and forthrightly that I could imagine what it felt like to be inside their lives. I had had the same reaction when reading Barbara Baynton, but had missed 'the insight which comes from truth when I went to the published fiction of her female contemporaries with their voices muffled by literary conven-tions. Those conventions celebrate life's pleasantries, whereas the non-fiction accounts frequently have a certain edge to them because the women are under genuine pressure. Their language conveys the pressure directly, instead of trying to give it the shape of emotions acceptable to the senti-mental 'women's fiction' of the nineteenth and early twentieth centuries. Paradoxically, the women who did not go to publishers continue to be readable long after most of the published prose has grown boringly outmoded.

The unpublished women deserve a wider hearing than they can get in the manuscript rooms of libraries, I decided, and that is why I have put together this collection, hoping that it sits on that unseen borderline where history meets literary criticism. As history, the letters and diaries are primary documents with social and cultural relevance, but I want them to be more than springboards for generalizations. Too much of that has gone on already. Later generations, with their own special needs, have generalized about 'pioneer women'. The important thing now is to get these women out of the categories and give them back their individuality. My comments in the book are designed to introduce the speaking voice, nothing more. Sometimes I have made small changes in the prose, dividing it into paragraphs or correcting the spelling when it obscures the meaning of a word or confuses the sense of things. The object is for the voices to come through authentically without turning into museum pieces accessible only to translators. These changes are described in the notes at the back of the book. Always my principle has been to let the women speak for themselves with a minimum of editorial fuss.

I cannot pretend invisibility, just the same. Selections had to be made, material arranged, a balance tried for among ages, backgrounds, and social positions even though that effort at balance had been foiled from the beginning by the widespread illiteracy. The bias toward English made matters worse by leaving the actual variety of nationalities and races unrepresented, and yet translations, however revealing as historical insight, could only obscure my attempt to find out what sort of expression women gave to their experiences in the bush when literary conventions were not interfering. Some material I excluded merely because there was not enough of it. A few pages from a diary, a single letter on its own, are fleeting glimpses of a life, and to pursue my enquiry, I needed fuller accounts, wider in scope. With the governesses, an exception could be made. Their limited correspondence fitted together into a group-portrait of women who came to Australia to do a particular kind of work and were reporting on their success, or lack thereof, to the one organization in London which had sent them all off to the colonies. Other women are arranged side by side when they wrote about parallel things – voyages, journeys overland, memories of the past. On the surface, this looks like a case of categorizing individuals according to experience. Actually, it is just as much a bid to resist precisely that temptation. Categories tell some things but not others.

Even the voyage, that one experience shared by all emigrant women whether on their way to city or the bush, could be so stunningly different that to speak of degrees of hardship seems an inadequate method of measurement. Naturally there were some hardships shared fairly evenly. For everyone the voyage was dislocating. It could hardly be otherwise. After all, the homeland and the new land were separated by something like 13,000 nautical miles, and most women knew there would be no going back. 'Farewell' meant forever. Most of the women had never been on a boat before, and the prospect of going to sea must have been daunting. They would have to make do with conditions which were cramped in the cabins and claustrophobic in steerage. Few passengers had anything approaching privacy, the food was boringly repetitive at best, and the voyage went on and on.

At mid-century, when the seven-month journeys of convict ships were a thing of the past, and one might book passage on a fleet clipper racing its way to Melbourne in an astonishing seventy days, the norm continued to be something in excess of one hundred days. Three months, four months, keeping family life intact, the children well . . . it must have been a trying initiation into emigrant life, trying for everyone, but more difficult for some than for others. Anna Cook opens this collection with her breezy shipboard journal chronicling her obvious delight in it all. The disadvantages of ship's life were a challenge to this immensely self-confident woman with her keen sense of fun and her high spirits. Forty years earlier, Ellen Moger's voyage had been hell. Time alone cannot explain the difference. Children continued to die during the journeys, and Mrs Cook notes the deaths of those on her passage. These were not her children, however, and that made all the difference.

Time in itself removed neither the painful nor the primitive. A date alone tells little. The piano Lucy Jones proudly took with her to Booroopki in 1883 looks more comically out-of-place than Annie Baxter's had in her hut at Yesabba in 1840. Photographs reinforce the point. A woman in 1910 looks admiringly into the camera of her parish priest, the endless demands of a primitive life showing in her weathered face and in the hands of her teenage daughter. That woman and Sarah Davenport would have understood each other, in spite of the sixty-year gap in their ages.

If this nameless woman had been Sarah Davenport's contemporary, she would have vanished when she died. No photographer was around to capture Mrs Davenport and her family on daguerreotype that day when

Even in the first years of this century, life in the bush could be primitive and exhausting. The face of this mother, the hands of her older daughter, the younger girl with her out-grown dress and bare feet – all bear testimony to a harsh life. In the album of the Brotherhood of the Good Shepherd in Dubbo, New South Wales, a priest has written of these parishioners: 'A Very Bushy Family'.

they set off for Yass in 1843. Nine years later, photographers had visited Australia, though none had yet set up a permanent business. Soon a few of the more adventurous among this new breed would begin carting their heavy cameras and cumbersome developing equipment through the bush, but they must have been an extraordinarily rare sight because none of the women in these letters and diaries ever mentions seeing a photographer – or even hearing of one. Annie Baxter did have her portrait painted a few times, and later in the century the Clifton family was photographed. Louisa Clifton, in fact, is the only one of these women whose likeness has come down to us in any form at all.

This is frustrating. Curiosity is aroused, and unsatisfied. What did these women look like? Do the conditions they describe match our reading of them? Lucy Jones writes 'hut' on her drawing of something that resembles a tent. What did Annie Baxter's 'hut' look like when she first arrived at Yesabba? What image did Penelope Selby see in her mind's eye when she wrote home to her sisters, 'Every time we remove our hut is worse'? Photographs would answer some of these questions and would add other dimensions to our reading of the accounts. Stylized though poses had to be while people and animals stood stock still in positions they could hold for second after slowly passing second, the fact remains that the faces in the photographs were the faces of actual women, and the places where they posed were the places where they lived. Photography is clearly akin to the writing of letters and diaries. All record the immediate, and draw their power directly from experience.

Photographs seem therefore the most appropriate illustrations for this book, especially photographs of women in their ordinary surroundings where they go about the business of their daily lives. The problem is that photographers did not go out into the bush to take pictures of women at their everyday tasks during the 1840s, and it was rare for them to do so during the two decades which followed, but most of the letters and diaries I have selected come from these scantily photographed years. Sketches were made during that period, of course, but they share the disadvantages of Victorian fiction, remaining for the most part within the confines of similar conventions. Even the work of someone as skilled as S. T. Gill has now paled into prettiness, predictable and perhaps insipid.

Striving for artistic effect, sketches falsify. Annie Baxter's, for example, are gentle, charming, and genteel. The life she records in her journal is none of these. As a well brought-up girl, she learned to draw, and she drew as she had learned. It was her writing which matured under the pressure of time and experience. Still, the sketches are interesting simply because they are hers. They are another way she had of imagining the bush and another way we have of imagining her, but because I am trying to keep that sense of immediacy which gives the letters and diaries such power, I have used no sketches other than those done by the women themselves.

Photographs seem preferable in spite of the problem with time. Their kinship to the mode of writing matters more than chronology, and besides, they offer another sort of opportunity for imagining women in the bush. They give a visual shape to those silent women who left no words. What we know about such women is what we guess when looking at their photographs. Rarely are their names recorded; dates and places are for the most part matters of conjecture. The photographs have survived haphazardly.

So have the letters and diaries. Sometimes, as one might expect, families have held on to them, and have then either lent them to libraries for copying or donated them outright. Even within families, however, the writing of women may have a strange history. The Davenports who continue to live in the vicinity of Wangaratta in northern Victoria are justly proud of their pioneer forebearers, and at some stage, a member of the family made a typescript of Sarah Davenport's reminiscences. A photocopy of that typescript was given to the La Trobe Library in Melbourne during the 1970s, and it was the photocopy, listed in *Women in Australia*, which I first read, unaware that in the meantime the original had come to the library as well.

Once I began looking closely at the transcript, I grew uneasy. Was it a hoax? It was written in standard English, with the occasional eccentricity of spelling or expression, and a decidedly odd notion of paragraphing. But Sarah Davenport, as she describes herself in the reminiscences, should not have been writing standard English. Her background amidst the mill workers of Manchester at the turn of the nineteenth century would have made the education assumed behind that prose unlikely unless the person had sought out special opportunities, and the opportunities Sarah Davenport remembers herself as seeking out are for work, not education. Such a stream of catastrophes runs through her account of life in Australia that I began to wonder whether I was in the presence of a parody of 'hard times down under'. The language and the experiences did not match: the voice was not authentic. Before I could decide whether to abandon the account, fascinating though it was, and to trust my strong suspicion of something being phoney, I had one of those strokes of luck which every once in a very long while brightens the dogged task of the researcher. I went to the opening of an exhibition at the La Trobe Library. The subject of the exhibition – 'Dreams of a Golden Harvest' – seemed unconnected to my own pursuits, but there in a glass case I saw the original of Mrs Davenport's reminiscences. The mystery was solved.

Sarah Davenport wrote exactly as I thought she must have. Whoever made the typescript presumably cleaned up the prose in the process. This meant encapsulating it within sentences which begin with a capital letter and finish with a full stop. Sarah Davenport's sentences were units of thought without benefit of such distinctions. More significantly, the whole manner of expression was changed. A dead baby who was 'throne in the sea' according to Mrs Davenport, was 'buried at sea' by her more genteel and better-educated transcriber. Furthermore, sections were omitted from the original, and in various ways these omissions obscured what was going on. Probably the most interesting of these changes occurred in a passage recording the trip from Sydney to the region of the Ovens River in what was later Victoria. This was a long, slow trip when the Davenports made it in 1843. For a woman, it involved a daily succession of difficulties as she looked out for the needs of her family. It also confronted her with problems simply because she was a woman, but this point was obscured when the transcript was made:

> There was a great deal of bad language among them, and fighting going on one with another. We never spoke to them but armed ourselves my husband with a small axe, and I with a carving knife. I was determined to defend myself, and was in that position till daylight. At last I heard them make up a robbery for the next night, so they disappeared. I heartily thanked God for preserving us from vilance.

Perhaps even before the transcript, someone had gone through this section (and only this section) of the diary with a blue pencil crossing out the words in which Mrs Davenport had made her specific vulnerability crystal-clear:

> they was a great deal of bad language used among them and fighting one among another and they was for pulling poor me from under the dray for their own brutal purpose we never spoke to them but we armed our selves my husband with a small axe and me with a carving knife   i felt determined to defend myself   we was in that Position till Daylight   i believe they wold have assallted me but one more humane resisted them   that was one cause of thair fighting   at last i heard them make up a robbery for the next night

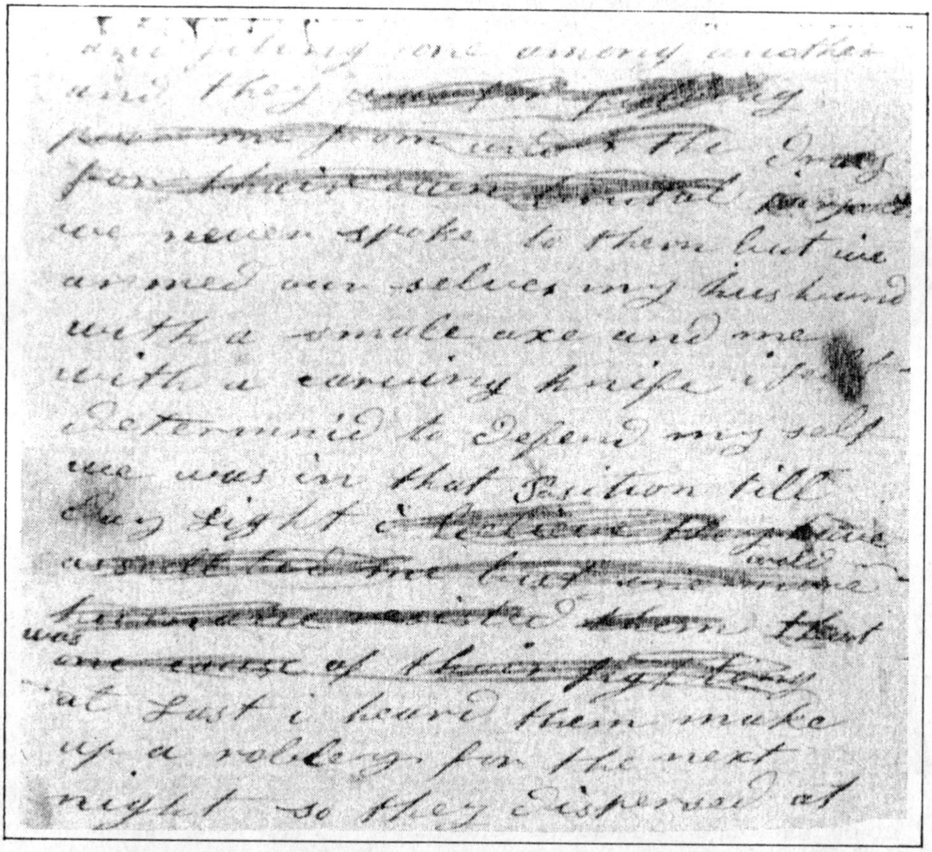

and fiting one among another
and they [illegible]
[illegible] from under the dray
for [illegible]
we never spoke to them but we
armed our selves my husband
with a smale axe and me
with a carving knife i [illegible]
determin'd to defend my self
we was in that Position till
day light [illegible]
[illegible]
was [illegible]
[illegible] of their fighting
at last i heard them make
up a robbery for the next
night so they dispersed at

We journeyed on till we came to a place called Liverpool. There we camped near a public house. The driver went into the public house and stopped inall night. They were a lot of ruffians and he was afraid of being robbed as he worked for himself. The dray and bullock were his own. We made our beds under the dray. The tarpaulin, forming a rude tent, our beds being on the ground underneath.

There was a great deal of bad language among them, and fighting going on one with another. We never spoke to them but armed ourselves my husband with a small axe, and I with a carving knife. I was determined to defend myself, and was in that position till daylight. At last I heard them make up a robbery for the next night, so they disappeared. I heartily thanked God for preserving us from vilance. Nothing more occured until we reached Berrima, and then we lost one of our bullocks, and my husband lost himself looking in an endeavour to find it, but meeting someone

The Davenport manuscript and typescript.

so they dispersed at that i hartley thanked god for preserving me from violance

Without knowing who made the typescript of the original reminiscences, or why it was made, it is reasonable to observe that the typescript turns Mrs Davenport into someone she was not. This seems a shame. Even if one recognizes the touchiness of later generations who want to feel comfortable about their rung on the social ladder, it does not seem right to legitimize the present by falsifying the past – and Sarah Davenport would, I suspect, be furious. She was who she was.

At least her family did hold on to those frail pages which must have cost her such labour to write. But what happened to women with no immediate family around them when they died? Although these are women who might well have had time to write, their words rarely survive. Ann Drysdale was one of the few exceptions. Middle-aged and single, this remarkable woman arrived from Scotland in 1840 to take up a run in the Geelong district of Victoria at a time when Melbourne itself was only five years old. She did have the advantage of being well-connected, however, and her diary became part of the Clyde Company Papers, with which it was subsequently published.

Ann Drysdale was one of the lucky ones whose diaries were given some attention. Annie Baxter was another, although it is difficult to see why. When she died on her farm at South Yan Yean, near Melbourne, in 1902, she was 88 years old and in the words of the solicitor who presented her will for probate, 'for many years past she lived separate and apart from her [second] husband'. Childless, with no relatives in Australia, she must have had some friend who appreciated her enough to take good care of thirty-two diaries and a sketchbook. For over three decades they vanished from sight and then in 1935 A. H. Spencer, of Melbourne's Hill of Content bookstore, offered them to Sir William Dixson. How Spencer got them or what Dixson paid for them remains a mystery. Fortunately for the rest of us, this extraordinary work went into the hands of a dedicated collector whose library now has its own unique place within the State Library of New South Wales.

A sketchbook belonging to Annie Baxter made an equally auspicious landing. Somehow it became part of the Ferguson collection, which went to the National Library in Canberra. When I was rummaging through the National Library's catalogue of manuscripts in 1982, looking under every conceivably relevant category I could dream up, I came across a card for

 The inside cover of one of Annie Baxter's sketchbooks with her drawing of what may be the homestead at Yesabba in the Macleay River District.

the sketchbook of a squatter's wife in the 1840s. That was all the information available, but it was enough to suggest relevance. I was totally unprepared for what I found. Here, without a doubt, was a sketchbook kept by Annie Baxter. The heading was plain: 'Yesabba, 1840', and there was the hand-writing, oh so familiar after hours and hours spent peering at a microfilm in my effort to read in Melbourne the diaries held at the Dixson in Sydney.

I was elated to discover the letters and sketches which are included in this book, and the librarians at the National Library were delighted to have the sketchbook properly attributed, but the discovery set me wondering. If thirty-two notebooks are in the Dixson, and a sketchbook belongs to the Ferguson collection, what else was there? And where is it? The survival of women's accounts has obviously been a matter of chance.

Of course the accounts themselves are about 'chance' in the double sense of 'opportunity' and 'accident'. The women went into the bush hoping for the chance to find some better life. Once embarked upon their venture, they were subject to unpredictable forces they could not possibly control. On the first day out from Liverpool, Sarah Davenport and her family were shipwrecked. When eventually they did get to Australia, the sister in New South Wales, whose apparent kindness and concern had enticed them into the bush, turned out to be a callous and rapacious creature who really cared nothing at all about the welfare of the Davenports, and was actually after labour which was not just cheap, but indeed free. Where Sarah Davenport had expected opportunity, she met with accidents and the accidents were usually nasty. Her life was remarkably difficult, but what she needed for it was what all the women needed, wherever they went: strong nerves. The bush was no place for the highly-strung woman, no place for a nervous lady.

Anna Cook and Ellen Moger

THE LONG WATER EXPEDITION HITHER

1883 *and* 1840

The bush was not the beginning. First came the expedition over water, and a strange time that was, with the heat and the cold, the whales and the icebergs and an albatross, the fear of fire and fever, and always, always, that sea with a will of its own. Crossing the Atlantic was nothing by comparison, a mere quarter of the distance, and yet they left the British Isles and came south, these women who would live in the bush.

The voyage was a kind of trial run for them, testing their initiative and adaptability and sheer staying power. Anna Cook loved the strangeness of it all when she and her family set sail on the *Scottish Hero* in 1883, bound for the North Queensland port of Rockhampton. She was happily surrounded by a large family: her husband Fred, her unmarried sister Emma, and her six children – Ettie, Florrie, Lottie, Bernard, Edward, and baby. It was all new and great fun, and she was not even sea-sick. The crowded boat reminded her of the Devonshire village of Torquay she was coming from, and in a way she managed to keep village life with her just by transferring it to the ship and then comparing all odd and exotic experiences at sea with what she knew at home. The strangeness was then no trouble, and she could write reassuringly to her mother as though she had not gone off into some utterly different world.

The details of cooking and organizing the family and chatting with shipmates took up her time and filled her thoughts. This does not mean that she was a plodding and unimaginative woman. Far from it. Her engaging sense of humour and flair for the dramatic are obvious in the way she writes. Her prose is vivacious, responsive, intimate, the prose of a woman who is enjoying herself. Trivialities cannot irritate unduly. Nothing ever upsets her dreadfully. The family and their well-being are what she cares about, and she is quite proud of how well she takes care of them. Her account is an unselfconscious tribute to her success.

on board *Scottish Hero* off Cape of Good Hope
14th December 1883

My dear Mother,
We are now about half-way on our journey, and I hope during the other half to have written a good long letter. It seems nothing to look back on the past six weeks, although to you it must be like a year. Well, I must commence from the time the Pilot left us at Weymouth. It was very exciting – two boats left Weymouth, one was a large fishing boat, the other a little punt with just one sail, and it blowing a good stiff breeze. Well, the small one arrived first, and the pilot being a big man was enough to send her to the bottom. So the pilot says, 'Now you'll promise and swear you won't drown me?' 'Yes sir.' So he went off with three hearty cheers, and that was the last face we saw until we sighted the Brazilian Coast.

The next day we were travelling towards the Atlantic, and the sea was getting stronger, and people's insides began to tumble about, and almost all the passengers were sick, both men and women. I was obliged to laugh, although I pitied them, because I have never been sick or ill since I came away. Edward and Lottie were not sick or Fred but the others had two days of it, and by that time we were out in the Atlantic. Oh, what splendid waves – so long and even. I thought I could never see anything so grand again.

Well, one day was pretty much the same as another until a washing day was started. The carpenter had made a couple dozen tubs out of meat and flour casks, and as the weather was getting warmer (it was never colder than when we left Gravesend) this great washday commenced on a Monday. Groups of women were seen, some standing, and some kneeling on deck. Then comes the question of hanging out. We had to put up our own line, and when that was up we didn't like hanging up the linen – until a Portsmouth woman says 'Here goes,' and her chemise and drawers went off in full sail, catching all the wind. How we did laugh to be sure. The Captain and doctor fairly choked – they watched us from the poop. Mine were hanging up just over the butcher's table, and when the purser went to serve out the meat, my drawers kept flapping in his face, and he said 'By Jove, I wish this woman's somewhere else'. I wasn't far off on my camp stool, and could not keep from laughing.

The next day was another excitement. The boxes were taken up – every box was brought up on deck, and then we had about three hours to look out what clothes were wanted for the Tropics. It would have made a capital picture if anyone could have sketched it. I see one man open a pot of jam and thrust his fist into it. Some had one thing, and some another. Presently up comes our tin bath with his sides well bent – however there was nothing particular damaged. The bottle of sherbet was smashed, and one pot of jam cracked, that was all. The other pot of jam had on a pair of gloves, the striped ones of Harry's. Oh dear I thought Emm would have gone off at them gloves, and the little bit of butter on my plate that was left from tea the day before we left – it was only about two ounces – however it was good, and we eked it out till Sunday. The onions we found very useful – in fact it would be a good plan to bring a few extra to sell.

The next day I went in for cooking because we can make anything we like and get it baked from 6 a.m. till 4 p.m., so with a tin of fresh mutton which I had I made a splendid pie, and Emma came to dinner, 'My word,' the folks did sniff, but that was their share. We are able to make up such nice little dinners and teas, although the meat is salt. We put it in fresh water and soak it well. The salt pork is delicious, much better than we get at Jeffry's, and we can have bacon every morning and fried bread. We first put some slices of bread into a dish, then the bacon, and the cook turns it out proper, but as the weather is getting warmer we shall have our breakfast on deck, as well as our other meals. It looks a little bit like Ansteys Cove to see the folks sitting about in groups.

Every day is pretty much the same. It is like being in a village. The time flies along while we are chatting, looking at this one and passing remarks about another. It's really astonishing what one can pick up from one another. There are all classes, all trades, and one or more from nearly every County, and every religion – in fact they are so mixed that the service on Sunday is given up because so few attended. So that Saturday and Sunday are exactly alike on deck.

The children were to have a school when we left the Channel, but the young man was very sick and ill for a long time, and it was given up. They have everything imaginable to amuse them, and they are as happy as the day is long. And they are long too – it is quite light at 4 a.m. until 8 p.m.

We had just entered the tropics when a cry of 'shark' – however I couldn't see it, but it followed us, and the sailor said it was a sign of death. And in less than 12 hours a young man fell down and died. I daresay Louie will remember seeing a sickly young man at the cabin door – it was him. He was buried the next day, on Florrie's birthday. Of course it was something fresh so at seven in the morning all hands were on deck that wished to be present, but not me. I don't think I could stand that at any price.

Now for poor Florrie's presents – the Captain gave her some muscatels and almonds, the steward a piece of cake, and a second class passenger some Osborne biscuits, and I made a jam roley for dinner, and a cake for tea. She invited Emma to dinner, and another single girl came to tea. So I don't think she came badly off with a ship's birthday.

Oh, the tropics – it is hot. We are sleeping without anything to cover us, and all night the perspiration is running off us. I get up about five, and by 7.30 all the children are on deck, and have breakfast. I generally take baby's water up and wash and dress her in the sun, but after all it is not as hot as I expected.

Now I must tell you about the glorious sunset – I quite believe it is the grandest sight I shall ever see. About a half an hour before the sun sets, the horizon changes into hundreds of hues, each line has a background of bright crimson gradually changing into every shade of red. Then a deep golden colour spreads over the whole sky, tipped with bright gold and red. 'Jerusalem the Golden', the hymn, seems to describe it a little, and that only gives a very faint idea. Just fancy, we can see 22 miles across, whichever way we look, so as we stand by the side of the ship we can see 44 miles of this glorious sky. Well, just in the centre is the sun itself, and this is too bright to look at, and presently it changes into a golden ball, then like a clear ball of fire, which gets smaller and smaller until it seems to sink into the sea. But the golden sky remains for two hours or more, with every shade of colour. I don't think any picture has ever had a true sunset, because there are so many changes in it, and the day before we crossed the line there was a distinct black line seen across it.

Crossing the line has caused much excitement. The single men caught a few soft fellows and told them it was lucky to be shaved as they were crossing, and they did shave them as bare as a child. Then one or two of them dressed up and walked up and down the deck representing old and new England, one in the Bush with his pockets full of money, the other at home starving, and their pockets hanging outside. I have been talking to see that the articles of agreement between the ship-owner and the commissioners are properly carried into effect, and to whom all complaints are to be made. One of the emigrants is usually appointed to assist the surgeon in seeing the rations served out, keeping order between decks, and to report generally on their conduct to the surgeon.

The steerage passengers are always put into messes of six, or such other number as may be determined on by the surgeon-superintendent, and are victualled according to the following scale per head :—

Bread ...... $\frac{3}{4}$ lb.	Daily.		Butter ...... 6 oz.	per week.
Flour ...... $\frac{1}{2}$ lb.			Mustard ..... $\frac{1}{2}$ oz.	
Meat ...... $\frac{1}{2}$ lb.*			Oatmeal ..... $\frac{1}{2}$ pint.	
Suet .... 1 oz.			Peas .... 1 pint.	
Water ... 3 qts.			Raisins....... $\frac{1}{2}$ lb.	
Cocoa...... 1 oz.	On alternate days.		Rice .... 1 lb.	
Coffee...... $\frac{1}{2}$ oz.			Sugar .... $\frac{3}{4}$ lb.	
Tea......... $\frac{1}{4}$ oz.			Vinegar ...... $\frac{1}{2}$ pint	

Potatoes $\frac{3}{4}$ lb. 4 days in the week, and when expended 1 lb. of rice to be substituted for 3 lbs. of potatoes.

Women receive the same rations as men ; children to receive rations in the proportion of two-thirds between 7 and 14 years ; and one-third between 1 and 7 years ; children under 12 months to be provided for by their parents.

The usual supply of medical comforts is also to be put on board for use in case of sickness, in the proportion of—for every 100 passengers, counting the children at the rates stated above, 10 lbs. of arrow root ; 50 lbs. of preserved beef; 400 pints of lemon juice, in stone one-gallon bottles, and 400 lbs. of sugar to mix with it; 60 lbs. of Scotch barley ; 18 bottles of port wine; 300 gallons of Meux, or Reid, or Barclay, or Whitbread & Co.'s stout, in $\frac{1}{2}$ hhds.; 50 gallons of rum.

The medical comforts to be issued as the surgeon shall deem proper. It is intended that women who may be nursing shall have a pint of porter each day; also, that if the water should be bad, an allowance of

* Prime new Irish East India beef and pork, and preserved meat, alternately.

T

In 1839 while Ellen Moger's children were dying 'for want of proper nourishment', *The Hand-Book for Australian Emigrants* was painting pictures of well-stocked larders and a range of 'medical comforts' available even to those passengers who travelled steerage.

some Cornish people who went out seven years ago, and have now been home for four months holiday. I think it was at Sydney they had been living, and when I told them where we came from they said they knew a young man from there called Yeo. And they know young Rossiter in Adelaide. There are several in the ship who know Torquay well – a Mrs MacKay has a cousin, a waiter at the Imperial. There is a family from Clifton knows Mrs Munro's sister with the invalid child.

That is how we spend our days on deck, for working with a baby is out of the question, and every afternoon a little after three hot water is served out to women who are nursing, so of course the teapot goes to work, and sometimes Emm comes down to join me. I have made up that red and white grenadine for Lottie, and the red twill frock for baby, and have cut up Emm's red shawl to make her another frock, and then she wears the little pink print frock Lizzie gave me, so she will last on till I get there, for I can assure you she is not a dying subject. Bernard has come to grief – one pair of his washing trousers were put over the side to drag, and a fish took a fancy to them, so I have cut up baby's grey frock that was made out of your dress, and made him another pair. We have lost five hats over so we shall have to buy as soon as we land. Emma has lost hers too.

There is a great deal of sickness on board during the voyage but measles is the only infectious thing at present. Bernard had them very slightly, and to prevent any of the others catching them the doctor said he could stay in the hospital. However that didn't take at all, so when I came back from hanging out my clothes he was on deck again, and there he lay all the day wrapped in a blanket. Fred slept with him in hospital one night. A little girl died with them – she took cold and was soon gone, and since then her little brother has died, so now the poor woman has lost both her children, but is expecting another shortly. The first baby that was born gets on very well, the next one died in three weeks, and now there are five waiting, daily expecting to be carried off into the women's hospital. It is laughable, for there are only three beds, and one of them is for the nurse. They are kept there a fortnight, so that is not bad.

You will be glad to hear that we get our stout every day. It looks so comical to see the women go to the dispensary every day at 12 o'clock. One man borrowed a baby and carried it to the doctor, and says 'You see, Sir, unless I have some stout I shall be obliged to wean this child.' So he had a drop – anything is done to make fun.

We have been making good headway for several days, and have seen some ships and steamers in the distance, and have sighted land three times, but not near enough to distinguish anything. The Island of Trinidad looks very pretty. The First Mate says it is exactly like an iceberg – it is not inhabited, but there are some splendid goats on it. After leaving that, there is nothing to be seen but birds and water, and the winds are driving us far out to sea on the Western Coast, until we sight South America, and so we keep up and down that coast for a whole week. We see plenty of Brazilian fishermen – their boats are very curious, two pieces of wood is all they stand on, and they have one sail up. Two boats came quite close to us, and behind the sail were two black men, and it seems as if they are fastened down in some way. The poor fellows couldn't understand all the shouting from the children, and seemed half afraid of us.

The next thing we see was the Medusa. Oh they are so pretty floating along just like a young duck. They are pale pink and the sea a beautiful blue, and you can't think how pretty the contrast is, but they float along too fast for us to distinguish any legs. The next day they were to be seen every five minutes. You see we are up on deck so early that we are glad to pass the time away in looking over the side of the ship.

I think I will give you the routine of one day, and every day is the same in this respect. Quite early a man shouts out 'All women and children on deck,' and by 8 o'clock breakfast is ready. The Captain of the mess fetches that. Fred is Captain one week, and Mr Holroyd, who is in the next berth, takes the next week. There are 33 messes, and as many as 10 or 12 adults to some messes. In ours there are 7 and we are number 19, so when they go for their food they wait their turn, and if not there, be served last. After breakfast the men wash up, and whatever dishes are used in fetching meat or soup or anything else, the Captain must keep clean.

After breakfast the men go below and bring the beds up on deck to air and well shake the blankets and sheets etc. Then they scrub the berth out and the portion of passage leading to it. Then they have to fetch whatever is given out on that day. If it is Monday, a man shouts 'Captains of Messes, for your cheese,' and they get a week's allowance, share out what is due to the other berth, and keep the rest. We are four and a half adults, they are three. The next thing is jam or marmalade, and the next flour, but that we get Monday and Wednesday, ½ pound to each adult; Tuesday preserved potatoes – I don't care much about them, but they make good potato cakes – pickles, coffee; Wednesday flour, suet, currants, raisins; Thursday preserved onions and carrots; Friday tea, sugar, butter and treacle; Saturday pepper, salt, mustard. So you see we have plenty of everything to use from.

Well, dinner time comes, punctually at 1 o'clock – Sunday fresh meat soup, and fresh tinned meat – not corned beef but actually roasted. We get that about 11 o'clock, and I generally make a nice meat pie, and they are good too, and if we want any potatoes we only have to put boiling water to them and mash them with butter, pepper and salt. Every other Sunday, and every other Thursday we can boil a pudding. The single men take the other turn, but we can always bake. After dinner the men wash up – all at one trough, pipes of hot water leading from the condensing house. Tea is fetched in the same way. All toast is made a half an hour before tea. Monday pea soup and pork, very good. Tuesday fresh meat and soup. Wednesday pea soup. Thursday fresh meat. Friday pea soup. Saturday salt beef. Bread and water is served out every day before breakfast.

We went on a very short allowance for a little while, and there was a bonny fuss. All the men went to the Captain and demanded their weight. They said the Purser was robbing them to line his own pockets at the other end, because whatever is left is sold by auction, and a commission is given to the purser. So the Captain went down and examined the stores, and found nine tanks of flour, besides several barrels. After that we had plenty, and an extra ¼ lb of flour. Now there is no stint of anything. I go to the officers steward every evening and get a nice cup of tea and a relish from the Captain's table. After a pig has been killed I get some good sausage meat and always a little to carry below.

During the very hot weather, after all the children were asleep I used to go up on deck and stay sometimes till twelve. You can't imagine how lovely the stars look and the dear old Orion – he is turned upside down – his head would be across Plentifords Hill, and his feet just over Rossiter's shop, but so clear – just like so many moons. Everything is turned round about since we crossed the line – even the sun travels another way – it rises in the East and travels North. Instead of travelling towards the Strand, it would go towards Tor. I can quite see now why all the seasons are so different.

The boxes have all been up again to get out warm clothing. We are now in the Indian Ocean. I don't wonder at that young gentleman being so cold coming from Africa. It is cold – the days are drawing in, and every day we get nearer Greenwich time until we pass the Cape, and we are sailing far far away from any land, the air is frosty and all the crew are looking out for icebergs. I do hope we shall see one. It is five weeks now since anyone had any meals on deck, but the children go up every day when it is fine, and skip or drive their hoops. In the evening all the men have their turn at singing. I have been all round the deck two or three times, and we sing 'I shall never forget the days when I was young'. We play touch wood, or do anything to keep warm – can't you picture us all scampering about like a lot of wild things?

It is wonderful how well all the children keep. Lottie is as rosy as an apple, in fact there is no difference in them – they are all fat and well. Ettie slipped down the other day and scalded her arm with some sago – she had been to get it boiled for baby. It is all right again now. Several have been very badly scalded – when the ship is rolling they slip down, sometimes with boiling soup or tea. Two or three have fallen down the hatchway. There is scarcely a day passes without some slight accident.

At last I have had the pleasure of seeing a whale – there were three to be seen. They send the water up so high, and they rise up a good piece out of the water. One was an immense thing, longer then the ship. I have seen two sharks – one was close by the side of the ship. They look to have such great heads, and as they rise near the surface they send up a very pale blue light. The birds are lovely. The boatswain and steward have caught one, and they measure from the tip of each wing 9 feet 9 inches across. They are called the 'Albatross'. I will send you home one of the feathers. There are hundreds flying about.

I wish every day you were here, although I should not like you to come in a sailing vessel – it is too long for anyone without children. I hear all the women say the time hangs so heavily on their hands – they have nothing to do. It is too cold to work, and some days it is impossible to write – it is roll, roll. If I am washing myself I lose the water, and when baby is sucking, it jerks it out of her mouth, and she gets so wild. It is laughable to hear Edward. If the ship is ever so steady, and he upsets anything, he says 'I couldn't help it – ship rocking', but he is such a good little fellow, always imitating the sailors. He gets a piece of rope and throws over the side of the bed – that he calls fishing. He ties his hat, or anything else, on one end, then he pretends to pull the sails up, or down – that he calls 'Rockhampton' because there is one particular rope that all the men are willing to pull, which means fair wind.

Fred has been on the forecastle and made a grand discovery – there are two young men from Kingston, one he knows very well – they are both going to Brisbane. I wish you would tell Mrs Lear if ever she thinks of coming out Mr Lear must apply for sailmaker's place and work his passage out. Our old sailmaker is 73, and for every death he gets something extra for making the shroud, and each time he says 'I am still living, and the oldest man on board.'

Every day at 12 o'clock, the Captain takes the distance of the sun through a queer looking glass, very much the shape of an iron rest. Then he puts down the longitude and latitude, and the miles we have travelled during 24 hours. Fred copies it, and if I send it home perhaps Miss Munro will trace it out and show you on a map the actual road we have been. I think it will be very interesting. We have been hundreds of miles out of our track one way and another, and have had some heavy seas to contend with, but it is a grand sight. One cannot help thinking how wonderful the sea is, to stand and see the waves like mountains. It looks every minute as if we must be covered.

The middle of the ship is deep down in a hollow. One night the carpenter came round to secure all port holes. He says 'It is a dirty night' and sure enough it was. I shall never forget it – just as the lights were hung up, the hatchways were put down, and presently we shipped tons of water. Oh what a force it came down above our heads. It swamped the quarter deck as well, but as it happened to be a fair wind it sent us through it like mad, doing just fourteen knots. Very few went to bed that night, and fewer slept. The captain assured us there was nothing to fear. He said it was not a real storm, but a very big sea running. At 4 o'clock in the morning, bang bang bang went something, and the upper and lower topsails were blown to shreds. Oh, thinks I, we are going now. As soon as ever I could, I went up on deck, and what a grand sight. One can never imagine what it is, and I for one am proud to have seen it. It looked exactly as if we had to go through a dark tunnel of water, but no, our *Scottish Hero* carries her head too high. She rides the waves most beautifully, and on we go. But downstairs it is so unpleasant – the hatchways are closed, and the poor children have nowhere to play. It is not so bad being below now as it was in the tropics when the rain came down like a river without one moment's notice – sometimes we were sitting down in the very midst of a meal, and before we could scramble up we were drenched. But after all it caused a good laugh.

Now I must begin to tell about Christmas – every day we are wondering what sort of dinner we shall have. The Captain told Florrie it would be an extra supply of salt jumbo – 'Oh,' she says, 'You mean Salt horse.' I must tell you the Captain takes a great fancy to Florrie, and the Doctor likes Ettie, and every Sunday they give them some dessert. Well, I am gone off my story. The day before Christmas, such a shouting 'Captains of Messes – for flour, currants, and raisins'. Each adult had ¾ lb extra, and a pound of fruit, a tin of condensed eggs, a tin of preserved carrots, a tin of onions, extra tea, jam and suet. Then we were told to get our puddings ready by 8 o'clock to boil all night. Then a man comes round to all the berths 'Will you give up your soup tomorrow and have your puddings boiled in fresh water, or have them boiled all night in salt water?' Everyone gave up the soup, and by 5 the next morning all the large puddings had to be ready, the small ones by 8. It would have done you good to see them, and the many different ways they were marked – some had a piece of wood tied to the string, some a button. One had a china doll, another a bunch of rags sewn to the bottom. Ours had a tin tally. Presently up comes the young women's puddings. Haloo – here comes a couple of icebergs – I never saw such whoppers. Even as early as five, all hands were stirring and very merry. At midnight the single men sang carols outside the Captain's cabin. They had two violins and two concertinas. They sang 'Christians Awake', 'While Shepherds watched', and 'Ring the bells of Heaven'. Several women were up getting their puddings ready, and we went up and walked about for a little while. It was raining a little so that rather spoilt our dance that we intended having.

Christmas Day it was raining and blowing hard until the evening when it cleared up, and everybody went on deck, although it was so cold. The Doctor sat in the hatchway and gave each child a packet of toffee and a handful of nuts. Then a scramble for nuts of all kinds, and biscuits. Sometimes when they thought another handful was coming, down comes a shower of flour and smothered everybody. It was all great fun. Some of the women went to the baker and got some flour and when the Captain least expected it, he had it proper.

Oh, I forgot to tell you how our dinner went off. We had fresh beef, potatoes, and a good plum pudding with brandy sauce – a double allowance of everything, and instead of plain bread it was currant bread for three days. Everybody had a tin of milk for each mess. Although I am allowed one a fortnight for baby, and as she doesn't take the bottle we have it in our tea. That is one thing I should advise anyone to take, and a box or two of red herrings. If you can't eat them you can make three [shillings] each on a long voyage when others have run out.

I have not been able to do any writing for several days – it has been such weather, at least not bad, only the wind was exactly at the back, and the ship was rocking night and day. I think the night before last it was worse than it has ever been – it was impossible to lie in bed without holding on; almost everybody got up. Our great barrel of water turned over and rolled along the passage and back again, the water going in all directions. My flour jumped off the shelf, a tin of onions marched off, the teapot jumped into bed and emptied its contents. Presently we heard the water rushing again and somebody else had lost a barrel of water, and our gutter that runs along the side of the ship was full of rice, treacle, from the stores. Now it is a dead calm.

Nothing particular happened since Christmas, until New Year's Day. On New Year's Eve there was a grand dress concert, given in the single men's apartments. A large bill was posted up just as it would be at home announcing the concert. However I couldn't go. Fred had knocked his leg again, and he went to bed. But for the sake of old times I stayed up with a few others, who were in a similar fix. About 11.30 the cannon was fired, and that continued until after 12. Then there were fireworks, ringing the bells, dancing and singing. It was all high day again for a time, then a few hours quiet, and all was astir again with their puddings. It was pretty much the same as Christmas Day, very rough and raining all day, and everybody was agreeable except the woman in the next berth to me – and she is a disagreeable thing – but I don't say much more to her than I am obliged. I can get on with every one else very well.

The first thing I heard this morning was that another little child has died through the night. They are expecting two more deaths, and goodness knows how many births. It will be a narrow squeak with some, but one thing I do hope, and that is that we shall not be kept in quarantine. Every morning the doctor and two constables come round and examine all the bunks, and scatter disinfecting powder, and fluid, all over the place, for they say there is every sign of sickness, especially as we are going to the two extremes from cold to heat.

Our diet has been changed a little every day – there is boiled tapioca served out, and about three times a week the children have boiled rice with eggs and milk in it. There is plenty to spare. Then in the place of salt beef we get fresh meat and can boil a pudding. We gave up soup as soon as the warm weather set in. Every day this week I have made some sort

In 1857 the Minter family posed for a photograph in their new garden at Mount Moriac, Victoria. One wonders how difficult it was for the mother to keep up appearances. Did she make those elaborate matching dresses for the three older girls? Is the baby wearing a Christening gown, and did the mother make it also?

of cake for tea, and twice have had a hot lunch. In the morning we have porridge – I save about a quart of it, chop some suet, enough for a pudding, about 4 onions, one egg, half pint of flour, salt and pepper to taste, and a little sago, mix all together and bake just the same as any other pudding, and just as wet as a baked pudding. Not too stiff. That is one lunch. The other is a meat pasty – just a snack for Emma. Another little cake is to roll out some pastry, lay a piece in the dish, put on a layer of currants, a little finely chopped suet, a little lemon peel, but as I have none I put marmalade, some spice, and sugar, put on the crust, and that makes a capital mince pie. All our cakes and pie crusts are made with suet. I must say it is the best suet that can be got for money.

Today is Sunday, all the children have their thin clothes on. You would be surprised to see what swells the folks are, but it does not matter what one wears as long as it is tidy. A large hat is very acceptable, for the sun is hot. Yesterday we were all marched up on deck at II o'clock, and the whole place was covered with brimstone and sulphur, the hatchways were closed as soon as the fire was put to it. The men ran like mad, or they would have been smothered. It was opened about an hour after, and the smoke came out like a chimney. Today it smells so sweet. I can't believe any sickness can come now.

An address has been presented to the Captain thanking him for his great kindness, and attention, during the voyage, and in it they told him that we had gone short of provisions many times, through no fault of his, but as soon as any complaint was made to him he saw that we had it back again. He is certainly a good man in every sense of the word.

The carpenter's son has carved such a handsome spoon for Ettie, and her name, the name of the ship, and his initials cut out at the back. This young man went to Queensland when he was three years old and his mother died on her passage out. His father told me it was the greatest trial he ever had when he set foot in Queensland with three little children. However he has worked hard up in the bush, given them a good education and this year they have been home to Bradford to see his brothers and sisters, and finding two sisters had gone to America they started off over there, stayed a month, and they are going back again quite disgusted with English ways; they say there is nothing there worth living for. The working class seems afraid to enjoy themselves. The young man works at the preserved meat trade and gets £1 a day. There are three parties in this ship going back. They cannot settle themselves in England, and each one is taking out a relation. I do hope we shall get on well, and be able to pay you a visit soon.

Anna Cook arrived in Australia with her exuberance intact. True, she loathed the depot at Rockhampton, calling it 'about the dirtiest place I ever put foot into', and she complained that 'the immigrants are huddled in there just like so many cattle'. The town itself she liked, with its tropical fruit trees and lovely mountains. Soon the Cooks were on a steamer bound for Brisbane, and before long they had found a new six-room house, made of pine and resting on four posts. It would not be finished for three weeks. Meanwhile, Fred had got himself 'a large job from the new Government Bank to fit it all up with venetian blinds', and the children had started to school where the girls 'go through a course of drilling to make them walk upright, and are made to speak properly, and Florrie says each one has to tell their own faults when the teacher asks who has been talking'. Whether the Cooks remained in this town close to Brisbane, or went 'up in the bush' where living – so Mrs Cook has already heard – is 'not half as bad as we imagine', this jaunty woman would have had the energy and the enthusiasm to keep on top of things.

Not so, Ellen Moger. No chatty letters came of her voyage to Adelaide forty years earlier. She was hallucinating, not writing. Even after she landed, seven weeks passed before she could bring herself to write to her parents, much as she wanted to reassure them, to let them know that she had arrived and all was well. It was not. Three of her four children had starved to death. How could she find words for that journey through hell?

She circles around the news, mixing the mundane with the terrible, trying to strike the right note, to create the appropriate voice for what she has to say. She can hold on to nothing as she writes. The letter is a mish-mash of perspectives, a confusion of narrative events, with sudden shifts of tone and feeling. Control seems too hard, the pressures towards disintegration too strong. These words are a mother's grief, and the grief is horrible. It will not let go.

Adelaide, Gouger Street
28th January 1840

My dear Parents,

I have very melancholy accounts to give, which I cannot do without great excitement to my feelings.

We landed at Holdfast Bay, about 7 miles from Adelaide (the ship being too large to go into port) on the 10th of December 1839, having been just four months to a day on the Great Deep. We had a safe, and many would say, a delightful voyage; but as regards myself, for the first five weeks I was scarcely able to move my head from my pillow with Sea-sickness, which brought me so low that I could render but very little assistance to the dear children, as I was obliged to be helped on deck by two persons, Edward and another Edward and the children suffered but little from sickness. But as we entered on a warmer climate, the dear children became relaxed (with the exception of Emily) gradually getting weaker and, for want of proper nourishment, became at last sorrowful spectacles to behold. They could eat none of the ship's provisions and our vessel was not like many that are sent out, provided with one or more cows for the accommodation of the sick; and, had I the voyage to take again, I would make that a first consideration as I firmly believe that the dear children would have lived, and much sickness been spared, had we experienced proper attention from our Doctor and been provided with a little natural nourishment.

Poor little Alfred was the first that died on the 30th of Oct, and on the 8th of Nov, dear Fanny went and three days after, on the 11th, the dear babe was taken from me. I scarcely know how I sustained the shock, though I was certain they could not recover, yet when poor Fanny went it over-powered me and from the weakness of my frame, reduced me to such a low nervous state that, for many weeks, I was not expected to survive. It seems I gave much trouble but knew nothing about it and, though I was quite conscious that the dear baby and Fanny were thrown overboard, I would still persist that the water could not retain them and that they were with me in the berth. I took strange fancies into my head and thought that Mother had said I should have her nice easy chair to sit up in and, if they would only lift me into it, I would soon get well. I had that chair of Mother's in my 'mind's eye' for many weeks and was continually talking about it.

I was bled and blistered, or rather, plastered, and continued in that weak state until within a week of landing. I think I never should have recovered at Sea – you can have no idea of the effect the sea has upon some constitutions. Mine, for instance. It was a sort of Sea Consumption. Our Captain took great notice of our children, when he saw them gradually wasting away and would send for them into his Cabin and give them portwine, almost daily. In fact, wine and water was the only nourishment they took for weeks and that was given them too late. I would advise everyone who came out for Australia to bring nourishing things with them and take in turn with what is allowed on board, for the change is so great and so sudden to what we have been accustomed that the constitution, unless very strong, sickens under it.

My dear Emily now seems more precious to us than ever, and I feel very thankful I did not leave her in England. Her health is not as good as formerly, having something Scurvy, the effects of Salt diet. She is also troubled with weak eyes, a complaint exceedingly common in this town, from the great degree of heat, light and dust.

It is now time to say a little about the country, after so much said of my frail self. I have given you but a poor description of our voyage from the fact that little transpired worthy of comment, for it was, I assure you, one continued scene of confusion. I will, however, give you a faint description of one day and you will then be able to judge of the rest.

The bell calls 'the watch' off at six o'clock in the morning when down comes the Steward to give out the rations for the day, 'Ho Mess!' (six persons comprise a Mess) for rice, biscuits, flour, suet and raisins, or such as it may be, reiterated through the ship, till one is stunned with the sound. Then comes such a rush of meagre looking visages till all are served. Then immediately follows the cry of 'boiling water'. Then there is such a scamper, with piles of soap, biscuits and slices of pork to roast at the Galley fire which, many having to wait full half an hour to accomplish, return metamorphosed into Blackamoors, with smut and smoke. When the great treat was over, those who were able to go, were ordered on deck to break-fast and there kept the whole of the day. Great was the difficulty to keep the emigrants above, not withstanding there was an awning to shelter them from the scorching sun.

The Doctor was a young and very austere man, and during the first half of the passage very careless and inattentive to the health of the passengers, till there were many alarming deaths, when he became more solicitous, respecting them.

During my last illness he appeared quite an altered man towards me, allowing me more brandy, arrowroot or whatever I could take. In turn, and as a recompense on my part it seems, I invited him (whilst in a state of delirium) to my wedding dinner of roast pig and turkey. I was in an odd way, as you may suppose, to take such fancies into my head.

We had thirty deaths during the voyage, besides a young gent, a cabin passenger, who was missing one morning at breakfast time, when it was discovered that he must have thrown himself from the porthole in his cabin. He was a man of very quiet and reserved habits and no cause could be assigned why he did the direful act.

But, to return to my description of the transactions of the day. Ere the sumptuous repast of biscuits and pork or biscuits and butter is over, down comes our Commander, the Dr, ordering all beds on deck, after which the ordinary deck cleaners commence their operations by throwing chlorides of lime and scouring out, which you may suppose is quite necessary, and with all they were in a sad state of filth, frequently finding vermin, but could not tell from whence they came. I spared no trouble to get fresh and clean changes of clothes for the dear children, whilst alive, but to no purpose. They were soon remarked as being the four nicest children on the Ship and this you can imagine caused no little jealousy amongst some of the mothers and there are not a few queer ones amongst them, I assure you.

Pardon this digression, my dear parents, for whilst I write, many thoughts of scenes and past trials enter my mind and frequently I feel as though I must throw away my pen, though I have much, very much I would tell you, nay, more than my poor weak spirits will enable me to recite. However, as I am enabled strength of body (I trust I shall of mind also), I experience more resignation to my circumstances. I have been under a Doctor Nash's attendance since we landed, for a month, and he ordered me strengthening medicine and port wine, which have wonderfully restored me. Edward was also laid by for more than a week since landing, but I am happy to say he is now regaining his strength. I fear I am covering my paper in my old style, sooner than I expected. I will, therefore, proceed to tell you many things in few words.

There were seasons on board when I could have wished and did wish that you were with me, to contemplate the beauty of the setting sun – its splendour was beyond description, and in a few moments you turn to behold the moon rising in silent majesty and shedding her glorious rays over the vast and mighty world of wonders. Whilst gazing on the beautiful scene you are, perhaps, interrupted by the sad tolling of a bell, informing you some poor victim to sickness and privation was about to be launched into a watery grave. Such events are not uncommon, but the mind, I assure you, soon becomes hardened and callous on board a ship.

No doubt, you are anxious to know how we like the country and what we are doing and I also am solicitous to inform you. At the same time, I am at a loss what to say, as there are two ways to represent the same case. One very flattering, or the reverse, but I wish you to know from me the plain truth as I would ought extenuate, or ought set down malice, but as far as my little knowledge will authorize, without embellishment, make a fair statement. To say I like the country would be false, for I do not. And I believe the English are greatly deceived with the many flattering accounts respecting the beauty of the country and fine salubrious air of South Australia. It is true we came in the heat of summer, but I write as I find it. The heat has been most intense and when attended by what is called the 'hot winds' and whirlpools of dust, which are like clouds of smoke, extending as far as the eye can reach, it causes an overpowering lassitude which I am unable to describe. When the rain comes it descends in torrents, we have not had much. Winter here is considered the growing season. At the present time everything is scorched up, or I should say bears the appearance of barreness for I have not yet seen anything to scorch. I asked Mr Brandis the other day where the beautiful geraniums grew that he sent such a fine account of to England, as having 'trampled under foot'. His reply was that they grew a few miles off in the country where, he said, everything bore a different aspect.

Bugs and fleas we have by thousands everywhere. Some nights I can get no rest for them. When we came first I was in that horrid place, the Square, and caught from 100 to 200 of a night and still they were swarming. Ants and mosquitoes are also very tiresome, these are a few of the comforts of 'Australia'.

The outer world mirrors the inner. All is desolation. Australia is dust and sickness, bug and fleas. Reports of the country's beauty have deceived. If the promised plentitude of geraniums is to be found, it is somewhere else, a 'few miles off' perhaps, not here. Mrs Cook might have possessed energy enough to ward off the summer's 'overpowering lassitude', but of course the sea claimed the hats of her children, not their bodies. However strong Mrs Moger may have been before her ordeal, the long water expedition has loosened her grip on life.

Ellen Moger's sense of self is bound up in motherhood, but her efforts to care for her family have been as resounding a failure as Anna Cook's were a success. Children for whom she had 'spared no trouble to get fresh and clean changes of clothes' were 'thrown overboard', as she says with stark directness. She refuses to soften death with evasive euphemisms, and will not be falsely consoled. Her efforts to be brave and honest make painful reading. Preoccupied with the counterpointing extremes of health and death, her account jumps about disjointedly, as though her mind will not hold steady. She tries to write enthusiastically about the splendour of the setting sun, but half way through the sentence, her mind is back on death again and she has introduced 'the sad tolling of a bell' into the set piece of her picture postcard description. A sentence which begins with what seems emotionally neutral comment about choosing a vessel provided with cows, suddenly announces for the first time the deaths of her children. The movement of her prose maps out her wilderness of lost connections.

While the emigrant voyage has inflicted change beyond endurance, Ellen Moger is not bitter about her children's deaths. She lets the ship's doctor off the hook and instead of blaming him, seems by implication to blame herself. A disquieting sense of inadequacy colours the account. If *she* had known more, been better prepared, the children would have lived. She is always self-abasing. She writes about her delirious fantasies in a rather mocking tone, as though they were the experiences of a frail creature whose mind had weakened into comic foolishness. Instead of being angry and railing against her outlandish circumstances, she sets up resignation as a goal.

Ellen Moger had been reduced to 'a low nervous state' well before she stepped off into heat-stricken South Australia. She was in no condition to be a pioneer woman. One wonders what happened to her and to the remnants of her family. Did her health improve? Did she see the geraniums in bloom? Did she survive?

FATIGUE AND BUSTLE AT AUSTRALIND

1841

Louisa Clifton had heard the talk for so long, all 'the torment and harrass about Australia'. It was dreadfully complicated and really depended on people outside her family because her father was considering more than a new home. Marshall Clifton was helping to organize a brand new colony in the wilderness, a dream of the better life.

Plans were drawn up in London, and a company formed. It would buy a large tract along the sparsely settled coast of Western Australia and sub-divide the land into allotments. A beautifully laid-out town, with spacious quarter-acre blocks, would be surrounded by one hundred-acre farms. The company's prospectus glowed with enthusiasm: 'It is hardly possible to conceive a finer situation for a Town, both with reference to sea and inland communication and other natural advantages.'

Utopia was at hand. Nature was plenitude. Fine fish abounded in the waters of the inlet, which was 'frequented by black swans, ducks, pelicans, cranes and other aquatic birds'. In this idyllic setting the town 'will extend over a space of 1,000 acres, exclusive of a reserve for public objects, such as quays, streets, squares, markets, churches, and public gardens'. The summits of the highest hills would be reserved for 'the intended College, Hospitals, Observatory, Pleasure Grounds for Park, Cattle Market, and Cemetery'. The town – and the colony – would be called 'Australind', the very name conjuring up notions of a richly profitable trade between the new Australian colony and the wealth of India. Best of all, Marshall Clifton would be the settlement's chief commissioner.

It all sounded marvellous. For the Cliftons it would be a real godsend, bringing financial safety to a family stretched beyond its circumstances. A pension of £600 per year did not go far in a household with fourteen children, even after a move to France where living was cheaper. For Louisa's father, the new job would be a wonderful opportunity. Marshall Clifton was an energetic man who needed something challenging to do with his talents. He had been only forty-five when he retired as Secretary to the Victualling Board of the British Admiralty in 1832. To be chief commissioner of the Western Australian Company would provide scope for his organizational skills, and in the new colony he could carry on the horticultural experiments which had earned him election as a Fellow of the Royal Society in 1820.

Louisa's mother would have less to look forward to, and more to regret. Elinor Clifton would have to leave her two eldest sons, Frank and Waller, who were now grown and would remain in England. Equally painful would be the separation from her own family of devout and closely-knit Quakers. Through them she was related to Elizabeth Fry and E. G. Wakefield, whose model colonies the experiment at Australind would follow. Mrs Clifton's family's home was Wandle House, Wandsworth, where her sisters still lived. It is to her cousin Priscilla and the relatives at Wandle House that Louisa most often turns when she thinks of England in her journal, and her mother must surely have done the same.

Twenty-five-year-old Louisa was less than sanguine about the move to Australia. The very subject could leave her feeling 'completely tempest-tossed.' When she heard that 'all has been settled about the Company', she wrote: 'I do not allow myself to think or speak of it, or rather I cannot; but an indescribable sadness comes over my mind at times; it is the shadow of the future coming to cloud my thoughts and feelings.' Still, she was a deeply religious young woman who tried to be as exacting a Quaker as her mother, and if God had marked out Australia for her destiny, she would go. Her mother was counting on her, as she very well knew. Indeed, during their last months in England when Louisa was being courted by Edward Kater, it was her mother's desperation which determined her not to accept the anticipated proposal of marriage. Succumbing to what looks very much like emotional blackmail, Louisa reassured her mother that she would go with the family: 'I chose Australia; dearest Mama's bitter tears have decided my wishes. I would rather break my heart than add one drop to her cup of sorrow and of care.'

As it happened, the choice did not arise. Kater behaved most strangely and ungallantly. His intentions had seemed so clear to everyone, and Louisa was led to believe that he would 'follow us out to Australind.' Shortly before they sailed, he told her that if he visited Australind it would be as 'a pleasant wedding trip' – and there was no suggestion that she would be the bride. She was dumbfounded: 'This took me back indeed,

No information seems to have survived about this portrait of Louisa Clifton, when it was painted, where or by whom. Probably it comes from before the time when the twenty-five-year-old Louisa lived in the tents of Australind. The elaborate hairdo, the dress designed to show off her fashionably delicate shoulders, look like reminders of the life she led in France and England.

and I did not know what to say, particularly as he had before pressed me to send him a sketch of our cottage, immediately on arriving, and which I had promised to do.' She accepted his gift of flower seeds for that mythical cottage, but now knew that thus had 'ended an acquaintance of – what shall I say? intense interest; would that it had never arisen. . . . I am always to be crossed in all my interests; this has been a final stroke; it will certainly preserve me from ever forming another.' There was, as she said, 'humiliation': 'my pride is wounded and indignant feelings aroused; but I had not believed there was anything serious until made to believe so by others, for I have learnt not to reckon on any man's affections nor to trust them.' And yet – six months later, when the first mail reached the Cliftons at Australind, Louisa would expect a letter from Kater, only to find herself miserably disappointed once more. By then, however, she would have plenty of distractions, including the attentive Mr Eliot, Resident Magistrate of Leschenault.

Leaving aside the entanglements of the heart, it is tempting to see the move to Australia as just what Louisa Clifton needed. She was showing signs of dwindling into the usefully unmarried daughter who could be depended on in a rather boringly predictable fashion. Nineteenth century gentility was threatening to close in. Her surviving journal, begun in France in early 1840, records a process of change which looks decidedly liberating from a twentieth century point of view. She had taken up her pen 'after an interregnum in my journal writing for two or three years' and had been 'led to do so by the reflection that if our destiny should be eventually to settle the other side of the world, it will be a sweet enjoyment to be able to recall with clearness the events and incidents of the time that remains to us in Europe.' There is nothing surprising or particularly noteworthy in what she writes. Her life and her language offer little more than a confirmation of middle-class English ways. When the journal follows her onto the sea and then to a new land, it becomes a record of change – of change in the patterns of everyday life, and change in the expectations about manners and mores. To read the Australian section of the journal is to watch an orderly English gentlewoman learn to live with confusion.

There was so much confusion, so many kinds. A week before the *Parkfield* sailed, it looked as if the entire Australind venture might disintegrate there and then. A Lieutenant Grey had arrived from Western Australia saying that the land purchased for the settlement had been resumed by the authorities and was no longer available. Grey added to the misery a claim that the area was a veritable Sahara anyway, and totally unsuitable. People who had eagerly bought up town sites and farm allotments now panicked and wanted their money back. In a last-ditch effort to avoid bankruptcy and to send the boatload of emigrants on their way, the directors of the company decided to move the whole enterprise three hundred miles north of Fremantle to Port Grey, as strongly suggested by the Lieutenant of the same name. Since the town planning had taken place in a London office rather than on the actual location, and people had bought their sites according to the office plans, it was all just a matter of changing labels on pieces of paper. The emigrants finally set sail on the *Parkfield* in December 1840, intending to stop at Port Leschenault to pick up the surveyors who had gone out ahead. This was a distinctly make-shift proposition, never really satisfactory, and the surveyors greeted it with dismay when the *Parkfield* arrived. Luckily, Marshall Clifton had kept his head during the pandemonium, and he managed to calm things down by getting permission for them to stay at the original site so that they would not have to sail up the coast in the vague search for somewhere else.

The Company's behaviour had been alarmingly amateurish, but for a moment the confusion was over. More would come in its place, and Louisa would record it day by day. Some confusion would be simply a matter of the physical mess which was part and parcel of life in tents and flimsy huts. Other kinds of confusion were more elusive, those confusions of the mind which could leave Louisa feeling blue – or exhilaratingly open to her unknown future in the land of hopeful promises.

Wednesday, 17th March 1841. Barque *Parkfield*
Under feelings of the most intense interest and excitement I take up my pen to write the account of this day; we are laying to within sight of the Australian shores. How can I describe the emotions of this moment?

About ½ past 5 the soul-reviving sound 'land in sight' rang from the mast-head; and then how every heart leapt for joy. I soon after went and joined all the party on deck, and there in the far horizon, in the grey colouring of coming twilight, loomed the faint outline of our adopted land. At a distance of 30 or 40 miles it rose high. The moment any eyes first rested on that 'dim discovered scene' was one the remembrance of which the longest life can never obliterate; none who have not known what it is to sigh, to long with sickening longing for land after a voyage of more than 3 months can fully understand with what ecstasy of feeling the first view and scent of land greets the weary senses.

A native fire has been distinguished on the shore tho' we are still distant, and we are almost laying to and standing off the land till daylight dawns. The motion has been very distressful all day and I have done very little and felt wretchedly uncomfortable. Mrs Gaudin went into hysterics on first seeing the coast; it is time she should display some feeling for she has not hitherto manifested much.

Thursday, 18th March 1841. *Parkfield*
A boat was soon descried coming off from the shore, and between 2 and 3 o'clock it reached us. It proved to be Capt Coffin, an American settler, who acts as pilot to ships coming in. The moment, I felt, was an anxious one to hear of the surveyors. Mrs Gaudin said not a word. Papa enquired after them and heard of their safety, but that poor Mr Gaudin was out of his mind, and had been so from first sailing. Papa immediately broke it to poor Mrs Gaudin whose distress was of course extreme. This sad intelligence produced a general feeling of gloom and sympathy. I had always dreaded and expected it, but the shock upset me, for the more we heard of him the more affecting appears the whole case.

About 6 in the evening we found ourselves in Leschenault Bay, within ½ mile of the shore, the sea perfectly smooth, the temperature more warm and balmy than can be described. We were all struck by the pretty aspect of the country at the mouth of the inlet and in parts along the shore. Masses of beautiful foliage grow down to the water's edge and in an opening of it we descried Mr Eliot's and Mr Stirling's little dwelling. Papa, Bob and two of the young men went ashore and found Mr Austen; then called upon Mr Stirling and Mr Eliot; heard that Australind is beautifully laid out. Everything here promises prosperity, and all excessively cut up at the change of site, which, as neither the *Stirling* nor the *Henry* have arrived, was before unknown to them. The excitement of this evening may be imagined.

Friday, 19th March 1841. *Parkfield*
Papa with Pearce, Mrs Gaudin, George Smith and Charles Bedingfeld went up to Australind at 7 in the morning and returned about ½ past 7. The description of Mr Gaudin's state is the most heartrending and

by the pretty aspect of the country at the mouth
of the inlet in parts along the shore masses of
beautiful foliage grow down to the water's
edge & in an opening of it we descried Mr. Eliot's
little dwelling. the remainder the coast axe
sand hills but there is vegetation upon them
trees every where seen beyond the hills in the
distance high reminding us forcibly of the
hill at Subiaco. The coloring as the sun began to
decline became exquisitely soft & delicate —
the hills robed in the brightest lakes & blues —
the sky reflecting every colour in the rainbow
yet so softly that every tint completely melted
in one another — I cannot easily cease to
remember the first Australian sunset
nor the feeling with which I viewed its
promising coasts the native fires burning
along the country the smoke of which however
we only saw — Papa Bob & two of the young
men went on shore. Found Mr. Austin
there called on Mr. Stirling & Mr. Elliott
heard that Australind is beautifully
laid out, every thing here promises
prosperity. but expensively cut up at
the change of site, which as neither the
Stirling nor the Henry have arrived
was before unknown to them —
The excitement this evening may
be imagined —

affecting I ever heard. He was lying nearly naked, dirty beyond everything, on a mattress in the corner of his tent. After some persuasion they induced him to wash and dress and see his wife. He appeared pleased to see her and talked, but a strange apathy and indifference seems to mark his aberration of mind. He said it was not fit for her to remain, so she came back, overcome with the awfulness of her position.

The evening was passed in hearing a glowing description of this lovely Australind and its vicinity. The meeting and disgraceful conduct of the surveying party under Mr Austen, his and his wife's sufferings on the voyage, poor Mr G.'s pitiable condition, and then summed up in regret on all sides that this is not to be our resting place. Mr Stirling, Lieutenant Nory, Mr Eliot, Mr Ommaney, Mr Onslow called in the morning and expatiated on the advantages of this colony, the impossibility of settling at Port Grey; they have all speculated on our arrival, and there is a general gloom at the disappointment in their expectations. Papa decides to go tomorrow to Perth to the Governor.

Saturday, 20th March 1841. *Parkfield*. Port Leschenault
A grey day; till these two days not a cloud has been seen for 6 months. A heavy rain drove us down from the poop very early and the weather looks threatening and windy. It is lightning vividly. How exquisite is the being at rest. I feel intuitively in high spirits.

2 of the natives, dressed up for the occasion, visited the ship this morning. They were both covered, but I was more shocked than I can express at their appearance. I never witnessed so affecting a sight as this display of the degradation of humanity. They do not look like human beings, so thin, so hideous, so filthy; oiled and painted, red faces and hair, and pieces of rush passed through their hair. They danced and distressed us still more; in fact I feel distressed at the idea of living among such a people, so low, so degraded a race.

Sunday, 21st March 1841. *Parkfield*. Leschenault
It blew too hard to enable the Capt to read the service on deck and we all therefore separated. The morning till ½ past 11 was very much interrupted by a visit from Dr Carpenter and one of the young surveyors, a Mr Harrison; the former I like, or at any rate feel disposed to like for dearest Priscy's sake, who met him on one of our Wednesday's parties and had a great deal of conversation and was pleased with him. Christina was not prepossessed in his favour. How clearly was the past brought to my

recollection by seeing one whom I had met in our dear English home. Mr H. is not pleasing nor gentlemanly.

The evening was passed in conversation on the natives and local interests; nevertheless I felt in a serious frame of mind and my spirit seemed to yearn for a corresponding disposition in circumstances around.

Monday, 22nd March 1841. *Parkfield*
I passed great part of the morning in making my noviciate in washing, an employment I expect often to be engaged in. I feel no desire to spare my self-indulgent nature; on the contrary I am only eager to humble it and to come down to the occupation most repugnant to it. There is too much selfishness, I fear, in my desire for refinement of every kind; it is a web that must be broken, for it partakes perhaps too largely of that which is only worldy, and producing dissatisfaction and vanity.

My mind has run spontaneously today upon Stanstead and its inmates; Anwell and Cat's Hill and those past days of pleasure, I believe; but they come up with heavy tread upon my memory and leave too deep a trace behind. A desolation of feeling has crept over me as I walked the deck this evening and surveyed the land before us. Dearest Priscy's society would at this moment have been of exquisite solace, for to her alone can I pour out all the weak, the foolish, perhaps the morbid feelings of the moment. But I will not encourage melancholy, for all is right and best. It is Providence who has brought us here, and for our happiness too, I do not doubt, and I therefore submit.

Tuesday, 23rd March 1841. Barque *Parkfield*
We breakfasted at 8 to start at 9 for Australind. The weather was most lovely and a fair Irish breeze carried us up quickly to the encampment. The scenery of the estuary gratified us extremely; the banks on each side beautifully wooded down to the water's edge, with foliage of varied tints even at this season of the year. Mama was charmed.

On arriving at the tents we were most warmly received by Mrs Austen and were astonished at the comfort and neatness of her tent. Fruit, wine, home-made bread and cakes were laid for us, and most refreshing and delicious we found that which we had so long desired to taste – good bread. The appearance of the camp struck us much; the tents distributed under large spreading trees, a hill covered with wood and bush rising behind. I never saw a more picturesque scene.

Thursday, 25th March 1841. *Parkfield*

According to appointment Mr Eliot and Mr Stirling came off to take us on shore about ½ past 10. Nothing could induce Mama to go ashore so we three, Ellen, Mary, and myself were obliged to go under Mr Gibson's escort, for he accompanied us. We landed at Bunbury, walked to the Giants' Causeway, a basalt formation at the point over which the sea was breaking, but it is not above 6 feet high so that there is nothing majestic or striking. Mr Northey and Onslow accompanied us.

We walked over the site for the town of Bunbury, a pretty situation for such a purpose. We then mounted the hills to the left of Mr Eliot's house, and were charmed with the exquisite view of the estuary, the hills beyond, dips and dells and knolls beautifully studded with large and picturesque trees forming the nearest landscape.

At length we arrived at Government House, situated on the summit of one of these high round knolls, commanding a lovely prospect, and tho' rude and rough in its construction, gave an idea of cheerfulness. A sofa, table, chairs, a small bookcase with books and writing materials in one corner, was all the furniture. A chimney-piece and fire-place for burning wood astonished us; the sides of the room whitewashed, the roof of thatch and high, the ceiling not having been built. Mr Northey showed me his collection of dried plants, and very kindly gave me a specimen of each kind.

After resting for some time we again set out. I again walked with Mr Eliot, Ellen with Mr Gibson, and Mr Stirling with Mary. We wandered through some sweet woods and were pleased with all we saw. We again returned to Mr E.'s and had some delicious bread and butter, which I did indeed enjoy and then came off to dinner; all four gentlemen; the Capt and his wife, Bob and his, had not returned from Australind. We sat down to a dinner so scanty and so bad that we were all made really uncomfortable, and did not conceal our indignation. The gentlemen were very agreeable and did not go off till after tea; their attention and kindness to us was most gentlemanlike and considerate.

I am destined to collect seeds and flowers. Mr E. gave me 62 packets of native seeds, collected by some famous botanist, a valuable present. I really enjoyed the excursion and felt quite at home with our new male friends, though I did not quite like our going alone.

Friday, 26th March 1841. *Parkfield*

Mr E. and Stirling having insisted on again coming off to take us for a walk, we could not resist the temptation of another agreeable excursion. Again Mama would not leave the ship so we again were obliged to go sans chaperone. Mr Gibson was of our party, which was the same as the day before. The weather was still more lovely than yesterday and I cannot forget the exquisite beauty of the colony.

We gently sailed up to the landing place, walked, (I with Mr Eliot) to Scott's farm, then to Capt Coffin's where we rested a few minutes and then wandered on along the banks of the picturesque Preston into the bush. We sat down by the edge of the ford while the gentlemen gathered the tea tree bark and then made calabashes from which we drank, as the water poured out from the bottoms. Having had a charming ramble we returned to Capt Coffin's where we found a delicious cold dinner laid out. He himself was piloting a ship and could not be there to entertain us, but which Mr Eliot did most kindly. I wished dear Priscy could have seen us and been with us; we three dining in an American settler cottage, with 4 comparatively strange friends.

Saturday, 27th March 1841. *Parkfield*
Many of our young men went ashore at 3 in the morning, to join Mr Stirling in a kangaroo hunt. Mr Eliot, however, true to his appointment came off about 11, and Mama, Christina, Ellen, Mary, and myself went off. We landed up the creek and walked to his house. The heat was too intense to walk out so we made Mr Eliot give us some work, pocket-handkerchiefs to hem. Mary and I attempted to sketch the lovely view from the verandah. We enjoyed the repose of the day; had a delicious bread and butter luncheon.

The hunting party arrived in detachments all the evening. Mr Stirling and Mr Onslow have just left us, having brought the fruits of their labour in the shape of a small kangaroo, as a present to Mama.

Sunday, 28th March 1841. Barque *Parkfield*
We had no reading; the sun being too hot to have it on deck. Meeting and reading with Mama as usual. Speculations all day as to Papa's return. A day of annoyance (a petty one) about the kangaroo and Mr Stirling not being invited to partake of it. About 5 o'clock a sail came in sight from the north, which proved to be a cutter. We of course immediately concluded that it was a government vessel, conveying Mr Hutt and Papa hitherto. Soon after, Bob with Mr Spence and many of the young men sailed off to meet her.

Sunset came on, a glorious one it was, the sky painted with every tint and hue of the most radiant rainbow; dark followed; a boat was heard alongside and in a moment Papa, Pearce and Mr Ommaney stepped on board. Our desire to remain here instead of going on to Port Grey has become irresistible. After the first feelings of joy at the safe termination of their hazardous Irish expedition had subsided, our anxiety to know the result of it became intense; all assembled in the cuddy, and tried to read in their countenances the decision. In half an hour hopes were crowned by hearing that the governor so entirely disapproved of the settlement being made on the inhospitable, barren, unknown coast contemplated, that Papa had taken upon himself the responsibility of remaining.

I cannot describe the joy I, in common with all our circle, felt. Two hours passed quickly in hearing the adventures of the travellers, the inter-course with the Governor, Perth, and the only drawback was Bob's absence and the anxiety about him. I retired to rest with a grateful heart, I trust, for this great favour. This place offers a home we never could have felt on an uncivilized uninhabited territory. Robert returned safely at 2 in the morning, having received despatches from the *Champion*, and rowed 4 and a ½ hours and almost failed in finding the *Parkfield*.

Monday, 29th March 1841. *Parkfield*
I passed an excited night without much rest; how did my spirit sink within me when at 6 this morning I heard Papa and Capt Whiteside in conversation, the latter expressing his opinion as to the safety of the anchorage at Port Grey and Papa's reply that [he] should proceed thither in accordance with his instructions. I felt calm, but discouraged indeed. After breakfast a thorough consultation held with the Capt and all; charts examined; Mr Hutt's letter read &c; and then it was decided by almost universal consent that Papa would take upon himself greater responsibility by going than by remaining, and that we are to remain here. What a renewal of hope and comfort to our tried and harassed feelings. Poor Papa has suffered sadly in the difficult position in which he has been placed by Capt Grey's abominable misrepresentations.

A very busy day, washing and ironing. Mr Eliot, Stirling, Mr Northey and Major Irwin who came down in the *Champion*, called. Mama explained the matter of the kangaroo and told them that the butcher had thrown it overboard today without anyone's knowledge.

Tuesday, 30th March 1841. Barque *Parkfield*

I have passed a day of considerable industry, activity and fatigue, having been engaged from 10 till our dinner at 4 in unpacking and repacking all my chests in preparation for our disembarkation and camping in a day or two. With the occupation of the muscular frame, how much the mind partakes in the energy of action; and to one who watches the process of the mind and feelings, it is singular to observe the variations, the totally different phases which characterise them at different times. This morning I felt bouyant; this evening thoughtful, associating myself with nothing round me.

On opening my desk today I met with a note of dearest Waller's written in the April of last year, the outpouring of a broken heart, and as I read it what a host of sad thoughts and recollections clouded my spirit. The faded flowers I gathered the last time I saw Wandle House, wore on that ever to be remembered Wednesday evening, the latter fell also into my hands; how strange that such apparently trifling relics of the past should possess so magical a power as to give a tone, a colouring to every idea and thought during a succession of hours. From these two incidents my present mood may be traced.

I met also with a note (which I had not before read) from dear Aunt M. Turner to dear Frank congratulating him on his marriage and requesting his choice of a present, and then added that 'a similar event to prevent Dear Louisa from quitting England would gladden my old heart'. Dear creature, the grave by this time has made her his prey and that probably was her last written note. I was affected by it and a train of thoughts I cannot express arose. I believe that was a wish entertained by many, but heaven decreed otherwise.

My feelings have been strangely buffeted the last two years; who can tell how deeply? I would not have had it otherwise, for with it all I possess a crowd of interesting and sweet associations and recollections that I would not part with for anything. As for marriage, I have always clearly seen there is a fatality which is insurmountable as to myself. In early life I had a strong prejudice against it, being persuaded that it is an unhappy state for a woman; as years have rolled on and I have increasingly needed a prop and support, a kindred heart, I have at times thought that it is a state in which I might have found the dependent happiness I have longed for. Now I am, I think, content with what is my apparent lot, and in drawing all my enjoyment from my own dear family circle I am resolved (for I have no inclination or power) to make no new friendship or interest. I am so often happy in the knowledge that I cannot again suffer as I have done in the severing of the ties of the affections. It cannot come again and I should be a fool indeed did I ever again place myself in a position of enduring what I have done.

Papa, Pearce, and some of the young men went up to Australind this morning to place some of the tents, and the wind is blowing so hard that they have not yet returned and I trust will not attempt it tonight. The *Napoleon*, laden with stock, the speculation of Mr Stirling and Mr Eliot, has arrived here this afternoon, and another whaler so that there are 4 vessels in company with us.

Wednesday, 31st March 1841. *Parkfield*
Passed the morning in setting to rights, work &c. A stupid day. I very stupid, not very well. It was not the *Napoleon* which came in yesterday, but the *Helen* with horses and stock from the Cape.

Friday, 2nd April 1841. *Parkfield*
Mrs Austen and Mrs Gaudin came down from Australind at 3 and dined with us. Mrs Austen returned in the evening, leaving Mrs G. to sleep here. Mrs A. [was] attired in the same dress as she wore at one of our soirées; and at the déjeuner, and [with a] white bonnet of flowers, [she] looked more than usually unladylike. The scenes in which she appeared in town were bought vividly before my mind.

Major Irwin, Mr Eliot and Mr Northey dined here; the two latter were my neighbours at the dinner table and made themselves very agreeable. With the former I had a great deal of conversation. There is something about him which amuses me excessively. From laughter however we came down to gravity and almost melancholy, as we talked of England, friends, separation, colonial life &c. He expressed many feelings which reminded me much of dear Waller, and the more I see of young men, the greater similarity I find in their sentiments on one point, that of sighing for an object, ties of affection, home interests &c.

His two little native boys came off in the evening; they were brought into the cuddy and tho' rather frightened at the large motley company, behaved extremely well. Guanga hung round Mr Eliot with a sweet confiding manner and then read the English alphabet clearly and boldly. Christina sang; they look astonished beyond measure, and listened most attentively but said little. It appeared too much for them.

 Place, date, and occasion can only be guessed at. The women, waiting while the cattle are watered, are too genteely dressed to be drovers' companions. Are they travelling in some commercial vehicle? Who lives in the hut on the hillside, and in the tent? Where does the road go?

Dr Carpenter in the midst of all this confusion and bustle began to write his home letters; one of which to his brother at Trinidad contained about 5 lines; he is the most heartless, conceited man I have ever met with.

Saturday, 3rd April 1841. *Parkfield*
Although I have not been at all well, this day has been a pleasant one. I enjoyed a quiet reading in my own room for an hour or two; the more delightful in proportion to the rarity of such an employment. I then went on deck alone to try and sketch the coast, but failed.

A very small party at dinner. Robert, Papa, Capt Whiteside and Dr Carpenter are dining at Government House. We have been sitting on deck watching the fires on shore near Shenton's store. The scene has been most beautiful, worthy the pencil of a Claude Lorraine; the moon and sky dazzlingly bright; the sea glistening and perfectly smooth; the outline of the shore dark and clear; the lurid flash and the curling grey and vermilion smoke of the fires throwing a bright redness over the scene, investing with a wildness congenial to the spot and exciting to the imagination.

Poor Mrs Gaudin's cup of sorrow is almost overflowing. Her maid Maria turns out to be thoroughly worthless, and she is obliged to discharge her; thus depriving her of the last comfort she could look to, that of having a confidential, comfortable attendant. She left us in very low spirits.

Sunday, 4th April 1841. *Parkfield*
A day of exquisite warmth and beauty. A very small party at the reading on deck; being the last day on board, I wished to take a sketch of the coast and attempted, but had no pleasure or success in it, feeling it to be an undesirable occupation for the day.

Monday, 5th April 1841. Australind
Papa was so discomposed at our decision not to accompany him to the encampment this morning, that at the expense of a great deal of exertion we resolved to go up at 1 o'clock, and about ½ past 1 we took leave of our kind friends the Whitesides and the barque *Parkfield*. Although exulting in the joy of getting ashore, my spirits forsook me at last; the remembrance of the first time I saw the ship, with whom and with what feelings, with the train of thoughts accompanying a review of the past, ran through my mind. I felt an oppression of spirit which I could not throw off, during our calm and scorching row and sail up the estuary. I made an effort to be chatty, but was silent; the last view of the *Parkfield* awakened too much thought and feeling.

I here transcribe a letter I wrote to dear Waller this night:

Tent, Australind
5th April 1841

I must attempt before I lie down for the first time in the bush, to give you some description of the picturesque romantic scenes in which we are now engaged. We have just made our beds on the ground, arranged our tent for the night, and with the moon shining brightly through the canvas over head, solemn stillness reigning around, except when broken by the merry laugh of gentlemen encamped round a log fire, the chirping of the grasshoppers and now and then the breaking of a wave upon the distant shore. You may fancy Mary and myself kneeling at a table we have rigged up in the centre of our abode, alternately writing and talking over this strange page in our history.

Papa with a party of young men came hither this morning and left Mary and me to follow with a boat load of goods &c later in the day. Mr Eliot and Mr Stirling went on board the *Parkfield* just as we were going and insisted upon taking us up in their boat, a proposition we readily agreed to rather than commit ourselves to the care of Dr Carpenter. We sailed almost all the way up this beautiful estuary, under a sky of surpassing beauty, the heat intense and scarcely a breath of wind. On arriving, we found our tent erected and two or 3 others scattered about, on the slope of a deep declivity a few hundred yards from the waterside, commanding a lovely view, surrounded by beautiful trees, but in a state of charming confusion, the sand, ankle deep, almost the only floor.

Our kind friends Mr E. and S. insisted upon getting everything to rights. We all went to work under a scorching sun to cut rushes for the carpet, turned everything out; they then spread them, arranged this table which with a nice English cover gives an air of comfort to the apartment; put up books; in fact, in the course of an hour or two we found ourselves in order. Mrs Austen then kindly came from her settlement with a loaf of bread and cold meat, a most acceptable present after the labours of the day.

An immense fire of branches was soon lighted on the level ground a little distance below our tent, water boiled, and tea made, and having fortunately got up our plate chest containing knives and forks, teacups &c, we sat down to a welcome repast, and with more comfort than we could have imagined possible. I wish you could have seen the interior of our new abode, some sitting on the ground, others on our mattresses rolled up; I making tea upon a gun case seated on a hassock in the midst. By degrees all the young men collected to this centre of comfort and sociability. I forgot to describe in due order a scene which amused us vastly. While we were engaged within, we found the Government Resident, the magistrate of the district, Mr Eliot and Mr Gibson, hard at work without, kneading dough to make damper, in other words, unleavened bread, which has since been baked in wood ashes, and promises to do justice to the skill of the manufacturers.

I cannot describe half of the amusing and curious incidents of the day nor convey to your mind an adequate idea of the picturesque appearance of a bush encampment in such a climate and with such scenery on all sides. Papa and Mr Plowes have a tent; Mr Eliot and Stirling and many others are by this time reposing on the bare ground, wrapped in blankets by the side of a large fire. We have just made our beds and are so completely tired that we are longing to lie down in them. The nights are extremely cold and we are beginning to feel very chilly, and the sand underneath strikes damp and cold. Mama, Ellen and all the party are to come up on Wednesday.

I find myself involuntarily providing against the motion of the sea, altho' we have been almost entirely at rest for the last fortnight. The delight of feeling still, relieved of the burden of preparation against pitching and rolling and a thousand other charms in being on terra firma again compensates most fully for the personal exertions which will be required for some months to come; and then the indescribable blessing of not going to Port Grey. I feel a sensation of 'home' in this place; civilization is partly known. There are only 3 or 4 settlers, but there is the truest hospitality and kindness, and instead of being out of the reach of any human beings, we here at once meet with a hearty welcome and with ready assistance and cooperation. I cannot tell you how truly kind Mr E. and S. have been. The former is a very agreeable gentlemanly man, and the latter is most pleasing, and tho' a colonist not less the gentleman. All is hushed and still and I must to my rest as we are to be up at 5 in the morning.

Yours,

L.C.

Monday, 17th May 1841. Australind

I began the week with a determination to be more than ever active and industrious, and having on Saturday night packed away all my extra possessions in my chest, I felt at liberty to begin washing Mama's and the children's things; what then was my dismay when going to my chest I discovered that the milk pan which had stood on it all night leaked, and a stream of milk had found its way into the chest and penetrated down to the very bottom, soaking a great portion of the clean linen I myself had laboured to make so, besides pieces, patterns, books &c. I felt quite in despair as I took one thing after another wet through, and was at last compelled to turn the whole contents on to the ground. I was occupied till dinner in drying and arranging my things, many of which were washed again, and a more fatiguing day I have seldom had, nor a more vexatious occupation; too tired to do anything in the evening.

Tuesday, 18th May 1841. Australind

A very beautiful day gladdens the spirits of uninteresting and hard

Tuesday 18th May 1841

A very beautiful day gladdens the spirits in spite of
uninteresting & hard occupation. So accustomed
experience with us from my various engagements
seldom have time to think of the weather with a
view to enjoying it - the heat was very oppressive.
tho the early morning extremely cold. I was again
occupied with the linen - I laid it all out,
dried that which was damp, packed all the children
into a flour cask & all the table linen & into another
large empty tub. & thus secured it all from
farther harm - this is the most satisfactory
end accomplished & I have nothing more to think
& two on that most worrying subject. Mr Eliot
& Mr Stirling had promised to dine here as to day
remain the night to accompany us on an ex
cursion up the Collie the following day. we waited
dinner some time. but they did not arrive &
then we received a note informing us they were
too much occupied with the newly arrived stock
to come up for some days to come - we all were
pleased to give up this boating trip. for myself
I was delighted. I have no inclination to expose
It is attended with so much fatigue. the country
is so similar every where I think that there is
nothing to tempt one beyond the precincts
our own picturesque encampment. besides
after so long a voyage so much unsettlement
I do sigh for rest & quiet enjoyment —
I have had dear Eleanor unto in my thoughts
of late. with sentiments of affection & interest

occupation, so I sometimes experience, although from my various engagements I seldom have time to think of the weather with a view to enjoying it. The heat was very oppressive, tho' the early morning extremely cold. I was again occupied with the linen. I laid it all out; dried that which was damp, packed all the children's into a flour cask, and all the table linen &c into another large empty tub and thus secured it all from further harm. This is the most satisfactory end accomplished and I have nothing more to think or do on that most worrying subject.

Mr Eliot and Mr Stirling had promised to dine here today and remain the night to accompany us on an excursion up the Collie the following day. We waited dinner some time, but they did not arrive, and then we received a note informing us that they were too much occupied with the newly arrived stock to come up for some days to come. We all were pleased to give up the boating trip; for myself I was delighted. I have no inclination to explore. It is attended with so much fatigue, and the country is so similar everywhere, I think there is nothing to tempt one beyond the precincts of our own picturesque encampment; besides after so long a voyage and so much unsettlement I do sigh for rest and quiet enjoyment.

Thursday, 20th May 1841. Australind
Chrissy washed in my tent while I repaired a dress &c. I forgot to mention my own feats in that way yesterday. I washed in the course of the morning all my last week's consumption of clothes besides other things, which I starched; made butter, and did vast other things, and the girls laugh at me as doing everything by magic. Mama and Ellen accompanied [the men who went to] the flat across the estuary to fetch the flock of sheep which Papa has bought of Capt Coffin. Miss Spencer and some of the children had preceded them some hours before. They landed upon the sand patch opposite this and enjoyed the view of this coast from that side of the water.

A party of gentlemen arrived about 4, the time our party relanded, and we were glad to find it was not the government resident party; a Capt Symers, Mr Tapson, Mr Onslow – the two former on their way to Perth. Mr Tapson, a sheep driver, in fact having brought up this late importation of sheep to Bunbury. Colonial Society! How little captivating or refined it is! Capt Symers is a rough but rather pleasing elderly man; Mr Tapson vulgar and unprepossessing, young, rough, and of course in dress, to English eyes anything but a gentleman. The want of gentlemanly dress is an additional friction to 'taste'. A very stupid dinner. I felt low-spirited and requiring to be drawn out rather than to exert myself in conversation. Fell silent. They went soon after dinner.

I forgot to mention a conversation Papa and I had with Dr Carpenter one night some days since. I was resolved to express what I thought of his indiscretion in telling Ellen her chest was affected and his unreasonableness in not taking any notice of her indisposition after the fuss he made about her one day, since which time he has never felt her pulse. The conversation was highly dissatisfactory. Papa had been on the subject of medicine with him and had told him some home truths. I could not but join in when the opportunity offered for expressing my feelings. Papa expressed his opinion (as I did mine) but was very sharp and stirred up the Dr's ire. Such conceit, self esteem, unreasonableness I could not imagine any sane person would display. The next morning he was very cold and distant. Mama had a conversation in which he repeated again the same folly as the night before; but Mama would not let it come to a quarrel, and since we have gone on smoothly. Ellen is now active and getting strong, tho' he says he never before had so intensely anxious a case or devoted more thought to it.

We had a very nice little meeting this morning. My spirits were softened much.

Friday, 21st May 1841
A different morning to that which I had planned; instead of letter writing and journal scribbling, I was engaged in collecting provisions &c for Papa's bush expedition. He, accompanied by Gordon Hamilton, started at two for Waringerup; Papa on the old horse, the baggage on one of poor Mr Plowes little ponies; it is so thin and out of condition that I thought it never could walk under the comparative light weight of the saddle bags.

The girls, Chrissy and I worked with Mama in the afternoon, a pleasant comfortable hour's quiet. I called on Mrs Gaudin and Mrs Williams, not having seen them since Sunday.

Mr Plowes dined with us. The conversation this evening was energetic in defence of Capt and Mrs Whiteside, on our part, against Mr Plowes and Bob, who believe Capt Coffin's account of the insincerity of Capt Whiteside in speaking slightingly and ungenerously of us to him, in fact convicting him of the most wanton tittle tattle. I and those who know him are convinced of his innocence. He is not the man to condescend to do so. Mr Plowes [was] always ungentlemanly to him, and his wife gives credence willingly to all the untruths told of them. We know the source. Mrs Whiteside knew how it would be and cautioned us against believing anything that was attributed to them. Miss Spencer is a second Mrs Greatham, a deep mischief maker, and we little know now to what an extent. The more I see of her the more do I distrust and recoil from her character.

Sunday, 23rd May 1841

Another Sunday has almost mingled with the past. The weather promised to be wet and stormy this morning till it cleared off about the time of our meeting, which was held in the marquee and joined by Mr Williams, Pearce and Bob; no one was willing to attend reading the service; a longer meeting, and chapters were substituted for it.

Mama, Christina, Ellen and I went down to the now almost sunken pier and sat on the rafters there talking over the delight of seeing dear Frank and Eleanor and speculating whether dearest aunts and others would ever be persuaded to come out. The sun flung a flood of light over the unruffled waters of the estuary and the plash of oars and the voices of the children, boys, and Mary, who paddled over to the other side were heard distinctly from their farthest distance. The thought of being joined by these we love lights up glowing hope and eager anticipation, but at present I seem not to be able to realise it.

On returning, I called on Mrs Gaudin and accompanied her and her husband to Mama's room. We afterwards all walked together to the site of our house and strolled about for an hour or two in the vicinity, sitting down here and there on the burnt or cut down stems of trees, which rather thickly bestrew the ground. Mrs Gaudin seemed quite to enjoy a walk for the first time and expressed herself as being happy in being with us; she looks better though her legs are not cured. Dr Carpenter has not yet returned from Mr Eliot's whither he went this morning. Mama read to me many of the little papers she has at times written, and Christina and Bob came and sat with us in her room.

The day has been a pleasant one. I have not felt my usual heaviness and stupor after dinner and have been reading and writing and hearing the children read. I wish to write many letters and have much to express to many, and yet I cannot bring sufficient resolution to the point of sitting down to begin. I never before experienced such an entire incapability of mental exertion; the sense of distance imposes a barrier to communication not as far as feelings are concerned, only in the verbal expression of them.

My heart is just as warm as ever, but my pen is frigid and powerless.

Waves are falling and breaking on the shore with a sound of proximity intimating the restless state of the ocean on the sea coast. It is a splendid but a mournful sound and that in more ways than one, by reminding one of the time passed upon it and by this heavy surging of its waters being a certain harbinger of approaching bad weather. Before a gale of wind this is generally or always announced to us in this way.

Gervase has been grievously offended by Miss Spencer's unkind treatment of him lately (without any cause) and her 'unladylike conduct' to him today. Mama has spoken to her about it, she requesting her to prevent her being insulted by his using such an expression. It has (this topic) elicited a great deal of information regarding her conduct and character, and it is sad to find how lightly it is esteemed by the boys and young men. She is wholly deficient in female delicacy of conduct or feeling and her influence upon the children and Lucy especially I do deeply deplore.

Monday, 24th May 1841
I felt brighter and more buoyant than usual, and have under the spur of this new energy determined to make drawing and collecting flowers the object and pursuit of my leisure hours. I am very eager to send home some sketches, but this I cannot do until I have acquired some progress in the art. Passed an hour with Mrs Gaudin in her tent. Read a few chapters of the 'Abbots' in the afternoon.

Tuesday, 25th May 1841
Papa, Ellen, Mary, Chrissie and Bob went for a walk to the Collie and started soon after breakfast and were out some hours, bringing home a quantity of very pretty flowers, many of which I pressed. I have not seen yet many which strike me as surpassingly pretty; all nature is, and must be, lovely and I love it wherever I meet with it, but I do not think it rivals her charms as displayed in England.

Papa thinks everything here superior. That opinion seems the result of a sanguine temperament to my judgment.

Wednesday, 26th May 1841
A busy morning looking over all household things in use. Chrissy and I accompanied Papa, Mama and some of the children down Coombanah Road which Papa had set some Indians to clear. It runs along the border of the estuary on the flat between our tents and the water. It is astonishing how much the hand of man improves nature (unless particularly picturesque),

throwing an air of interest upon a scene otherwise tame and unstriking. A distance of half a mile I should think has been cleared of bushes and trees which are left in lines on each side of the road which is very wide, and being still green with vegetation looks tempting for a ride on horseback. It is wooded down on the water's edge, but not with many pretty trees, the banksia prevailing, which is particularly ugly. We sat down on the trunk of a fallen tree while Papa used his hatchet in opening in parts a peep of the waters of the inlet looking now rather angry, now bright and blue, as the squalls which we have had frequently today play upon or pass over its surface.

We returned upon the higher bank or crescent, calling upon Mrs Clarke whose tent is placed some distance beyond the surveyors'. Her baby is still sadly delicate and she suffering much with sore legs and weak eyes, of which she is gradually losing the sight. She is so patient and contented that I felt we might learn a lesson from her. Clarke, who is a surveyor (of a lower kind) is now employed under the Company.

Met Mr Gibson and Gordon and chatted with them. The young men rarely ever see us. I must confess they do not contribute to our pleasure, for when we do meet it is quite an arduous task to make them converse. Mr Treene, Mr Durlacher and Mr Greenside dined with us. The Dr who had been sent for yesterday to Scott's to see a poor woman dangerously ill after her confinement, returned, but having dined, drank tea with the children. I had a very bad headache which obliged me to go to bed directly after dinner.

Mr Durlacher, a very short but exceedingly handsome young man, made himself very agreeable and pleased Mama by telling his history, wherefore here, and for how long; everyone I find to whom I have hitherto conversed on their prospects have unanimously the same wish to return to England as soon as their circumstances permit, and even a tear stood in Mr Durlacher's bright blue eyes when he spoke of a return to his own country. He told his age which I was astonished to learn is only 20.

Mr Greenside is wonderfully like Edward Bell, but less goodlooking. He is very pleasing and there is an air of melancholy about him which excites interest; he too is quite a youth. Mr Thomson is rather better but has suffered much with rheumatic gout for some days. Two of the young surveyors have never even had a tent to sleep under, their only covering at night being a rick-cloth covering some of their goods open at each end and presenting an air of discomfort no one can imagine but those initiated into the scenes of settling life.

Would that dearest Priscy could look in upon us; as we sat on that broken down tree in Coombanah Road we tried to realize the possibility of her and dearest Aunts coming out and I thought of one wish in childhood of being 'old maids' and living together in some pretty little retired cottage in the country. Our youthful dreams might be realized here in some measure, but I dare not give myself up to the delusive hope of ever seeing those beloved friends of my childhood in this land. I have been too often cheated by hope's syren smiles to listen to her winning suggestions more.

Papa took Miss Spencer and Lucy with him to the Point, such we call Shenton's, at the entrance of the inlet, close by Mr Eliot's. He called upon Mr E who wished to come up, yet declined doing so. It is an age since we saw him. We quite long for a visit. I wonder how dear Priscy would have liked him. I think she must have liked, though she would not probably admire him.

Thursday, 27th May 1841
A showery disconsolate day. I did not get up till near 11, having woke with a bad headache. I read in bed for an hour, a treat I enjoyed much. Meeting as usual; worked a little, wrote and wandered about. I felt unstrung and stupefied.

Heavy showers of rain and squall of wind from time to time all day; nothing of interest occurred save another proof of the Austins' unprincipled and unjustifiable conduct. Mr Gaudin sent for his paint-box which was left safely in the store when they came up to this encampment. Part of the tray and a few broken paints were all that was returned of it; they having been found under a tree, the box broken open and two pieces and a bottle of liquid carmine, valued at £10 taken. Mrs Austin found it, and it is not uncharitable to say considering what a woman she is that it was wantonly destroyed by her; her malice and evil temper would not be credited did we not live on the spot and know the truth of her infamous conduct. Altogether I have never heard of a more hateful woman than she. Poor Mr Austin may be mean-spirited and weak, but she who rules over with iron hand is chargeable with all the vice of their proceedings.

I am still amusing myself with the 'Abbots', but do not lose myself in absorbing interest as in younger days.

Friday, 28th May 1841. Australind Tents
The first birth in Australind took place today, one of the workmen's wives,

Stallard, has a boy. Passed the morning in writing a long letter to Aunt Kate, the first since my departure from England, a relief having broken the ice as regards letter writing. My powers of writing seem completely frozen.

Saturday, 29th May 1841

After the unsettled day of yesterday the bright beaming still weather of this day has been particularly acceptable and I availed [myself] of it by attempting in earnest to make a sketch of Mama's tent. So I took a chair and all the paraphernalia of drawing to a suitable spot between her hut and the inlet and there I enjoyed repose till the heat of the sun drove me to take shelter under her roof, and I arranged my painting concerns snugly by the door and took a view of the estuary before me, and succeeded, tho' wretchedly, better than I had expected. I am so anxious to send to dearest Frank and Waller and Priscy a few sketches of our present encampment ere thatched sheds take the place of tents and the marquees.

The store house was expected to be entirely completed, the roof was not however wholly thatched. Nevertheless the dinner Papa had promised to all the workmen on the occasion of the first building being erected in Australind took place at 3 o'clock, and we all went in when they, their wives and children, were assembled round the long and capital table erected for the purpose. They sat down about 40, I think. Morgan the head carpenter at top, Hough the thatcher at bottom. Kangaroo soup, kangaroo pies and steaks, pork, beef, pease pudding, and suet puddings composed the fare, and most excellent it proved to be, doing justice to Usher and Whitely's exertions. Papa allowed no spirits: beer, colonial and Barclay's porter only. Everything was conducted with great decorum, and to the universal satisfaction of the parties assembled. The men sat till 10 o'clock, and sang solos, choruses &c displaying considerable talk and knowledge. Absalom sings beautifully, as do several others.

Monday, 31st May 1841

A day of extreme fatigue and bustle, unpacking china, glass, lamps &c for tomorrow. Did not feel at all well, and the labours of the day and arrangement of the dinner party felt very burdensome. I recollect doing nothing but unpack this day, and have therefore no more to mention. Very stormy weather and promising ill for tomorrow.

Tuesday, 1st June 1841

A fine calm morning led us to hope and expect that the weather was settling and fine. The morning was accordingly passed in extreme activity; making tarts and custards, bills of fare and other arrangements for the fête, this being the Anniversary of the founding of the Colony.

The scene in our room was truly ludicrous and I think I must name a few of the contents of our comely apartment. Before it was in any way arranged, we had the satisfaction of being requested to admit Mr Greenside &c to get out some more surveying concerns from the box under our bed. This discomposed me considerably, but I was obliged to submit to the painful ordeal, and they took out the box and we are now happily quit of it altogether. All the paraphernalia of pastry and custard making, grinding coffee, ironing, making fromage and cheese, casks of peas, brandy, sugar and other stores, barometers, wearing apparel, books, boxes and loose books, milk pans, sieves, and dairy apparatus in every direction. Having no other table than the top of my drawers, baskets of dirty linen, music books I had opened for fear of wet, flowers, medicines, starch; in fact there is hardly a thing that can be thought of that is not to be found in my room, mine, especially, being at the entrance.

After a day of extreme exertion, we dressed and were ready to receive Mr and Mrs Ommaney, Mr Eliot, Little and Onslow who arrived about half-past 4. The weather began to look threatening. The Gaudins and the Williams arrived about 6, and by degrees all the gentlemen in the colony. We had no sooner assembled than a shower of rain commenced, more violent and fierce than we have seen since the first storm. It continued so long that we gave up all hopes of either getting down to the store house or when there of having any dinner. A stove in the open air and no shelter presented a formidable obstacle to the serving up of a handsome dinner for 38 people. At length it began a little to subside, and clogs and cloaks and shawls having been obtained, the ladies were handed through the rain and water to the dinner room.

Mr Eliot took me and I sat between him and Mr Ommaney. As the whole roof had not been thatched the rain dripped through the canvas thrown over the aperture and the table and plates wetted and it obliged all the ladies to sit high up the table at the top, so that poor Robert was left at the bottom with the children, Miss S., and our stupid young men, while Pearce had a delightful place at the end, Papa and Mama sitting opposite in the centre of the table.

The dinner was capitally arranged notwithstanding the unpropitious weather, offering luxuries to our colonial friends hitherto certainly not

Why was this photograph taken? The man is not holding the axe like one used to woodchopping and the well-dressed woman sitting among the logs is surely part of the joke. Place and date unknown.

known here. We had a very agreeable day. Mr Eliot as usual very agreeable, rather more exclusive in his conversation with me than I wished. But I was in hopes I had obtained the first contribution to our Australind Museum in the form of some skins of beautiful birds that he begged me to accept, but on my proposing so to appropriate them, he declined giving them; only wishing them to be a personal gift. He is a very droll person and I cannot quite understand him; truly and thoroughly amiable in the best and highest sense, and gentlemanly in every feeling; very melancholy, making himself out to be selfish and indolent, but in reality far removed from either. I should think a strange mixture of the grave and gay. He said he has become quite a fatalist since we came, [and] as he always brings rain and disasters with him, almost doubted whether to come today. He goes however by his own account frequently to his favourite resort on the top of a hill near his house to catch a view of Australind and its tents, the possibility of which he has only lately discovered and which he eagerly avails of.

Miss Spencer was in a regular passion at having the children by her side, which Mama had particularly told her was not to be the case. The consequence was she was little noticed, the gentlemen opposite being too much engaged among themselves to make an effort to amuse her. Mr Plowes was completely tipsy when he came and became so madly so that after leaving the table he threw logs of wood at the pantry tent and was so violent that many were alarmed till he was taken to his own tent.

All the others joined us in the marquee at tea and we had a very sociable evening in conversation and looking at Henry and F. Bell's drawings and my scrap book. My thoughts were so much in the past; this day year, the first of my residence in James St, and so much with dear P. and others who were with us the last party we had that I was obliged to exert myself to perform the civilities of the occasion.

Mrs Ommaney was very poorly all the evening, having caught a chill in the long water expedition hither. Mrs William in her wedding dress looked unusually well, and Christina very sweet; Mrs Gaudin most disagreeable and irrational, I think.

We did not leave and separate till half-past 12; rain falling in torrents all the evening; our tent in a sad state of wet; thunder and lightning soon came on; rain such as no one can imagine who has not lived in this climate; the night has been a truly awful one; the whole artillery of the heavens concentrated apparently high in the air overhead; lightning streaming like fire through the thin canvas over us; rain descending in sheets of water; wind at times sweeping with uncontrollable force against and around us. We did not undress entirely, but putting on our flannel gowns, lay down; Ellen's bed so completely drenched that she placed one tolerably dry mattress on the ground by my bed and covering herself over with damp blankets and shawls prepared for a sleepless night. My bed was wet and damp, but I found it acceptable nevertheless, being dead tired.

Gervase and Pearce stayed with us till 3. Papa slept in his tent and Mrs Ommaney with Mama. A few intervals of death-like awe-full dark silence only increased the sublimity and tangible idea of their agitation and power. I felt nervous, but trustful and calm, calling to mind our deliverance on the sea and the present proximity of the same merciful arm. I had once almost dozed when an explosion, as of an hundred cannons, roused me with a speed which precluded the possibility of my getting any sleep again, so that I did not for one moment lose myself all night and rose soon after 7. The worst storm took place at half-past 5. I never heard wind or rain equalled, or heavier thunder and lightning; the darkness too was so thick that we hailed the dawn of day with delight.

No future settlers can suffer what we do; for when others come they will find things made for them and our experience available. Friends in England should be made acquainted with the dangers of this Australian coast in this season. A fatal grievance prevails on the point and I feel horrified to think of people blindly coming out at any time of year, to be exposed to such awful weather as this. Had we come one month later, I know not what we could have done, and as for Port Grey we should not have been alive had we been there now.

Wednesday morning, 2nd June
Breakfasted in the store house being a pouring cold day. Mary is quite poorly from the effects of a chill and damp. Lucy is in bed in Mama's room from the same; everybody and everything looks indescribably wretched; all work stopped; the first beam in our tent placed and standing alone: so much for tent life.

Sunday, 6th June 1841
We have not long finished the service of the day through which I have gone with heaviness of spirit. The religious condition of the settlement grieves me much, inasmuch as the people seem to be a flock without a shepherd. None of the workmen attend and but few of the settlers, and it has become

a dead letter and form without sermon, without even the communion service as formerly; under these circumstances is there not something for us to do? This is a question which very frequently forces itself upon my mind, and a heavy burden it brings upon my spirit; and yet what can we do? or I individually?

Could Mama's meeting house be erected, an afternoon meeting might be the means of drawing a few together for the purpose of public worship and instruction, and Mama has this morning been expressing her wish to engage some of the carpenters to work at its erection during their leisure hours which they now devote to those of the settlers who require their assistance in building. Were we free from all opposition in all matters of this kind, how feasible a plan would this be; but to propose it is difficult, and alas, I as much as ever shrink from the opposing spirit with which all efforts will be met with on the subject. How often have I to mourn over my total want of efficiency in actively coming forward in matters of religious usefulness. I cannot; altho' my desire, my deepest desire, is to see truth prevail in myself and around me. I often think of Mrs Fry's exhortation 'to be fervent in spirit serving the Lord'; labouring in the ample fields spread before us, with great zeal according to his will and requirements; and yet – I sit down and do nothing.

Mama has been reading to me her journal of the last week which led to a few remarks on her part on the beauty of this climate, country &c and her conviction that did people come with intention and wish, as she did, to make it her 'home', there would be found happiness and enjoyment in it. I disagreed with many of her opinions, but she would not hear them, knowing, she said, how and why we differed, and it was therefore useless to say a word on the subject. I have been distressed, for differing in opinion never need destroy sympathy, and if I meet not with it in her, where now can I look for or find it?

The rain is descending in torrents on my rick cloth where I am writing; heavy thunder rolls on in the distance; the ocean breaking on the sea shore makes the very ground tremble. This is the heaviest settled rain we have had and it is very cold and damp and discomforting to a degree. The marquee was so wet during reading that soon after they adjourned to the store, which tho' crowded with stores is a shelter, and there they have kindled a fire of banksia cones which burn beautifully and as bright as coal. Usher tells me there is not the slightest prospect of our getting any dinner, the rain, as long as it continues so heavy, almost extinguishing the fire.

The storm increasing in violence, I here broke off the thread of my narrative and accompanied Ellen into the store, where I found the whole party and George and Valentine Smith sitting on the casks and packages around a vacant place in the centre on which a bright fire was blazing and imparting an air of comfort which nothing but a fire can do in such weather as this.

I wish I could give any conception of the scene this afternoon and evening; the former I passed in reading Richmond's *Annals of the Poor*, a work I always peruse and reperuse with pleasure; Christina and Ellen, perched upon the top of some packages at some distance from the centre of attraction, read also; the rain still falling in floods. A pot of pork was placed over our fire, the only thing that could be cooked under existing circumstances, but which we found with the addition of rice a very acceptable break in the day's monotony. A plank was laid across some boxes, and Pearce carved, while all the rest of the party scattered about on the piled up luggage and on a chair or two near the fire, broke their fast with considerable industry and gratification; Usher in attendance with his frying pan, supplied us with excellent fritters. Our meal being at an end, Mama and Mary occupied themselves in frying pancakes for the servants, and we thought of the amusement it would afford our beloved absentees could they see Mama dexterously throwing the fritters on Sunday in such a place and in such circumstances. I think this has been the strangest of the strange scenes we have witnessed; every day seems to bring with it new and droll combinations; they pass before us like stage scenes or the varying pictures of a magic lantern.

All very sleepy and tired all the evening. Chrissy and I and some others suffer much from the wood smoke, our eyes are quite dissolved. Pearce slept in the store, his own tent being deluged. We had the pleasure of getting into thoroughly damp and wet beds. I slept in my flannel gown, and passed a disturbed night in consequence of the rushing noise of the water running on and in and through our tent, and the violent irritation on my ankles from mosquito bites. The inflammation extends over a surface as large as a crown piece, and a large blister often rises in the centre.

Of Thursday, Friday and Saturday, 3rd, 4th and 5th June I have omitted to say anything; the marquee having been torn in the preceding gale, it was lowered and we were obliged to make the store our place of resort during those three days. The large space, long table (boards placed on casks) and the sense of security it afforded, combined to make the change rather agreeable. We always had a banksia cone fire burning at one end on the ground.

Thursday was a day of almost incessant rain, attended by awful squalls of wind, which increasing towards night, we removed all our mattresses in: Ellen's and mine placed on the table, Miss Spencer's on chairs, the children's and Mary's on boxes and the ground, and Robert and Christina's at the farther corner of the room. We could not prevail on Papa and Mama to take shelter with us, and I passed anxious intervals lest the trees close to their room would give way, the wind was so tremendous. Friday night we also slept there, returning to our tent on Saturday, the weather having then moderated. The greatest drawback to living in the store is the dirt, the sand being very loose, and without either rushes or boards a constant source of discomfort.

Poor Charles Bedingfeld met with a sad accident on Saturday; while using an axe in clearing Coombanah Road, the tool slipt and cut the side and ball of the foot in a frightful manner. The loss of blood was considerable before the Dr effected the dressing. He was conveyed to Mr Gibson's cottage on a shutter, and I fear will be laid up there for some weeks. We saw the shoe through which the instrument had passed; a sole as hard as wood was completely cut thro'.

Monday, 7th June 1841

A calm fine morning revived my spirits after the depressing weather of the last week, and I set busily to work, to washing and various household occupations; unpacked and repacked my teak chest to get out something from the bottom, a long and fatiguing operation. Worked a little with Mama in the afternoon.

The interval between dinner and tea I was idle enough to pass on my bed with Ellen talking over the past &c. Dr Carpenter more cheerful than of late. All went out at 10 to see an old tree burn, which being in the line of road and too near Pearce's store, was given over to the flames. The sight was a very interesting and picturesque one and reminded [me] of Cooper's description of the backwoods on fire in the 'Prairie' or 'Last of the Mohicans'; I forget which. We did not see it fall, tho' apparently only supported by a shell work of charred wood, and it is even now standing, though a breath of wind would, one would imagine, lay it low. Lightning at a distance made us fear a storm, but we have passed a quiet night, distant thunder this morning being all that we have heard of the anticipated thunderstorm.

Thursday, 10th June 1841

Since Monday my time has been occupied much by writing, copying parts of my journal, in order that I might send the original to Pris.

Mr Greenside completed his house on Tuesday; it is a neat little dwelling consisting of two rooms, roof and sides, thatched, and two windows on each side. It is the neatest hut yet built. He most kindly came down and pressed us girls to take possession of it till our building is completed and was very urgent in his request. I of course could not think of keeping him out of it.

I was returned from a stroll in the bush with Rachel, having separated from others who were taking a walk, when Mary and Pearce met me with a packet of letters in his hand. It was a moment of delight and fear, mingled feelings.

Tuesday, 15th June 1841. Australind

Like yesterday I feel totally unsettled, indolent and dull. The weather is so depressing to the spirits. The influence of rain, when dwelling in tents without internal order and domestic comfort and arrangement is particularly depressing. My room in the 'hut' being nearly completed, I feel all the unsettlement of an approaching move, and am waiting most anxiously for the completing of the brick floor to begin moving in all my things. Small as it is for 3 large people (being 15 feet by 11 only) yet I anticipate the change with considerable satisfaction. The wretched wet and dirt of our rush ground, the damp and wet of the rick cloth, more or less everything under it makes me long to get out of it.

I have been reading Alison for an hour or two this morning, and that is the extent of my occupation. At other times I have been wandering about and standing at the edge of the estuary watching the heavy showers of rain sweep in heavy mist across its waters. Every sound, whether of breeze or of wave only seemed to touch some triste chord, so I returned resolved to dispel melancholy thoughts (a difficult task at times). I am thankful and contented in the present and my hopes lie in the future.

Yesterday I spoke with Charles Bedingfeld who was enjoying sunshine and air for the first time since his accident. His foot is going well, but he looks thin and pale. There has been again a disturbance with Miss S., the old story, falsifying, mischief making &c. Papa had a serious talk with her; he will not allow her to leave to go to Perth, but said he should send her back to her uncle. She was in dismay at that suggestion and apologised and implored so hard to remain that it has been overlooked and made up.

I do trust there will be no more difficulty.

Wednesday, 16th June 1841

A notable day and one that will be long remembered, that of getting into a house again, and a termination put to living in tents. Slight as this cottage is, being only formed of thin planks with a rush thatching as roof and ceiling, a floor composed of a layer of bricks packed close and tight together upon the sand, the sense of comfort and enjoyment I feel in taking possession of it can only be imagined by those who have lived as we have for 3 months. Papa obtained from Mr Thomson some windows for each of the rooms; they are large for the size of them, and open down the centre in the true cottage style. This is a luxury I especially enjoy, and I can scarcely do anything but gratify the childish gratification I feel in looking through glass again. The view of the estuary from this cheerful sash is always a pretty scene.

I sent up my bed yesterday hoping to have got in last night, and had the pleasure consequently of making my bed on some chairs in the tent. The night was very boisterous, and I rejoiced to think it would be the last of exposure to wet and fear that we should be unhoused. By the assistance of Papa, Pearce &c we had all our things removed in and arranged by 3, when Pearce lighted a cone fire on the floor, to dry the wet sand on the bricks and the rushes which make the room feel very damp and cold.

I had several visitors, much to my annoyance. Mrs Gaudin came up, which discomposed me. I cannot fancy a person intruding at such times. Mr Gaudin and she dined with us; he is far more idiotic than I imagined. Some people still say that his peculiarities are faults of the heart and disposition, not head. I am not of that opinion, but I do agree with Christina in thinking him truly disagreeable.

A very windy, wet evening. The cold in the store is considerable when the wind is high. It blows through the open chinks of the boarding and the open space under the roof. The blinding smoke from the cone fire on the sand in the centre of the little space we have to sit in, is almost more disagreeable than the evil it is intended to obviate. I have been anticipating retiring early to enjoy my new room, but in consequence of the bad weather we did not break up till 12, and then I gave up my bed to Chrissie, placing my mattress upon my teak chest with boxes at the end to make it long enough. Pearce stuffed the open space under the roof all along with dirty clothes which served to keep out a portion of the wind. Pearce and Robert slept in the store.

I could not help comparing this night with the first Mary and I passed on our landing here. I cared not for the cry of the wild dog which woke me this night, except as being distressed to lose the poor goose which he carried off, a sense of security lulling my heretofore watchful senses. I never can forget those first nights of tent life. This spot was then a wild untrodden wilderness; bushes, zamia, brushwood and small trees thickly covering the soil which is now quite cleared; the dining marquee then just being erected seemed to me a most lovely spot, and I felt it too much so to like to leave the immediate vicinity of our own tent, and then when night came and we were left to ourselves; Papa and the two boys at some distance from us; all hushed; no one stirring, and then to hear in the dead stillness of night a wild cry like a wild beast, and presently pat, pat, round the tent, then the canvas shook as the creature sniffed against it and scratched in the hay which filled an open packing case. My heart beat when I tried to allay Mary's terror, lest it was a native coming in; for I was just as frightened, tho' I pretended to be quite calm. But after some demur as to what could be done we resolved to peep out and call Papa; that was an alarming moment. I feared to espy either man or dog. The latter it clearly was, for it yelped again and ran down to the shore where we fancied we heard him jump and catch the fish which rise to the surface of the water by the bright moonlight. The frequency of the nocturnal visits of these wild dogs since then proves beyond doubt that there was that night but the canvas between one of them and our faces, as we lay on the ground close to it; and when I think how lonely we were, how easily he might have come in at the entrance of the tent, what our personal feelings were in the security of our abode, I wonder we were not more intensely frightened than we were.

All this, and we have suffered much from nervousness since, is, I am thankful to say, past. Tent life, that strange scene in our history, is over. It will always be a singular episode to look back upon. I wish I could more minutely have portrayed some of its peculiarities, drolleries, discomforts. My journal does no justice to it in any way. During that period the necessities of life occupied so much time, thought, and fatigue, rendering unavailable any leisure hours, that I could not enter into every detail, and when I did write I only hastily expressed what I felt at the moment, instead of narrating events as they occurred.

Thursday, 17th June 1841

While getting up, a report was brought me that my beautiful yellow Wandle

House hen had been eaten by a wild dog, and it was soon to my extreme vexation and pain verified by Mary Ann's bringing me the wings and feathers, which too truly proved its fate. She perched on the same tree as usual to which our rick cloth had been attached and I can only suppose that the tree which reclined very much was accessible to the footsteps of the detestable dog. So all things that are valued come to an end, and alone of my [fowls] remain 2 only and 1 rabbit out of the 4. A very depressing day in other respects was rendered the more so by this loss. I so prized that hen especially, living remembrance of dear Wandle House.

Friday, 18th June 1841
Again a depressing day; nothing but domestic disarrangements...

Saturday, 19th June
A very busy day; moving again, glass, china and hundreds of things off the shelf in the store, to give the trestles of it to the surveying department. At other times hard at work at Pearce's shepherd's plaid colonial shirt. I sat up till 1 to complete it. Papa and Mama retired and we sat round the fire talking, drowning the sound of the wind and rain till 12. Chrissy slept with Ellen, not well, with face ache.

An excitement prevailed throughout the encampment in consequence of Louisa Lamb (Clarks' servant, who came out with them) having been missed since yesterday in the middle of the day. She left the washtub suddenly and has not since been found. Natives and other people have been in quest of her but have been unsuccessful.

Sunday, 20th June 1841
Pearce attended our meeting; reading afterwards, no sermon. Mrs Stallard returned thanks after her confinement.

A very lovely hot June day indeed. We strolled about with Mrs Gaudin till she went on the water with some of the young men. After wandering with Mama and all down Coombanah Road, Chrissie, Bob, Pearce and I accompanied Papa, Mr Treene, Valentine Smith to Aylesbury Hill, Mount Cameron, down to the swamp, home. The former is a sweet spot commanding a view which, if not intercepted by foliage, would be almost panoramic; the distant country and even the nearer valleys clothed with trees always reminds me of French views. Robert killed a small yellow, very venomous snake. He cut off its head and it continued to move and the mouth to open for a long time afterwards. In the tea tree swamp we found the tree I have heard described. It is 42 feet in circumference at the base and is a venerable monument of antiquity affording a fine subject for a sketch.

Parties have been out all day in search of poor Louisa Lamb. Our shepherd Thomas who led his sheep down to the Brunswick in search was led by the barking of his dog to the spot where she was sitting too exhausted to move. He led her home in a state of dreadful thirst and exhaustion, having tasted no water or food since Friday. Mama went down to Clarks' to see her, but she covered her face with her hands and cried bitterly and did not wish to be seen. She wandered into the wood accidentally, she says, and lost her way. She could not have lived another night; the two last she passed in the hollow trunk of a burnt tree. There is no doubt, I think, of her being a little deranged; she has been so before and her conduct has been so strange at times that it would appear to me more than probable that she intended to destroy herself. She has said more than once she intended to do so to her friend Mrs Barclay.

A sad event has just taken place to our poultry. Robert by mistake for swans has shot Ellen's beautiful goose.

Monday, 21st June 1841
A quiet morning reading, writing and arranging various things. After lunch I walked with Papa and Chrissie down Coombanah Road. Worked in the afternoon.

Pearce and a large body of gentlemen were sent to the sand patch opposite to proceed to the store which a native informs Papa has been broken up by some Indians, and 3 casks of flour stolen. The night was very rainy and they did not come home to supper at 10. Some of the men who had been separated from them while chasing the delinquents, Troublehouse, Chapman and Wemar, returned knowing nothing of them. They crossed again to the sand patch. Later Papa fancied he heard the gun fired as a signal to send a boat. Not finding them, tho' dark as Erebus and raining hard, they proceeded down to Bunbury for them.

Dr Carpenter was sent for at 10 to see Mrs Macashen, Mr Eliot's shepherd's wife whom he has several times seen. It was quite a dangerous undertaking to cross the Collie such a night as this without a native or companion. The ford is nearly a mile across the 2 mouths of the river, halfway out into the estuary and at this time of the year the water reaches to the top of the saddle. Dr Carpenter is accustomed to these expeditions now. I pitied the poor creature whose pulse was to be felt by such a pair of hands as his are now; they are entirely black and covered with tar and

On a road to Bundaberg, Queensland, 1904.

sores and disgusting to the last degree. It is no matter of joke now; were I the lady of the house never should he sit down at my table in such a state.

Tuesday, 22nd June 1841
Began with the little girls French lessons and Worsley, Latin, as Dr Carpenter seems entirely to have discontinued any thought whatever of him. The wooden parlour being completed we moved a table and chairs in and dined there; it is a long room, bricked, 3 windows in it; the width of course the same as our bedroom. The night was inclement, and we felt it delightful to be under shelter and out of the uncomfortable store. A rather sleepy party.

Wednesday, 23rd June 1841
Washed all the morning after having attended to the children. Took a turn after lunch. Rain coming on, we sat in the parlour, working, reading aloud the life of Archbishop Usher. My fingers being sore I read the stories out of our annual all the evening. Neither felt well nor bright.

Thursday, 24th June 1841
We were much disturbed by voices in the dining room till 2 or 3 o'clock in the night, and recognising Pearce and Bob's I only imagined they were sitting up on account of the wind and rain. I was roused however early this morning by hearing Mr Plowes go into the dining room and ask Pearce if he had heard the news. This we soon found was the cheering intelligence received by a boat sent up on purpose by Mr Shenton and which arrived late in the night, that the *Vixen* with letters from the Governor and our packet of letters had arrived in the bay. Papa and Pearce immediately went down, altho' a strong gale was blowing. They did not expect to return tonight, but being unable to get the mails in consequence of the wind and sea, they returned to dinner at 5, having sailed up in an incredibly short space of time. We are destined to be tried about our letters. The ship – the *Trusty* – has been unable to land her mails for 3 weeks, and now the letters are in the bay, we still are unable to get them. A quantity of *Times* newspapers came with the Governor's despatches, and we have had great pleasure in perusing them.

Midsummer day in England; a squally midwinter's day with us. This day last year the haymaking party at Wandle House has occupied my thoughts much and has led me to dwell necessarily on those who shared in and those who contrived the enjoyment of that delightful day.

Friday, 25th June 1841

Again a very unsettled squally day, so much so that it was deemed unadvisable for Pearce to go down for the packets, and for the same reason we conclude Mr Plowes has not made his appearance with them. This is truly tantalising and unsettling. I have not felt very well, cold and comfortless.

Saturday, 26th June 1841. Australind

The winds have at length subsided after weeks of more or less boisterous restlessness, and the calm morning enabled Pearce to go down to Bunbury in his boat immediately after breakfast to bring back our long expected, long wished for despatches. I exerted myself industriously all the morning to get through all the necessary occupations of the day that I might be free to give myself up wholly to the anticipated most delightful but saddening enjoyment. At half-past 4 he arrived. As I watched the plash of his oars upon the surface of the sleeping estuary, while yet a long distance off, the excitement of hope, fear and joy alternately occupied my feelings, producing sensations which a 6 months absence from, and now communication with, the beloved ones far off can alone produce. We met him at the water's edge, and accompanied him with his prodigious parcel to the parlour with eager and trembling steps. Many of the young men stood around and received the scanty supply of letters for them, while many had the bitter disappointment of finding none for them. Amongst these were the Gaudins, Mr Greensill and others. How I felt for them. We all opened and read ours to ourselves.

This morning, 27th June 1841, I awoke to a new era in my mental existence. I lay many hours awake last night in thinking over the contents of my letters as well as of those mentioned in them, and then upon the past as connected with one individual whose unsought for appearance upon the stage of our existence has been fraught with pain and keen annoyance. I now for the first time am truly and completely and sincerely disenchanted of that most delusive of all expectations, that of meeting with consistency, sincerity and what I must denominate real probity of feeling and conduct among men.

It is a sorrowful truth of learn, the lessons of which are tedious in their process, long to be acquired and always dearly bought. This has been my experience and most especially in the trying circumstances of E. K.'s acquaintance. I was compelled to believe that his winning, uncommon and tender kindness and interest was sincere and indicative of more. I found it was compatible with other views; but yet there was a vagueness and mystery hanging over our last intercourse that I confess I could not unravel, and tho' I have not been so foolishly blinded as to connect him with the future, there has been sufficient uncertainty to make imagination call up possible (but not probable) occurrences after our departure, and in these speculations and surmises upon what the truth may be, there is always infallibly mixed with them much of the mind's own coining.

It was but a few days ago that Ellen and I were talking over this subject, and she expressed her expectation that we should probably hear from him. I could not accede to that belief, but I said I felt confident he would go down to Wandsworth, would long to talk to Waller and know something of us and that at any rate he would have received my books, which I never intended or wished as a remembrance of me, only a gift which I thought appropriate to his feelings, and trusted might be beneficial to him. My only and last desire for him, but not one of these expectations have been realised, he has *not* called on my aunts, not apparently expressed any interest, and *not* received my books. I freely confess I have been hurt and astonished at the 2 former derelictions, but such is the world.

My confidence is painfully and lastingly gone in men and now I have done with them. I most sincerely believe there is no such being to be found on earth as a *truly sincere and faithful* man. Love is all a selfish gratification of amour propre; friendship exists but in name; a froth, a flutter of the feelings, it may be, but extinquished by the same warmth that fanned; profession against spectre of unreal sentiments and expressions; in fact all centres in self, in vanity.

I seem now waked from a dear dream, for I once had confiding feelings, and insincerity and heartless profession were the last things I dreamt of looking for in the world around me; too confident in others or rather too much confiding in them. My sad mistake has been that I have manifested too much of the confidence I felt myself, the sentiment of all others the strongest in my own bosom. I am undeceived now; the illusions of early confiding youth are past. I am roused to a different set of thoughts, appreciations, expectations and hopes.

Here I am, the other side of the world from home, severed from my dearest companions, my freshest feelings withered, the sweet mists of life torn from my eyes, with nought to look upon in the world but coldness, dissimulation, selfishness; and yet tho' the surface is sore tossed and troubled, I trust the undercurrent is less ruffled, and [am] calmly dependent upon our heavenly father, in whom only I desire to centre all my affections.

The present occupies my powers, the future (not as concerns this world) all my hopes.

What will dear P. argue from the fact that this day I have not had the courage to look at my flowers, almost in blossom. Every other day I have visited them many times and passed many a 10 minutes in watching and tending them. Were it not that English plants are rarities here, and I wish an English garden, I would never see them again. They only touch a chord striking painful recollections, injured pride, public exposure, trifled feelings; these one would never willingly summon to the memory, and I court oblivion as I once courted reminiscences of the past.

1st July 1841. The Cottage, Australind
After determining to send my journal up to the day of despatching our letters, I am inclined to change my intention after reading the foregoing entry, for it may give an erroneous impression of my conclusions on the subject therein discussed. It is the ebullition of surprise and disappointment on being deceived in a person's professions of interest, as manifested by E. K.'s conduct after leaving. There is no personal feeling.

I have enjoyed the last few days writing and doing little beside. The evenings are so beautifully moonlit that Ellen and Chrissy have walked with me after dinner up and down the flat, separately, and I have enjoyed talking. The letters have given rise to so much conversation on people and things that interest me. My thoughts rest much in England today; but I am stupid in writing.

2nd July 1841. The Cottage
A soft grey day; after my usual walk after breakfast, feeding my chicks &c I again sat down to writing, finished my letters to Eleanor, Aunt Kate &c.

Houblehouse and another Indian were brought up here, Chapman having turned King's evidence and given up his accomplices in stealing flour out of the store. William Hooper brought the poor creatures to Papa. Their distress and terror appeared great. After trying to elicit as much as possible from them, Papa determined to send them down to Mr Eliot, and he to proceed thither himself tomorrow to be present at their examination.

Some of them will be sent, I fear, to Rottnest; a dreadful punishment it is; their heads are shaved and they become convicts in fact; but being deprived of liberty and independence so dear to wild man, they soon die of broken hearts. If this be true, what an affecting thought. Tho' punishment for all crime is necessary, yet how much mercy should be shown to this poor race to whom but one talent seems to have been given. When will justice appear upon earth? Not I fear while white man who professes Christianity falls so far short of acting up to its first principles. I cannot help liking these poor people, especially the children.

A squall of wind and rain is so awful at this moment that as I write alone in my room I could almost feel nervous. The roar of the wind is quite stunning and the estuary is entirely concealed by the floods of rain. How thankful I feel that we are under the roof. The rain streams through the children's room from under the door: an awful flash of lightning, and a peal of thunder roars overhead. This is the worst storm I think we have seen. It is now a little subsided for an instant, and the white waves of the estuary are seen again. Thunder, and how the wind sweeps thro' the trees. I shall prepare to make my exit to the dining room. It has been blowing tremendously all the morning.

3rd July
A wild dog was shot by Hoskin the night before last, the same no doubt which has committed so many depredations upon our live stock. He was not much benefited by his good cheer, for [such] a miserable, half-starved wretch I never saw; of a large size (if fat) with but very little hair, having we conclude had the mange. The tail is bushy at the end; it is a very unpleasant looking animal, and [I] would imagine it to be savage; in packs they say [it] will attack, but not singly.

Saturday, 10th July 1841
I am surprised to find it so long a time since I wrote my journal. Since then I have been much engaged and interested in taking sketches, when the weather has permitted, and filling them up in the evening.

Papa and Pearce went down to Bunbury on Tuesday 6th, to superintend the disembarkation of the *Henry's* goods. That night was a tremendous one. The wind appeared to us to be heavier than we have heard it; it may be that the sound is increased by the proximity of trees, but to our ears it appeared unusually heavy, as was the rain, lightning and thunder. On Wednesday morning, to prove how good an anchorage is Leschanault Bay, the *Henry* and the whaler have ridden the gale out quite safely, and the Capt of the former says, he is perfectly satisfied with it, and he is capable of judging, for since he has been there the weather has at times been very heavy and the sea tremendous. The goods have hitherto been safely landed on the Point, so we call Shenton's locality. Pearce took down a tent, and

 In the middle of a desolate Western Australia landscape, the Irwins erected a neat home for themselves in the 1880s, and Kate Isabel Irwin stands proudly at the gate.

there they have lived; Papa sometimes sleeping at Shenton's.

At intervals we have had lovely sunshine and warmth. Thursday was particularly soft, grey and delicious. We have passed our time very pleasantly between drawing and reading Nichol's *Solar System* out loud of an evening. Mrs Williams, in her husband's absence, passed one evening here. She is so active, cheerful and amiable that I am quite grieved I ever said anything unkind of her.

Poor Mrs Gaudin is in dreadful spirits. Her husband's state is so distressing; he repeats to everyone in the settlement everything that passes between them, or whatever he hears from anyone, so that the young men are as intimately acquainted with her wardrobe and other people's affairs as with their own, and his language is so bad that we have been cautioned not to let the children go where they could meet with him. He is highly objectionable and disgusting to everyone. Mrs Williams on hearing that he has said something false and most objectionable of her habits to the young men and to us, told Mrs Gaudin of it before him, and said she never would admit him to her hut again; and then afterwards informed her of his conduct and proceedings; she never before could open her eyes to the truth, but now is sadly upset. She ought not to live with him. He is not fit to take care of himself or her, and I think he ought to be sent back to his friends. He makes himself useful in plan drawing however, tho' so deficient in general sense.

I have had book shelves put up in my room and am made so comfortable by it. Everything becomes very mouldy tho' in my room, as much as in a tent. Shoes, books everything under my bed immediately shew signs of it.

I forget to mention that poor Mrs Macashen died, I think on Monday last. The next day she was buried at Bunbury, the ground being the burial ground of the future church there. Dr Carpenter went down to it. I have been much distressed at this event for she has left 3 young children and apparently might have recovered. [Dr Carpenter] says first one thing, then another; in fact, but I will not say more on a subject so trying and distressing as that connected with him. How could we get another medical man? If Mr Davids would but come out. I cannot mention several proofs of Dr C.'s more than inefficiency. I would as soon employ one of our own settlers in cases of illness. I confess his living with us is becoming more and more trying.

Sunday, 11th July 1841

A sweet day. After the morning services, the latter of which was not well attended, many being absent &c, we all walked some way down Coombanah Road, Gordon with us, and some of the party accompanied Papa and Mama to Aylesbury Hill. She has taken a really long walk without injury. I accompanied Mama at 3 to Whiley's cottage, where we propose holding the scripture reading every Sunday afternoon. Not many attended, but those that did appeared interested and could not fail to be so.

She began [with] the Bible, and as several present were reading men, she explained her views of the account (Mosaic) of the Creation, and the present system of geology so as to make them entirely agree. For many minds have been thrown into doubt by the apparent discrepancy between the facts evolved by the progress of science and the written word of God. Her remarks were highly interesting and clear, and I like her plan of endeavouring to show that the God of grace is the God of nature also . . . .

Here the journal stops. That seems a pity. Louisa Clifton was a sharply intelligent observer with decided opinions about people and the way they behaved. To follow the entire history of Australind through her eyes would be fascinating, especially since she was at the centre of that history, short though it was. Two years after the journal finishes, the Western Australian Company ceased operation and began a long and laborious task of liquidating the assets of a ghost town.

Confusion . . . in the beginning, and the end. Emigrants were left stranded in the bush with no money and no one to employ them. Most moved on, but not the Cliftons. The collapse of the dream must have been deeply discouraging after all their effort, all that sacrifice. Marshall Clifton was again without a job, and the Admiralty pension would need to be stretched very cautiously indeed in this remote region where so much had to be imported.

At least Louisa had left home by then. To the surprise of no one who has read her journal, she married Mr George Eliot in June 1842. The Eliots also remained in the vicinity of Australind, and the proper young lady who reluctantly learned how to do her own washing and to eat kangaroo soup, took on the special fatigue of motherhood.

Annie Baxter's sketch of this tidy homestead, with its garden and outhouses and fenced paddocks, looks far too established to be Yesabba. Even the man carrying water in buckets slung across his shoulders is picturesque. The conventions of a lady's sketch book do not accommodate drudgery.

Annie Baxter
'DOING RUSTIC SO WELL':
LETTERS TO HENRIETTA

1840

> 'A journal is a delightful thing − if properly kept; it reminds
> us of dear very dear old times & friends − Now in a strange
> country with scarcely a familiar face near me, I look into you,
> my journal, and trace the love, the affection of hundreds...'

Annie Baxter liked that sense of being loved by hundreds. She wanted to
be special. As a bride of seventeen, the vivacious and well-bred Annie had
sailed to Australia with her husband. Andrew Baxter, three years older
than his wife, was one of the officers guarding convicts on the *Augusta
Jessie*. He was himself a penniless lieutenant on his way to join the 50th
Regiment in Van Diemen's Land. Annie had married him, as she admitted,
when 'I was only bent on pique.' They were an ill-matched pair, and soon
the refrain began, 'Ah! No one can half conceive the horrors of an unhappy
marriage − but those who experience it − '

At least Launceston in 1834 could provide distractions for the young
Mrs Baxter. Here was a familiar world of social privilege where days were
visits and band concerts and gossip, and nights were dinners and balls. If
her husband did not admire her, there were other men to pay court − on
her terms. Richard Dry, later to become the first Tasmanian-born citizen
knighted by Queen Victoria, was her frequent companion. Together they
talked about books and people. Such friendships were flattering and pleasant; the problem of Baxter remained.

Annie hoped to keep her unhappiness to herself: 'My journal: I allways
come to you to enumerate all my grievances! No one shares the secrets of
my heart as you do − & why? Because your pages, like my little troubles,
will never be *seen*!' She must have exaggerated this concealment of her
'little troubles'. Baxter often spent his nights as well as his days away from
home, ostensibly at the Barracks with his fellow officers. By 1838 his wife
was complaining that he 'is becoming what he was before marriage − and
what gentlemen call "a pleasant fellow" − smokes all day − drinks at

night, & can sing as long as any of them – ' Her own circle of friends could not have been oblivious to her plight, particularly after she offered to show Richard Dry her journal. Still, she liked to think of herself as the silent sufferer: 'It is so repulsive to someone with my feeling to put up with what I do – yet nobody shall know it – '

If this dramatic gesturing was not quite true, it was certainly under-standable. Annie Baxter was highly romantic, and she refused to accept a pitiable role, such as that of neglected wife. Over the years she discovered that her gift for words could serve well in her determination to be signifi-cant. She talked, and she wrote. Her journal became a source of pride. Beginning with Richard Dry, the men who were her intimates read the journal. It was Annie's self in words, an autobiography which would even-tually extend to at least thirty-six volumes with more than 800,000 words. This is a prodigious amount of writing, and neither the quantity nor the quality suggests the work of a dilettante.

Between 1834 and 1865 while she was writing the thirty-two volumes which survive, Annie Baxter carried on a voluminous correspondence with her family and many friends. In 1840 when her English friend Henrietta asked for a description of bush life, Annie replied with a sequence of carefully composed letters. Today they seem much livelier and more readable than most of the accounts then being published in the British press. One of the best-known of these publications was Mrs Kirkland's reminiscence of her sojourn in north-west Victoria. This straightforward story of 'what happened, when, and where', was printed under the title 'Life in the Australian Bush in 1841. By a Lady.' It was included in the 1845 edition of Chambers' 'Miscellany of Useful and Entertaining Tracts', and was of the 'useful' variety, earnest amd instructive. Annie Baxter refused to be so serious. She could see the humour in pioneer life. Even when portraying an existence as arduous as Mrs Kirkland's, she would be entertaining. If she could manage this, her reader would admire her high spirits, courage, and determination; otherwise Henrietta might well feel sorry for the girl-hood friend now sunk in poverty at the end of the earth. Annie Baxter chose and controlled her material with skill. The letters do not read like first drafts, and it seems appropriate that she should have preserved copies in the sketchbook where she made her pencil drawings. Together, the letters and drawings make life in the Macleay River District of New South Wales seem a picturesque venture, whimsical if not always charming. Only occasionally is a note of bitterness heard.

The Baxters had moved to the Macleay in August, 1839. The year before, Baxter had been transferred from Van Dieman's Land to Sydney. At this time the government was making areas beyond the nineteen counties available for settlement. Grazing land could be leased for an annual licence of £10. A number of army officers were selling their commissions and taking up runs in the vicinity of the Macleay River, north-west of Port MacQuarie. Baxter joined their ranks.

Leaving Sydney did not bother Annie. After Launceston it seemed expensive and gauche. It was the alternative she did not like: 'I suppose that about the end of next week we shall have to leave Sydney for the bush – what I shall do there God only knows! I shall be so miserable – no books to read! or any person near me that I care about –.' A few days after this entry, she is hoping to go to India, but it's the bush for Annie Baxter, and she begins to think about it in a way one might well expect from a woman who came to Australia as a soldier's wife, with no thought of becoming a settler: 'I will go into the bush, make my fortune, and sail for old England!'

The Baxters made no fortune. They would have been amazingly lucky to do so. They were setting up a cattle station without knowing anything about cattle. They had no capital. The £525 spent on stock came from Annie's uncle, who appears to have inherited the family wealth when her father died. The times themselves were unpropitious: New South Wales was plummeting into economic depression. From the first, the Baxters faced a difficult struggle at long odds, but when Annie wrote to Henrietta she covered her 'little troubles' with humour and never gave way to self-pity. There would be no moaning from this lady in the bush.

Yesabba
January 1840

And so you really & truly wish to know what a bush life is! I'm not very au fait at such descriptions, but I'll try –

A bush life! oh! 'tis the most rustic thing you can possibly imagine – almost approaching barbarism – but to commence –

The time at which Mr Baxter took it into his head to settle, was August '39 – We had no house or hut of any kind of our own, nor had we even fixed on one particular spot to erect any – A friend of our's & a Bachelor, (what excellent persons this poor neglected, despised race are!) offered us his cottage until we should have our own – so to it we went – Very soon after, we pitched our slab hut on a pretty flat, close to a nice creek of fresh water –

I entered my hut, when only half the bark roof was on – and to add to our discomfiture, it rained almost incessantly for the first three weeks – It certainly was most ludicrous to see the Oposum skin rug nailed up to a rafter, to keep out the rain – We had two rooms – separated by a large Meg Merrilies shawl – The one was our bed-room – the other, sitting-room kitchen & all – We might almost have done without the kitchen – as you will say when I tell you what we had to cook –

Everything was most exorbitantly high when we 'squatted' (i.e. settling on Government land & not purchasing it –) and we determined not to get into debt – so we commenced feeding ourselves on Corn-meal – Now this is most excellent food for young chickens, but unfortunately we are not of this denomination; therefore we all began to look uncommonly thin – Baxter not being very strong, could stand it but a short time – and flour being £75 per ton, the next thing was to be considered *what* we could eat – 'Rice is low,' said my spouse, 'we will send for some rice; we can mix that with corn-meal, and I dare say it will be very wholesome'! We tried to fancy this wholesome food, and had nearly done so, when one day a friend came in – We of course asked him if there were any news – 'None of any consequence,' said he, '*only* rice is high'! Now this to us was very important, and I shall never forget the look of utter dismay that Baxter put on at this intelligence – enough to say 'We're done for!'

The rice came – we eat it with coarse sugar, & no milk – and altho' we did not find it improve our condition, 'twas pleasing to know that it agreed with others – to witness – the mice, cats etc – I really cannot tell you the millions that fed on our *Rice*!

At last our cows began to increase – and the dairy was made – but we had no person to make the butter and cheese – excepting our overseer's wife – who had a natural taste for the dairying & all that appertained to it – as you will see by the following circumstance – They lived a little *up* the creek – Now after making the butter, Mrs Webster used to wash it at the creek – I remarked one morning to the Milkman, that there should be a great quantity more butter than there was – 'Oh Ma'am, when Mrs Webster washes it, she lets it go thro' her fingers, and it then runs *up* the creek!' For a few minutes I was quite puzzled – for I never remembered in all my geographical studies to have heard of things of their own free accord, floating against a current – At last I understood that our fair friend allowed the butter to run *up* the creek into her hut, and then *down* her throat – so I dispensed with her churning, and commenced doing it myself – I succeeded pretty well – but oh! the labour! Often whilst busy in my dairy, have I cried, and wished I had been born a dairy-maid!

'Perhaps,' thought I to myself, 'I might have grown too stout in this very healthy district, unless I had had some severe exercise!'

About this time a young friend came down with her Mother to remain at her brother's – they were great additions to our small community – Mrs McLeod, who has been 18 years in the Colonies, is very well-informed & clever – but having known me in my 'better days', was quite astonished at the way in which I worked – and said I had more to do, than she ever had – This was a consolation! My next one was, that she pronounced my cheeses to be some of the best Colonial ones, she had ever tasted – And the greatest of all is seeing our Cousin, Mrs Kemp, with her nine children, & constantly no woman servant – Certainly her husband is a great help to her in her house, for between you and I, he is very old-womanish in his ways –

Then Philosophy too comes to my aid – What a blessing it is to be philosophical! In this way I will end the first letter – wishing you every happiness out of the Bush! I remain always

AMB

Yesabba
February 1840

Have you ever read 'Montacrite'? If not, do so – for it is very much our style of life in the Wilderness of N.S. Wales – The only very material difference is, that the writer speaks of servants in America being termed 'Helps' – whereas, I maintain that those of this Colony are, 'No Helps'! – These, being prisoners, have but one idea & this is how to get married, and settled – & pretty settlements some of them make – I had one who neither *could*, or *would*, do anything, altho' she should! – excessively dirty and wishing continually to argue with one into her own peculiarly nice habits & ways – These women are the pests of the country, they are such idling, tattling persons –

When my daily business was over, I used to go sometimes for a ride on a favourite Mare – Miss M. McLeod & I had taken an agreeable ride one evening & were returning, when we climbed up a steep bank to come home more quickly – My horse put her foot on a loose root when on top of the bank nearly, and she and I very pleasantly rolled back twice together – Poor thing! I thought she was killed – Marion screamed out 'Oh! she's killed!' and I in an equally sonorous voice said 'No, I'm not!' Over ran Baxter and first remarked 'I suppose you have broken her knees!' His anxiety was for Jessie – my Mare – Marion's & mine for – myself – Had I been hurt *more* than I was, it had been all the same, for no medical aid was to be procured, excepting a Mr M–n – this worthy person had been once wardsman in the Hospital at Port Macquarie, and this was his warrant for practising on we poor mortals – This Esculapius was called in, and after feeling my pulse, nodding his head significantly, and making use of the name of some tremendous nerve or other, determined on bleeding me – and so I was blooded with a penknife! Oh! ye nervous ladies, never come to the bush – I soon recovered – and *Dr* M– said, it was owing entirely to his medical treatment!

I had begun to keep poultry – but somehow or other my young turkeys died always, and altho' I reared plenty of chickens, they disappeared when fit to kill – Baxter said that our Overseer's poultry-yard thrived invariably better than mine! Many is the time I have cried with vexation & heat together – The idea of nearly killing oneself with warmth, and then to be told that everybody's poultry thrives better than yours! However, I do think that Overseer's poultry are something like a Midshipman's pigs – namely, never die! altho' he may have them for dinner constantly, still *his* never suffer –

Our sitting room served us for parlour, kitchen etc – In the bush, we have immense fire places – and a carpet hung across this served for a partition for our kitchen – I remember one day we had a large piece of beef roasting – the chimney smoked furiously – and we were putting up with this, for the sake of a *fresh* morsel of beef!! The old man who was turning it, kept on running out every now & then to breathe the fresh air – altogether it was enviable – when in came three visitors, one of them a lady – I do suppose she thought I cried with delight to see her – for my eyes were full of tears from the smoke! I asked them to remain however & partake of it, which they did –

My first kangaroo hunt in this country, was very entertaining – My beautiful greyhound, Ada, and another favourite dog took after some 'flying does' – and I rode off at a gallop after them – My friends could not follow for laughing at me – I never recollect taking so many leaps, in my anxiety to come in at the death – but I did not for all my trouble –

Captain Sturt says in his account of New South Wales, that a person may lie in the open air without being annoyed by insects of any kind! – Surely times have altered very much, for we have all sorts of knats, mosquitoes etc besides sundry indoor companions – people do differ tho' sometimes, and I hope for comfort's sake, that Captain Sturt was never bitten as I have been! Baxter often talks of your sending away your cup of tea at breakfast one morning, because you spied a fly in it! Why, I've had numberless flies in mine, and I take them out one by one with such coolness! And thank Providence at the same time, that my cup of tea remains!

After tea we generally retire – so I shall close my second letter to you, having arrived as far in the day –

AMB

Yesabba
April 1840

I this month had the pleasure of seeing a very old, and esteemed friend – who came down on a visit to Port Macquarie, and came all this way to see me in the bush! With him was a most delightful person, a medical gentleman – My friend was so much pleased with 'Yesabba' – and very entertained with my doing 'Rustic' so well – I promised to go down to the settlement to see Mrs Smith (our visitor's wife), and Dr Mollison (our other guest) asked us to remain at his house –

We went – and were very kindly received by our host – 'Twas this trip that introduced me to the élite of this 'Aristocratic district' – About 7 miles from the settlement, is a pretty estate, called 'Lake Innes', belonging to a very generous, hospitable person, named Major Innes – He formerly belonged to the 3rd Buffs – that Regiment which might take London by *surprise* – being allowed the entrée thro' Temple Bar, without *even* asking the Lord Mayor's permission! Is it then to be wondered at, that one of that favoured Corps, should wish to 'astonish the Natives' of this country?

Mrs Innes has a great quantity of her Native/Scotch/pride – fond of pomp & power! She likes, for instance, to send in a carriage and four, to take visitors out to the Lake, to pay homage to her, prior to her calling on them – However, she called on me, and I was from home at the time –

but next day, Mr & Mrs Smith, Dr Mollison, Baxter & I, went out to dine with them – We had a sumptuous repast – and servants, jostling one another, to try and help you first – Mrs Innes took us into every corner & crevice of the house, which she seems to think a curiosity, and so it is, in the wilds of Australia – but only a snug cottage in the country at home – We returned to the settlement in the evening –

I did not remain more than 4 days away from Yesabba – and found all my pets glad to see me again – You must know that I spoil every animal with fondling them – Horses, dogs, fowls – all follow me – I can tame anything, excepting myself – After being any time by yourself in the bush, you become attached to anything that looks kindly on you – and I feel this especially, having been always a 'Pet', myself – How variable is life! But I thank Heaven to have received an English education, that is, I'm fond of reading, – (passionately so) – working too – and I've almost sufficient good sense to see that whatever be our Station in this world, it has pleased our Wise creator to place us there – and altho' I do occasionally feel inclined to grumble, I always conclude that 'All is for the best', as it is –

The Blacks have been a source of considerable entertainment to us – I like them – and think, if properly managed, they may be of much service to settlers – They assisted us in many things – even in eating our *Rice*! They never intrude either – and so prove themselves much more mannerly than I am – having taken up your time with this scrawl –

AMB

Yesabba
May 1840

I finished my last with comments on the Blacks, and in the fullness of my heart, I commended their extreme shyness & good manners – Eh bien! A few days back, five *strange* blacks, that is to say most uncivilized, came to pay me a most unexpected, and I must say, setting hospitality aside, unwelcome visit – They insisted on coming into my hut, and touching everything – they had even introduced their heads behind the 'Meg Merrilies' shawl, when Ada growled at them from her bed (which is always close to mine!) – This rather undermined their courage – Miss McLeod, who was with me, determined on returning home – so I accompanied her –

You remember, dearest Henrietta, that you used all to say, I never knew fear! no more I do – it must be a terrible thing –

This is a page from a letter to Henrietta which Annie Baxter copied into her sketch-book, along with the pencilled drawings included in this chapter. Like her journal, the sketchbook was shown to favoured admirers. One of them wrote a lengthy tribute in return, beginning: 'This book was lent me to read by the charming owner [on] 19th January 1845 reader she is a most interesting creature and were you to meet her in the bush, the romantic part by the lake, a drawing of which is in these pages, you might call to your imagination without its being a very fertile one that a second Eve had arisen in these new parts.' Underneath these effusions, in Annie Baxter's hand and with her initials, is her response: 'The above was written by a kind friend but very great flatterer(?).' She has gone over the originally pencilled entry of the admirer with her own pen and ink. He may have offered discretion; she chose permanence.

To put my friends on their good behaviour, I asked them to go with us – it is only 2½ miles – This they refused, but said, they were going too, by and by, (a very indefinite time!) and would see me home –

We certainly did walk rather fast – and I spied my visitors, as I was returning – they however, did not come with me – so I was left to my own ruminations as I sauntered back –

Fond as I am of society & the beau monde, do you believe me when I say I feel happy at times, loitering by our creek by myself – occasionally sitting down and musing – Yes! I admire the bush for this – It makes us love our creator – We have so much to be thankful for, constantly – We hear trees, and limbs of trees, falling around us, yet we pass unhurt! I often say inwardly 'Lord, what is man, that thou art so mindful of him?' –

We have some pretty nature flowers here but I am unfortunately no Botanist – All that I do with them is to dry some in blotting paper – and collect others to adorn my most humble dwelling – A friend of mine wishes me to imagine myself on a gypsying party, all the time I'm in the Wilderness – I tell her 'no' – She says I am very discontented – She has a purchased farm, nice cottage, and on the high road to the settlement – she is very *resigned* – N'importe, le bon temps viendra – and with it your Rustic sister, to tell you all my tales by your warm fireside – Until then, addio,

AMB

Annie Baxter copied no more letters to Henrietta into the sketchbook. Perhaps they began to seem as coyly artificial as her neighbour's airy notion of pretending to be on a 'gypsying party'. Whatever the reason, the self-consciously literary endeavour stopped, while the journal went on.

Annie Baxter

'BUT WHAT, OH, WHAT CAN I DO?':
JOURNAL AT YESABBA

1843-4

Annie Baxter's enthusiasm for bush life is unexpected. Not many years earlier, she had been a well-bred young lady in an English boarding school, and her life had been that of her class. Even transplantation to Australia could be managed without undue disruption because she was after all still moving within the British Empire's military society. It was a society she knew well, for she was the daughter, sister, and wife of English army officers. In Launceston, her days could be spent doing much the same things as she had done in provincial English towns. What mattered were social engagements, spiced with flirtations and affairs of the heart.

Bush life for such a woman was an alien world, and yet from the moment Annie Baxter arrived at Yesabba, she was as keenly involved as her husband in the effort to create there a workable cattle station. She took pride in being able to use well those limited resources that chanced to be at hand, and was delighted when the seasoned squatter, Mrs McLeod, seemed on her first visit 'quite astonished that we should have such a snug hut'. During the first few months, Annie was also busy setting up a garden, the dairy, and a poultry-yard. Soon she was planting Tasmanian apple seeds and 'native raspberries'. As she worried over her chickens, turkeys, ducks and guinea fowl, she dreamed of making money of her own.

Fortunately for her sense of well-being, Annie Baxter loved the out-of-doors. On a rise near the house, she created a 'bower', where she could read and talk with her friends. In the morning she often went for a swim – which she called a 'bogy' – in the cold waters of Dongai Creek. For entertainment she had her greyhounds, and she watched with glee as the favoured Ada – a gift from Richard Dry – raced after kangaroos.

But . . . there were trials. Churning butter could leave her 'so fagged, that I don't know what to do with myself'. Then, the chickens got into the dairy and 'pecked my cheeses terribly, it's a very great nuisance after all my work – but everything goes wrong with me in this country'. There were so many problems which hard work alone could not solve. The world often seemed to hold more than Annie's fair share of antagonists. Someone strangled her Spanish hen. Ticks attacked her old dog, Spring, and after suffering a great deal, he died. Rain fell incessantly, and the dairy gave way with the wet. Such weather 'puts a stop to all work on the farm – nobody seems to be busy except the fleas and the frogs'.

Deteriorating health made everything seem worse. Annie complained of having 'the rheumatism in my face & head, for the which I've tried leeches'. Her throat and neck became so 'terribly swelled and red' that she could eat nothing. With some consternation she diagnosed herself: 'I do really & verily believe it is scurvy! I allways imagined only dirty people had that complaint but I'm sure it cannot be, for nobody ever was more particular than I am –' After the fall from Jessie mentioned in her letter to Henrietta, she may have had one of her four miscarriages – none of which she describes explicitly. Certainly her injuries were more serious than the rather jaunty tone of her letter would suggest. In the journal, she confided; 'It is God's mercy only that saved me – my arm is much bruised – my internal bruises are worse – my stomach pains me when I move at all –' Understandably, her spirits sank with the pain, and eight days later, the gloom still had not lifted: 'I'm getting better, but am still *but* so-so . . . Well! if ever mortal was to be pitied it is me! I'm so perfectly miserable in this vile bush, without a rational companion to speak to –'

The bruises healed, the bush seemed less vile, but she was still without 'a rational companion', and her uncompanionable husband was growing less and less tolerable. He was a general liability. Annie could treat comically 'the interesting squabble between Baxter and Mrs Webster – shall I ever forget it? Never – to see the former white as a ghost with rage, the latter red a turkey-cock – he walking majestically – she at a hand-gallop – both muttering as they went! 'twas more than good, 'twas exquisite!' When Baxter spent the Sabbath flailing about at all and sundry, however, his wife found nothing to amuse:

> 15th March 1840 – Sunday   What a Sabbath has been passed in this house! I can allmost affirm that not an hour of today has gone bye, without Baxter's horrible blasphemy! – he struck Supple and Scotchy – and swore at me – I care about as much for that as I do for him – not one straw – Nothing in this world will ever make me even esteem him! I positively hate him – his presence is loathesome to me – and as soon as ever I *can* get away, I will – and never return to him again!

 Annie Baxter thought Lake Yambuck was 'one of the most picturesque scenes on the coast', and the picturesque landscape is obviously what she wanted to draw, although we might wish that she had sketched the interior of her home, a subject which appealed to few artists or photographers.

Such moments of furious denunciation might have passed if it had not been for an incident two months after that desecrated Sabbath.

Annie's servant woman arranged for her mistress to come upon Baxter having sexual intercourse with another woman. A black woman. Annie was mortally offended. Part of the reaction was undoubtedly racial, but what she saw was something many pioneer wives must at least have known about. Annie's response must have been unusually defiant: she forbade her husband her bed forever. Years later, when she had finally made all the arrangements to leave Baxter permanently, his tearful protestations of devoted love were obliterated by her memory of that day in 1840:

> Really, had I not know the man, it would have made me wretched to see any person in such distress! but in the present case, I could scarely refrain from downright laughter . . . A man who, eight years ago, I found making a Lubra his mistress! Of whom my own servants complained to me! Love, indeed!

She went on to recall the strong-minded action she had taken, telling him, 'and with a registered Oath, that he must consent to take *for ever*, one bed, and I another; or else, I would go to my Uncle'.

Money was her weapon in this sexual battle. Baxter could not afford for Annie's uncle to know about their marriage. That uncle had already paid for the cattle at Yesabba, and Baxter was looking forward to the time when Annie would share a large inheritance with her brother William and sister Harriet. Any disclosure removing the financial props provided by Annie's family would ruin Baxter. Annie had a keen sense of her power:

> We were poor at the time, & I very well knew nobody in the Universe could manage better than I: so I gave him his choice – He consented; and no doubt thought, that in time, I should alter my mind; – he little knew me! Je ne change – qu'je mourant – Oh! nobody will ever know the bitter temptations & Trials I've had – the offers sotto voce, that I've had – and refused – No! if I loved, I would give up heart & soul – but not because I merely had to contend with Poverty, unkindness, & even brutality! These, what are they? mere nothings – I knew my health was going; my life wasting – yet it was myself who had made all this misery – I had no one to accuse of it but myself! Well, years have passed, and still I have been to the man I married only a *friend*. This, I have been; studying his whims, looking after his affairs, and in all but the *one* instance, a good wife.

The one instance involved Robert Massie, a Commissioner of Crown Lands. Soon after his arrival in the Macleay River District in August 1842, he and the Baxters travelled together to New England. Amidst the social frivolities of the Armidale races, Massie and Annie Baxter became lovers. Her husband must have been suspicious about what was going on; when he read Annie's journal, he knew. Not surprisingly, he destroyed the journal and the love affair. Massie, on the other hand, kept the journal Annie had characteristically lent to her intimate friend, and now, thanks to husband and lover, the volumes covering July 1841-July 1843 have vanished. Presumably under pressure from Baxter, but without explanation to Annie, Massie did relinquish his mistress. His aloof manner, cool and apparently uncaring, dismayed Annie. Years later, when she had left Baxter, the Commissioner wrote protestations of deep love, telling her that he had tailored his behaviour to suit her good. Perhaps – but Annie didn't see matters that way in her final months at Yesabba.

Yesabba, July 1843
I think I had written about thirty pages at the other end of this book, when one day my amiable consort tore them all out! Nothing could have much more annoyed me altho' if he had asked me to read it, I would (notwithstanding a few pieces of abuse of him) have shown it him – not so! He went while I was in the settlement and made a second key to my drawer, read my journal – and replaced it – in the meanest manner possible – This, he may see with all my heart – and I trust he will like it –

My N. England trip was described in it – Perhaps the happiest tour I may ever make! How often I recall those wet, dismal days! Certainly the society one is in, makes the day gloomy, or cheerful – for I never felt anything but the latter on that occasion –

Since my return, however, I have had a 'glorious' season of discontent – After my return to Port Macquarie, I went to stay a week at Captain Joblings' – this was in April – I certainly was very happy! We had such nice walks & such a ride! I felt then, that it would not last – it was in Horne's words 'that night, 'twas heavenly; But 'tis past!'

Eh bien – the morning Mr Baxter made his appearance, and said he had come down for me – I had previously promised Messrs Massie & Montgomery to go up with them – this was *not* to be – so that when they came to breakfast I told them so – I shall ever remember Mr Massie's look which this occasioned – He seemed to believe that I had always intended not to go with them – this was most erroneous – indeed I had too much anticipated it! For my rides to the settlement are always one continued *row* the whole way – I remained at Mr Freeman's that night – and Maria accompanied us home the next day – After she had left, commenced the most terrible disturbance I ever witnessed – Still I continued to plod on in the path of duty! Oh! If I had loved a man with my whole soul, I should have hated him after such an outbreak! How much worse so then when I entertain such thorough contempt for him!

Maria came back again the following week – and I was obliged to send for her Papa to take her home – I could not bear that a girl so young should hear the dreadful language that was made use of by her Uncle – He struck me several times and even threatened & attempted to cut my throat – Really I sometimes wish he had! for the torture of my mind is scarcely bearable at times – I know, that my old presentiment will be verified yet – I shall die wretchedly!

Captain Briggs offered me a place in his house if I would go – but I knew how ill he could afford it – & therefore remained – I firmly believe that no woman of the *lowest* description ever had more abuse than I have – And yet positively he has the audacity to wish me to behave as a *wife* should! He told Captain Briggs that I had left his bed without rhyme, or reason – How well he knows to the contrary! I wrote to William saying that my health required change of air – and asked him to lodge my passage money in Mr Miller's hands but it will be nine months before that can be –

Mrs McLeod is come to the settlement to live – A day or two previous to her arrival, Mr A. McLeod & Baxter had a quarrel – In the first instance the former was certainly in the wrong – but he received so much abuse, that I don't wonder at its ending in the way it did, in Mr McLeod kicking his *friend*! The latter called him 'In my pay'! Now until Captain Briggs explained this a little I positively did not understand him – I even said, 'You know, I never have money to make presents to anyone!' He then vented his spleen on Mr Massie, and sent word that he wished him to discontinue his visits here! so that I have never seen, or heard, anything of him since we parted at Yarloowa! How I look forward to seeing him at home, where my word & looks will not be censured – and where I can say how much I esteem him as a dear friend and one whose advice I would take sooner, than any one else in the world –

If Baxter could only have heard him so frequently taking his part and blaming me! but it does not signify talking – they shall not be named together –

July   I went last week to the settlement, as Margaret McLeod came up for me – In the following day Baxter came down too – altho' he said he should not leave home for a week, if at all – This was because he heard the Commissioner had gone down – Why, he must be an idiot to think that his continued watching would prevent my seeing Mr Massie if I chose! Nothing on earth should – if I intended otherwise – However, he met with a very cool reception from Mrs McLeod – and she kindly offered me to stay with her, until I heard from home – and tried all she could, to prevent my returning to Yesabba with Baxter – *Everybody* tried their persuasive powers for the same purpose – but No! Fool that I am, without advice from one quarter, I have returned!

I am making my clothes to go – but I often think, I never shall wear them, for so happy a purpose! This may be from my low spirits – but I have strange ideas sometimes – At times Baxter says the day I go, will be his last! at others he wishes me to send him various things from England – And now he is continually annoying me to sleep with him again before I leave – Now this is a most *knavish* idea – He knows very well that after having had four miscarriages and not having for so long a time been in the way of having more – that I should naturally be *enceinte* immediately – He would then lay it to my conduct on board a ship going home – But I had the advice from one older party than myself – on no account to humour him in this – There was no occasion for giving in – for I am not of a prostitute disposition – & this would be mere prostitution –

I feel so sorry at leaving this place (associations have rendered it dear to me) And if Mr P. Stephen purchases it, I will ask him to let me *rebuy* it again – and if I should never see it again! Why my thoughts will waking & sleeping revert to the happy warm days I've enjoyed here –

My mind frequently dwells on a lovely spot which we passed going to N. England – it was a beautiful bend of the McLeay – and Mr Massie & I had advanced before the rest of the party – I recollect saying, 'How I would like to live here with my horse, my dog, & a black boy to shoot & fish for me!!' My companion's remark amused me considerably at the time –

23rd July   Mr P. Stephen was here yesterday and only left this morning – He brought me a most kind letter from Mr Muller – in which he offers to cash me a bill on England for £100 – It is indeed a kindness I could never have expected from him and which I shall always remember with gratitude –

Mr Stephen will not agree to give what we want, so Baxter will not sell it – He however thinks of going to Port Phillip to sell some bullocks, and pay what he owes down here – Margaret has sent me some songs & patterns of collars (or 'colors' as she spells it!!) It is very thoughtful of her, & I will teach her to spell the word, for her trouble –

Last evening a most curious thing occured – We had walked up the range after a cow, and being steep we sat down on a tree to rest for a time – I for fun began to howl like a Native dog – when to our surprise one of them came out of the scrub, and answered me twice! This fact would be considered too marvellous for truth – so I shall not mention it –

Mr Salwey has been up staying four days – The rain brought in a flood, and he could not cross the creek – One day while he was here, Baxter flew in such a rage and abused Mrs McLeod & the whole _____ tribe with all his heart!

Somehow, all the interest I took in this book, is gone! I can scarcely find a word to put in it –

Friday   I don't know what day of the month it is! On Sunday last I looked once more thro' Byron. This day week while Baxter was out, I took his horse and went over to Sherwood to see Marion whom I heard was ill – Capt Campbell was there – and wished to ride home with me, but I declined the honor – He paid us a visit on Sunday – He told me that Capt Briggs had found my portrait – and just as I went in they were arguing whether he should see it, or not – I am in much better spirits the last day or two – why – I don't know – exactly – unless mes châteaux en Espagne excites me a little – Hélas! ils ne viendront jamais!

Mr P. Stephen was here last week – and he and Baxter cannot agree about the station – we think of selling it in another quarter. I shall not be able to leave before October I fear –

Wednesday   I certainly know the day of the week – and that is all – I have no idea as to the day of the month – It signifies now very little to me what it is so that it passes. How some day I may wish for an hour only of time which I feel now delighted to have done with –

Baxter has gone down today to the Settlement – and very loathe he was to do so – His principal delight now is to run about after me – and it makes me perfectly disgusted with him – When I've conversation it is exceedingly *chaste*!

He believes that I will live with him as husband – altho' I do so constantly tell him to the contrary – but his density surpasses everything I ever saw –

I had a long letter from dear Harriet – She tells me not to wait for my 'butter and cheese money' to come home – but to draw on her or William for it – At times I feel quite au despoir – I know if I went to Mrs McLeod's it would cause so much talk & there has been so much of that already –

We have had an immensity of rain lately – to add to the delight of being caged in the bush! Baxter wished very much that I should have gone to Glencoe with him and have remained there until his return – but I know it was only Jealousy which prompted the offer – and besides which I preferred remaining at home – The other morning while I was dressing he asked me if I would not like to have *one* child? I said 'No, I would never have a child by a father I destested!' 'Then whom would you like it to be?' said he – How often I think of a day in which it was said to me 'You would not mind having two children would you?'

William is going abroad again – I trust it may be here – for I should then return here & somehow I cannot endure leaving it – for 'where the treasure is, there will your heart be also' –

3rd of September   So much have I adventured by travelling – I rode over to Sherwood today, and had a long chat with dear Captain Briggs – He has a wretched time of it, poor fellow! He can neither go across the river, nor can anybody come to him – He commends me for coming back from the settlement with my husband – so that in this instance, thank God, I acted rightly –

Yesterday a man went from this, and brought me a basket which has been away some time, but no word accompanied it – If I lose this one friendship, I am indeed wretched! Perhaps my Uncle may come to my aid – I hope so –

Oh! that I had never come to this place! I will, if I go home, tell my Uncle I would rather have £3,000 now, than the £20,000 at his death – for I can then assist those I love and be comparatively happy – I shall never be entirely so again –

Miss Jobling was telling Margaret how very much D.P.M. was in love with me – that she had never seen such perfect idolatry! Yes! he was very fond of me, and studied my whims in every way – but being *in Love*, and Loving, are two separate things – How well I recollect his quizzing me about R.Y. and saying what a pity it was – this, until the other day, rather amused me – but I was then told, there *had been* truth in the Quiz – altho' never the remotest on my side – Well he is handsome & gentlemanly – yet I could never be in love with him –

Mrs McLeod wrote to me, and speaks very harshly of Baxter – She still begs of me to go down and leave this place – but I cannot –

I have one of *Miss Grey's* buttons attached to a locket, and which I value extremely – I was looking at it today & thinking of the time it was given – those were the Halcyon days –

Baxter wished me not to mention to any of my friends at home what has occurred between us – I will not just name it, but if I am asked any questions, I shall answer the truth – Harriet says, 'It will be a relief to your mind, so tell me all your disagreeables; of which I fear, you have too many' – Nobody knows the half – I would be ashamed to name them –

There was a letter from Mr Salwey today – He says he is thankful for our kindness to a sick colt we have been nursing for him – Baxter wishes to get him for *me*, nominally – what would he say if he knew – I had refused him? But I was obliged to send dear old Crockford home – so I will have nothing to do with any more – The creature altho' unbroken, eats thistles out of my hand!

The other morning Mr Baxter was going to *burn* the *History of Scotland* – I told him, I would thank him to leave *my* books alone – He said I had no business to receive presents – so I can quote this, if he hears about the colt – Had it been a good horse, I would have taken it and given it to Mr Massie –

Baxter intends taking a chère amie to Port Fairy with him – I hope she may keep him there & I told him they would be welcome to all the stock – We have now upwards of 900 head of cattle – and about 16 Horses & Mares – and I suppose I shall never have the benefit of *one* of them, even – The two Mares, I wished left with Isabella & Annie on thirds – but Baxter insists on taking them – Poor Jessie – I would like her to be well treated!

4th Monday This morning the Stockman told me that I 'had a down' on him for telling his Master tales about me! And that he heard I was over at the Commissioner's yesterday – To think of a Convict being made a spy on my actions is too much of a good thing – I have a great mind to speak to Captain Briggs about it –

In 1844 the Baxters left Yesabba for Yambuck in the Port Fairy District of Victoria.
There they started over again, but built this homestead which looks promisingly
substantial, if rather stark in its newness.

9th Saturday   On Monday Messrs Robertson and Baxter returned – the former quitted again on Wednesday – He wishes his brother to buy our station and seems much pleased with it himself –

On Tuesday Mrs Kemp passed the day with me – She can be very agreeable when she pleases – Wednesday a Mr Innsborough called – He is originally from N. England but has been for six weeks nearly on his travels from one station to another. He is one of three brothers, who some twelve months back, rode up the McLeay – Having lost their way, they became much starved – and at last had recourse to killing one of their horses – they remained 7 days eating him – and then carried his shoes up to N. England with them!

On Thursday Baxter exchanged Percy for a small Mare – since christened Baby Blake. He rode her over to Kempsy with Gusty Kemp & I – Mr P. Stephen was there – I rather think he is smitten there with Mrs Hall – She is very pretty and has seen much trouble!

We returned very late – I saw Magistrate feeding by Dandingalon – and when I reached home found there letters from Mrs McLeod, Marion and Isabella. Marion gives me an idea of N. England & its people – She says she likes Mr Baker – that he nearly won her heart for the way in which he talked of me – I did not know I was so great a favorite with him – How I remember him leaning over my chair at 'Armidale' – and the looks it occasioned! It seems that my new acquaintance remembers me better than my old one!

Marion makes it as an express request that I will speak to her brother when I see him – I shall – and what is more, not one of the family shall know the reason *why* I cut him – I think too Mrs McLeod has her notions on the subject – for she said 'You know best whether to forgive him, or not – but it would make us all so happy if you could.'

15th Friday   On Monday last, I received a note from Margaret, and some lollypops too! Last week I had three books sent up – They were *The Bishop's Daughter* – *Emma de Lissan* and *Klopstock's Memoirs* – The latter work I admired excessively! I never heard of him previously, altho' he is the 'Milton' of Germany, but this is from being unacquainted with their language – His letters to his wife, and hers to him are very beautiful – How they loved each other, 'twas earthly, and Heavenly! Would to God mine could have been the same for my husband! What ecstasy such feeling must be! On dit that 'stolen sweets are sweetest'! I doubt it – I should prefer uninterrupted intercourse –

On Tuesday Mr McLeod came over – I met him as if we had never quarreled – He had started to go home, when a thunderstorm came on, and he returned – and did not leave until the next morning –

Thursday (yesterday) we received a note from Mr Salwey, containing very distressing news about Mr B. Baxter's bill for £120 – this, it appears, will not be paid by the said person! It will involve us sadly – it cannot be avoided I suppose – but this I know is my private opinion, that he is a complete swindler – after owing the money for 7 years, to give a bill that he *knew* he could not honor!

So this morning early Baxter started for the Hastings to sell the station for any money. After luncheon, Captain Campbell rode a part of the way to Dungee with me – I went all the way – Mrs Hasker was very glad to see me – The reason she would not speak to Baxter was, that 'no man who struck a woman, deserved ever to be spoken to by man or woman again!' I asked her who *said* he struck me – She said 'Jeffries, he saw him!'

When I returned Blogg brought me a note from dear Captain Briggs – He says he will try and come over on Sunday, and see me – I do like him, and I can tell him all my troubles, and am sure to meet with a sympathizing friend –

On Sunday Captain Campbell is to dine, and remain all night, at Major Kemp's – I recollect Dr Mollison telling me of the night he remained there – sitting on the verandah wishing for daylight to bring him down to our Station – how that day too, he waited under a tree for Maria & I to go to bathe, and stoutly maintained that we were two hours away!

I was settling Mrs Johnson's account yesterday, & she was telling me that Mrs Rudder had told her to make haste back, as she expected her accouchement immediately! This is only the 13th! And the poor children have positively scarcely a mouthful to eat – this is tempting Providence indeed! *Why* do they have any more? I remember telling my pretty little friend Mrs C. F. that she must not have any more children – She answered quaintly, 'But how is it possible for married persons to avoid it?' Just as if the bare ceremony of matrimony was to be the cause of myriads starving!

16th Saturday   I had a visit from Mrs Hasker today – She was quite pleased with the alteration in the place –

I was writing to Captain Briggs a note to accompany two books – Many a tear has it cost me to make up my mind to what I have penned – it may be for the best but it has been to me a bitter trial – I feel now perfectly broken hearted and alone! and I shall go into the bush at Port Fairy, & try

& do my duty, so far as to get Baxter out of debt – this is *all* I can do – People when they see me with my face flushed with anxiety and intensity of feeling, think me one of the laughing, gay throng!

Tomorrow ends my comparative enjoyment in having my journal to write in! I cannot yet get over the delight I feel in putting down only a *part* of my miseries!

17th Sunday   It was raining all the earlier part of the day, and I had been busy thinking over 'the Past, the Present, and the Future', when the dogs commenced barking in earnest – I asked if any person was coming, and was told a gentleman was there – and a stranger! My *native* politeness, would not allow of his remaining outside, so I sent to ask him in – He appeared – very young – and goodlooking – such fine blue eyes – He sat down to luncheon, & said he was going up to Major Kemp's – He however, to make my story short, knew the Bremers, and so many persons that I knew – We became acquainted in a very short time – and he said it was Providence had directed him here – He is coming down to settle, and says he would like to buy this station – he *may* yet – His name is Benjamin – and he has only been out a week from England – altho' so young, (21) he is married and has two children! He sat for some time with me, and then proceeded to Major Kemp's – He will return on Tuesday – John Bremer is going to marry Miss Lewis – He has bought Mr Lewis' station – Silly boy! She is neither clever, sensible or accomplished – this for the bush!

18th Monday   In the forenoon Mr Baxter returned alone – It rained very much –

23rd Saturday   Yesterday Mr Baxter rode up to Major Kemp's – On his return, he saw his saddle, (which Blogg had brought up on a horse of Mr Salwey's) without the stirrups – He dashed the saddle on the ground, and threatened to give me 'a d____d good *hiding*' if I smiled – I took up the rake and gave him a rap with it, but not before he had struck me – I sent down by Blogg all the papers of import to Mrs McLeod, and not one shall he see again until I get my journal back –

24th Sunday   Mr McLeod brought me a letter from my dearest Uncle – He says William was very nearly coming to Sydney but will not now – I, however, think he will come *for* me –

I had three notes from Mrs, Margaret, and Marion McLeod – they are all expressive of much affection in their separate way – the latter girl is *truly good* – as her Mother justly observes – I don't exactly comprehend Margaret's note but will ask the 'Public Slave' what it means –

Percy Stephen is my beau ideal of a boy – He is so good hearted, unaffected, and candid – I could love him so dearly in 'William style'! His advice too was excellent – and I'll take much of it –

30th Saturday   Late this evening, Dr Carlyle & Mr Salwey rode up – the latter, good soul, brought me a letter from my darling William – and one from Harriet – The former writes in his own dear way, and tells me all I wished to know – Poor Bessie, is still ill – and is to undergo an operation in the thigh – They fear it will be of little service –

Harriet says my Uncle has just been to see her, for the first time since she was married – He said when looking over the house, 'All we want now, is dear Old Nan!' God bless him – He little knows what the same person is suffering now –

Poor Constance! Alas! that a girl so beloved by one so worthy of her, should have been so unfortunate! Harriet says she has had a child – by some married man – A man who would betray the trust of *such* a girl, does not deserve the name! How I have seen that same dear girl idolized by more than one – From my very soul I pity & feel for her – and I don't love her one iota the less! We are all subjected to trials in some way, and God help her, hers must be a bitter one indeed – She was the most remarkably ladylike woman, I have ever met – and all gentleness & placidity – My Uncle has settled some money on dear Hal & says her children are better brought up, than any he ever saw – He is living at Harpendon, and in Town, Eaton Square –

2nd of October – Monday   Messrs McLeod & H. Hill were here – they remained to tea, and then went to Dandingalon – The latter wishes himself in the Army again – He is not the only one – Mr Salwey took down Waterloo for Marion to come up & stay with me – I shall return with her for a few days – altho' Mr Baxter says most positively *not* – He said I only wished to go down, to be with Mr Salwey!!

8th Saturday   This morning to my great astonishment & delight in walked dear Marion – I was so happy to see the sweet girl; for she is in truth my beau ideal of a womanly disposition – We had nearly all day to ourselves as Baxter had gone to see the road party.

12th Wednesday   Messrs McLeod & Baxter, Marion & I, rode down to the settlement today – We dined at the Freeman's – and reached town in very good time – We found them all well, and glad to see us –

14th Friday   This evening there was a Quadrille – In the morning tho', when I was sleeping, Marion came running up to tell me that Mr Baker was down – He is as great a favourite with her, as with me – She too sees thro' his character – In the afternoon he called, and was asked to come in the evening –

Isabella and Annie came after dinner – then Mrs G. and the two Misses Innes – They are all exceedingly tall – The younger one, is in ill health, and looks so deadly pale – They both have such fine hair! This, *I* always observe, as I have so little of my own – We dressed, and made our appearance – where we found congregated the following party – Mistresses Gordon, Evans, Purves & Gorman – Misses Johnstone, Fattorini, Innes, Jobling – Mrs Gorman to my fancy, was the nicest looking in the room – Marion stoops so much, but she is a fine girl – and has so amiable an expression – Isabella looked pretty; but wants style – she is a very ladylike girl – Mrs Evans is so extremely thin, her shoulders are as pointed as my remark! Mrs Gordon has the look of a woman who has been in tolerable society, and is *still* very good-looking – Mrs Purves is too stout for an interesting bride, altho' I have no doubt she is an agreeable person – her spouse is rather of the same denomination –

But the male part, (the *Lords*, I mean, of the creation) require my attention – First then came Major Innes – decidedly the most gentlemanly, and handsomest man in the room – Messrs P. & H. McKay – McKenzie, Gorman, Halloran, Evans–Baker, Duff, M. & A. McLeod, Salwey, Baxter, Montgomerie and Robertson –

Mr Montgomerie is after Messrs Massie, Graham, and Stephen, the nicest person I know in the district – He has caught a good deal of the manière of the first of these – and of course improved by it – This reminds me, that Mr A. McLeod told me that some persons were complaining of being 'taken in', by my old friend – If he thought to alter my opinion, he was much mistaken – I shall, if even we never meet again, always entertain the same ideas of my *singularly* gentlemanly friend –

To resume my account of the entertainment – We danced and played, and went into supper about 12 o'clock – It was tastily laid out – After supper commenced the Bagpipes and reels – and Mr Duff danced some queer dance by himself – Mr Salwey & Maggy were carrying on their flirtation thro' me! The cows and horses were canvassed etc – pieces of honeysuckle flying about – and all *very* polite things said – Alas! they were lost on the party they were intended for!

Mr Baker was causing much amusement, at the expense of poor Miss Fattorini – this young person is a strange compound – She *appears* so witless – and all who know her say, it is complete Vanity! She is French, yet has not the *taking* manners of that lively Nation – She appears clever, yet deficient in common sense – Her singing was intolerable – Mr & Mrs Evans sang very well together – Their opinions seem altered – for *she* says now, that 'a bush hut with Herbert, would be happiness'! They are going immediately to the Goulborn, where he has obtained some situation – Mr Mackenzie is gone to China by the last steamer – I could not avoid thinking of the remark that this person made on the ladies the last party we were at together – and hope that he has entertained a better opinion of this –

When Mrs McLeod asked Mr Baker to come in the evening, he said he was afraid he would not be able – As he was sitting next to me I said 'Yes, come – for there will be some rather nice persons here – especially pretty girls' – He said 'Well I *will* come – but I should be far happier talking with you, one hour, than dancing with all the others!' This compliment I fully appreciated, as he really during the evening, talked more sensibly than I ever heard him – The party broke up, and all left, excepting the Misses Innes – and Jobling –

I had to take such a dose of laudanum during the evening.

Sunday afternoon, Margaret, Mr McLeod & I went to hear Mr Purves – I do not like his preaching at all; there is such a sameness in it – and too much gesticulation – I was so sorry to see Messrs McLean, Baker and Baxter come in just as the service was over – I gave the latter such a lecture on it –

17th Monday   Mr McLeod & I left town – we went over to Yarloowa – and found all there well – and looking as neat & pretty as ever – Dear Mrs Jobling is a person of whom I should never tire – Annie made me a present today – Isabella gave me such a very pretty bag on Friday – We remained to dinner – Baxter then joined us and after saying adieu to Yarloowa we rode on to the Plains – We reached the Mill very late – Mr Freeman was from home – attending a trial which is going on in Port Macquarie – between Mr R. Middleton and his brother's wife – From all I can hear, it appears a very disgraceful affair – and had I been in the lady's place

I would not have mentioned it, altho' seriously aggrieved – I don't know *what* I should do hardly in such a case – Were it a man for whom I had a regard, I think I should hate him – and if on the contrary, I should feel so disgusted, that I should lose all power, and remain quite in his possession –

Maria is grown very big – She is not a *nice* girl – I mean this literally – I wonder how she & others, can endure this country without cleanliness!

On Tuesday we came home – Dear Ada was ready to meet me – my dear pet! I don't know whether I should love a child *much* better – Talking of these, while I was down, a woman at Mrs McLeod's had a premature confinement and we saw the poor little creature – I should suppose that mine was as large, altho' I did not see it – Its little hands and feet looked too large for the remainder of its body – Strange – what thoughts it engendered in me – I looked at it – and thought, supposing it had been the child of some idolized father; every hope centred on it – and then to lose it! My soul would have been bowed down to the grave – The bare idea made me wretched – All my warmest best feelings are smothered and lost – and so let them remain – God knows best what is for me – and to his Almightly power I daily pray for that peace which the world cannot give –

In the evening I was returning from bathing, when Messrs Carlyle and P. Stephen rode up – I am always so very glad to see the latter – The former complains bitterly of his treatment at 'Elsinore' – They nearly starved him –

19th Wednesday   Mr Carlyle left this morning – Mr Stephen went as far as Dandingalon, and then returned – dear boy – I like him better than ever, for what he said today about an absent friend –

20th Thursday   Mr Stephen and Baxter went to Kempsy – and I've been happy alone – Mr Stephen gave me a pretty whip –

21st Friday   Baxter returned this morning – he says that Captain Campbell was in a most terrible state of drunkenness yesterday –

Dear old England is in a most tumultuous state – and Ireland still worse! – What will become of our beautiful country, and its poorer classes? What misery those have known out here, who never heard it mentioned before – Oh! that I could leave nearly all, and go to some little nook, and be happy!

Monday   Yesterday a note came from the settlement which obliged Baxter to go down today – Accordingly he started very early – I rode over to Sherwood – The good soul there, is looking so very care worn! I remained some time telling him all the news that I could recollect – I like to go

there – it reminds me of happier times – Mr McLeod was here on Saturday – I was saying what a very nice boy Percy Stephen was! He said quite
crossly 'Rather an old boy now –!' On our way up from the settlement I
was saying how glad Mrs McLeod would be if he would marry some nice
person – and how much I advised it – He asked me if I thought he would
make a kind husband? I said what I thought 'Yes! but a very jealous one!'
'Oh! you remark then that I'm jealous' – said he – 'I have tried so much
to overcome it, and other feelings, but I find I cannot!' This was extremely
unpleasant to me – but I turned it off –

How I fly from one subject to another! I had just returned from Sherwood, when Messrs Benjamin and Cameron called – The dray soon after
arrived with the 'Wife & children' – I walked to the gate to bring her in!
She is tall & shabby looking – not her dress; for that was quite superior to
mine – Very dark – with woolly hair – and to end my portrait, continually
says 'Mrs Baxter', and can only look men in the face! A broad Cork accent
and anything but ladylike – I remembered Mr Baker's words, 'I hope
Baxter will not think of introducing *his* wife to her!'

They remained but a very short time, and then proceeded to 'Upper
Dungee' – I do not by any means envy the situation of that Primitive
mile! – only 10 children – and no servants! People seem to think that I
hate children –

The garden is looking very pretty just now – and really in tolerable
order – Mr Stephen says that the Commissioner's looks so very well – He
had a rose in his coat from there –

Fishing has commenced and promises well – We had some good herrings
and perch a day or two ago – If persons could only spare time, and were
sportsmen, the game is plentiful in this district –

Tuesday   The Black is to be executed today in the settlement – I wonder
whether the unhappy man really knows right from wrong?

I am so glad that my Uncle is home now at Harpendon; dear Ada will
have such a snug place of it – I fancy I see the pet running about the
lawns, and spoiled more than now even, *if* that can be –

I rode up to Dungee this morning – trying to see the Mares – Mrs
Hasker was as busy as usual – After I returned I was obliged to lie down,
my head being so bad –

Eh bien! I must go to bed now – I begin to really like the Bible – and
when reading it every night, admire the beauties especially of the Old

Testament – I often wish that I had somebody with me, who would like it too – Altho' Baxter has laughed at me for reading it, I still continue to do so – and notwithstanding my prayers being inferior in words to those there expressed – still they are as fervent, and I trust that my Heavenly Father will hear them and forgive my iniquities – We are all liable to sin – and my unfortunate disposition leads me astray where others would be safe – It has been my misfortune to have had no Mother to control & counsel me – but it is too late now – I'm wretched –

25th Wednesday   Today I have heard of a most shocking occurence – the death of Mr J. McLean – The poor fellow committed suicide – It appears that ever since we left the settlement, he had been drinking very much – on the Saturday, however, he was becoming sober – (He had gone to bed, and the Major remained with him until he fell asleep) – when Bruce left the room, and took the light away – He must have awoke soon after, and finding himself alone, have felt frightened – The poor soul nearly severed his arm with a razor; his temple too, he cut – and his throat – He lingered until the next (Sunday) Evening – It is awful indeed to think of a man in his prime – with money and friends – hurrying himself into the presence of his God – May we hope that he is *allowed* into that presence?

Drink! what does it not cause a man to do? It unfits him for society either at his own home, or abroad – It puts him on a level with the brutes – And in this Colony, whoever *once* gives way to it, will never (unless by a most superhuman force) get the better of it – It is painful to fancy all this – & yet are there not so many instances of it? Talented young men – the very élite of any society, we see giving way to this odious dissipation! Many is the heart-ache their friends at home are spared by not being eye witnesses of this – They become perfectly maddened by intoxication – Even the lowest of men lose all respect for them – and indeed in *some* instances it is 'Hail fellow! well met!' with the commonest persons – Of what use has been their education – and their abilities! All to be buried in drink! – Baxter who returned today, says that Messrs Graham and Baker were quite as tipsy – and were racing, when both had falls – I wish it had been into some water – They both had left the settlement when Mr McLean died – I hope it may be a lesson to them, but Je m'en doute –

27th Friday   Messrs Gorham & Baker came to dinner with us yesterday – they are on their way to N. England – They left this morning after break-fast for Wobbra – They are both very strange mortals – yet I like them both –

The lake at Yambuck almost consoled Annie Baxter for her exile from 'our own bright Isle'. On the back of this sketch, she wrote: 'sometimes this very beautiful sheet of water is completely covered with Birds of all kinds, and the various notes emitted by them produce a sound so harmonious and sweet that astonishes, and together with the whole harmony of the scene tends greatly to produce reverie of the most soothing and lulling description'.

I had such an affectionate note from dear Marion – I cannot think how it is that she is not more admired – for to me she appears so very *loveable* – The remark made this morning, about my looking so *clean* quite amused me – The Commissioner will be back very soon – and I trust free from debt – He will then be happy –

7th of November Tuesday   I have been so busy at work lately, that my journal has become more of a Monthly Calendar – I don't think the less tho' – for my daily, hourly, thoughts are still fixed on the same subject – People tell me I'm becoming quite stout! – the fact is, my mind is now *made-up* – besides which I'm looking forward to seeing my darling brother – I feel *sure* that he will soon come out – I should be so happy to live with him out here – I had rather that, for a few years, than go home – Somehow, this country with all its *disagreeables* (how well I remember my lesson – would to Heaven I were taking another now!) has become endeared to me – Every tree almost about here, has its association – and as to the hut, oh! I do love it –

Lately I have taken to bathing before breakfast – and I find it so extremely refreshing – The days have been very sultry – it makes me feel at night so haggard and care-worn! I lie down just before tea, and invariably, when I rise to go to the next room, [I find] that my thoughts have been running riot, and my cheeks are wet with tears – This, to a woman is great relief –

Miss Brodie has been to see me on her way to Moonaba and returning to the Plains – She is about to leave the district – I like her for her sincerity very much –

Mr McLeod called on the way down to the settlement – He was saying 'What is the good of having a Commissioner for this district, when he is *never* at home – I could do all the riding he has to do, in a fortnight!'

'Very probably,' I said – 'but his writing is not so easily done by all!' By this timely repartee I shall not be in future subjected to hear an esteemed friend abused –

Kate Kearney has foaled – Badger made his appearance on the 25th of last month – We have him now shut in a stall, and he already does credit to my nursing!

On Sunday we received such an impertinent note from Mrs Kemp which I answered – Baxter says too tamely – not so – kind words turn away wrath –

Baxter has been over twice to Sherwood – I am very pleased at this –

Harry Freeman was up here – I never was more tired of anybody's company – he talks so incessantly! I recollect once saying in his Mother's company, that two cousins should never be allowed to marry – as their children were generally idiotic – She then said that she and her husband were cousins –

At another time some person, talking of another, said, 'Oh! he is *cranky*!' 'Ah! ah!' said Mrs Freeman, 'you talk of this, and that one being *cranky*, but you none of you seem to think *my* two boys so, *yet they are!*' After this speech *she* laughed outright – and *I* began to feel the tears rolling down my face! – Different *Doctors* have different opinions – That a Mother should laugh at the want of intellect, or *any* failing in her child seems to me so truly unnatural – I am called *cold* by some – Let them *think* and *say* so – but I could not be so to my child! How glad I am that I have none!

'I thought you a cold coquette until I knew you better, but I now see, that you have obtained a mastery over most violent passions – and believe me, all who love you will do so the more, for the struggle' – this was written by a person who has seen and studied mankind – to me – I may now say *but* 'One struggle more' –

14th Tuesday   I have been worked & fagged near to death – for my servants took it into their heads to walk off without rhyme or reason – breaking their contract etc – The man was taken before the Commissioner & Captain Briggs, and sentenced *to be fined* £2 – This is to pay me for my Slavery – Oh! Justice – I had formed a better opinion of Mr Massie, than that private pique should interfere with public duty!

Baxter left this afternoon for Mr Graham's – He was to ride down with Mr McLeod – this latter person has commenced his old trade of talking about me – I heard yesterday a speech – The person spoken of is *living* – and it was only because on former occasions the one talked of was *dead*, that I forgave Mr McL.'s speeches – The second offence is unpardonable – Both parties were so truly, immeasurably above himself, that he is & was jealous –

I have been reading over some of Harriet's letters – and they make me wretched – I know so well, that she will fret at not hearing from me, and yet I cannot bring myself to do so –

I answered my Uncle's letter – and drew on him – Misfortunes never come singly – and so in the midst of them we are fined – for not having paid our License – It serves us very rightly, but it comes hard, these times –

Maria is returned to Sherwood – I hope she may be of service to her Papa now, for he is in a sad plight –

Marion writes to me very affectionately – She is recommending Margaret 'change of air & scene' – (a fit of discontent has come on, and then this is the best cure! –) I think Margaret is smitten with Mr Salwey – So Yesabba is to be the scene of *In-action* for a month – I had rather have seen Marion, but never mind – 'better luck next time' –

Mr Massie has not brought down Crockford – I wonder where he is! I don't think *sold* – My large Mare has a foal very like him –

I have my watch again – and I like to hear it ticking – it is companionable – and yet you have no trouble in making answers to it –

16th Thursday   I rode over to Sherwood, and stayed a short time – Maria looked pale, but better looking than I ever saw her – She told me a funny story about Miss Brodie & Captain Beadon – They have both left the district, so it matters little what is said –

Captain Briggs was going over to Yarrowal to see Mr Massie – poor Crockford is lamed very sadly – for life, it is thought – I wish I had him to pet –

Reading *Ernest* again – I like it better every time I peruse it – it is admirably written – Valerie is such a good character – and so womanly – I have my favorite Byron, out again – Margaret says she has never read his works, as she always understood they were not correct – What can be more exquisite than his language! it makes up for some little *queer* sentences now and then –

17th Friday   I had been very busy arranging and sorting, when I spied Capt Campbell coming – I never did feel more cross! (excepting, always the day 'My Mrs Cheers' called) – Well! now I can feel amused at our extreme coolness to the poor intruder –

I did not even go inside the doors while he was here; but waited outside in the sun! He remarked it; & I said 'People may say I encourage *you* to come – and there is one opinion I care for – so I intend being prudish' – He rode on to 'Upper Dungee' – and I rather think is remaining there tonight, as he has not yet returned – I took Cocky out to feed, and I picked up some raspberries – I have lived on them for 4 days – and with cream & sugar they are not very unpalatable –

How shocked they would be in England to think of my having been days together, on a Station in the bush, without a woman servant! Thanks to Providence, I am without fear – and nobody has attempted to harm, or molest me – excepting those who should have known better –

It appears that Percy Stephen's attraction at Kempsy is a girl named Kitty, with the alias of 'Marchioness' – The same who was (*figuratively* speaking?) 'turned up' by Captain Briggs and Mr Massie –

I'm afraid 'the Marchioness' has met with a 'Dick Swiveller' in many respects –

I never heard a place with as much 'Slang' in it, as this District – every other word nearly is some 'Colonialism' – (pardon the word!) I wonder if ever this will be read by the person to whom I gave my other notebooks? I hope so – I hear that the Commissioners are to [be] put out of Office – I trust it may not be true – I should sincerely sympathize in Mr Massie's case; as he is trying so much to get out of debt – & is only enabled to do so by his present situation –

Mr Smythe says that some gentlemen in New England are waiting to horse whip Mr Baker when he goes up! I would pity the first man who attempts it –

We were talking today of marriages – Capt Campbell said 'I am buying Briggs' cattle and Gun; he had better sell me his daughter' – I said he could not do better – He says he does not like very young men; they require to see the World, before they can be agreeable & truly companionable! – I said that at all events, no person need be ashamed of *age* – but that I knew *some* young men, who had more *natural* knowledge of the World, than all the old gentlemen put together –

It is very late – and I now rise so early, that I become sadly jaded by Night – I feel as tho' I could put my head ＿＿ eh bien! What I said on the beach one day – but the answer! oh! when shall I hear those words again? Never –

24th of November – Saturday   I drew for my £40 – as I wanted to buy some really necessary articles – out of it, I've had to pay £14 for the License – £2.15 assessment and £8 – to redeem Clarion so that I shall yet remain without much that I actually want –

We have two new Servants – the man seems a very good one – the woman is taken up with a perfect squaller of a child – Never was there a more odiously cross child born, I do truely believe –

I quizzed Mr Salwey well on his affaire de coeur – well knowing all the time it was Gammon – One day he went fast asleep, and I was sitting by him working – when all of a sudden he burst out laughing – It was a dream! Happy creature to be even happy in his dreams!

Mrs Reid says that not hearing from me for so long a time, she began as usual to imagine every misery that could be in this world, to have fallen to my lot – Much, very much, has – yet I have been spared many misfortunes – for this, how sincerely I thank God – How *he* whispers comfort, when all else seems failing – Prosperity has more temptation and we are called from the good *intentions* often – by a busy world – God is good, and forgives us – but oh! 'tis adversity that draws us *closer* to our Creator – and we then feel, that if all in the world forsake us, *He* will not, – and yet with such a *help*, with such a *friend*, I feel lonely! I rise before the sun – and toil on all day with one thing and the other, to avoid my thoughts – yet I cannot help being wretched – It is a terrible thing to feel *Alone* in the world! –

On Sunday last there was a Kangaroo hunt – when Tray (Ada's Grand-daughter) distinguished herself – 'Good blood'! as Major Innes said of me –

Mr McLeod was here on Saturday – remained all night, and went to call on Mrs Kemp on Sunday – He and Baxter are thinking of going to Port Phillip over land, via New England – they will be about 1 month on their journey – I wish them joy –

I was reading some paragraph about Spring Rice, which reminded me of his 'Chère amie' Mrs Davies – She made him give her husband a good situation in V.D. Land, and she remained in England – All of a sudden she made her appearance in the colony – and as it was only a *whisper*, about her acquaintance with her friend at home, of course everybody called on her – I recollect going with Mrs Wellman – The latter was very pompous when with strangers, and Mrs Davies when we were announced was very evidently sitting in a studied & becoming attitude – She was half reclining on a pretty couch – and elegantly dressed – She was *not* good looking, altho' very attractive – Fascinating, but not *loveable* –

Mrs Wellman was much disgusted, at her not getting up to receive us – and when she said in certainly a sweet deep voice 'Excuse me not rising' – the look of astonishment still more increased on my companion's face – Mr Dry came to take us home – and I remember his observation to me afterwards –

Eh! bien – time passed on; and in about 8 months, madame was very evidently en famille – One day, or rather evening, I was sitting alone, when Mr Dry passed on horseback and called out – 'Come here Mrs Baxter, I have such a piece of scandal for you; but no! I am to tell you that Mrs Wellman wishes to see you' – He dismounted – I put on my bonnet, and off we sauntered – it was a lovely evening, and Mrs Wellman was in her Verandah – She gave a start when she saw me – and looked as if she thought Mr Dry in de trop –

'Oh! it's a bargain, Mrs Wellman', said he – 'I would not intrude for the world on *such* a piece of news' – & off he went – and then she began to ask what I thought had happened – I told her I had no idea – it all ended in her saying that Mrs Davies had had a child and that she and her servant had made away with it – Dr Seccombe had gone down on hearing it – and reported it to the Police Magistrate, Major Wentworth – a private investigation had taken place – and it was arranged that Mrs Davies should take her passage home in the next vessel – How often I took her part after-wards in Coteries of ladies – altho' I well knew that she had said to a friend of mine, 'Mrs Baxter is too *voluptuous* looking for a wife – what a chère amie she would make' – It was a nice speech to make – poor creature!

What very strange things I have seen, and met with in my travels thro' life – I had been about 13 months in V.D. Land when a Mr and Mrs G. Horne came out – Everybody called – and every one said to me 'You will find a rival in her!' For all that, I called – she was about 2 years older than me – with an extremely pretty face – Her eyes were certainly beautiful – and her mouth and teeth – *perfect* – She was too embonpoint to have a good figure – but the tout ensemble was good – Nobody could please her, but me! She wished us to be inseparable – Now altho' I was young (18) and giddy; still I saw thro' *her* Vivacity in a minute – yet I liked her – for like all of her caste, she was kind hearted, generous, and hospitable –

All went on well – until she fell in love with Mr J. S. – She never thought of concealing it – so that we all thought they were talking 'Platonics' – Never shall I forget going one morning to stay the day with his sister, when she said in her quiet way, 'What do you think I found in John's room this morning – why, one of Mrs G. Horne's Nightgowns & a Night cap – They were made up in a parcel – and she has evidently forgotten them – what shall I do with them?' I recommended her to return them in a brown paper – and say nothing more about them – This she did – and of course, thus ended their intimacy –

Mine was quite as amusing – I went up one evening to see her when her husband was from home – Her own room door was closed – and as I never venture into my most intimate friend's room without knocking, I did so at hers – 'Who's there', said she – 'It is me, but don't hurry out, I'll take a book' – at the same time I was moving off, when I heard her say 'Come back, Henry, it is *only* Mrs Baxter' – 'Oh! I had rather meet anybody than her' – said a voice I knew well – (it was not Mr G. Horne's!) – Thinking I was going into the room lately occupied by his fair friend, and himself, Mr H. A. shot thro' another and as I had moved off, *we met*! I cannot portray his manly face, at this moment – Such friends as we were – so well did we always understand each other! and to meet in this way! – He sat down and placing his hands before his face said, 'Oh! I wish all the world had met me, *but* you!' I spoke to him for a long time – told him how well he knew that I was no prude, and therefore he would understand all I said to him – I entreated him to go to Mrs Horne – and say 'Adieu' – He did – and when he returned he said all that he *felt*, I'm convinced – In a week he sailed for Port Phillip –

I then told her that she was the only one to blame – she knew her fascinations – and said that our acquaintance must end then – She begged that I would go the next evening, as I had promised, to a small party there – or her husband would fancy something wrong – so I agreed to go –

It will scarcely be credited – but on the following evening, she took me into the room, and shewing me a beautiful diamond ring said, 'Dearest Mrs Baxter – I'm going to ask you a last favor – Henry gave me this ring – I love him, and *will* wear it – I told George *you* gave it to me, will you not say you did?' I told her, I pitied her from my soul – that she must know how very wrongly she had acted – but that about the ring, I would say nothing –

When Mr Horne met me, he said that the ring was too costly to give away, and that I did very wrong to part with it – His wife was close to us – and I answered that altho' it was a very handsome ring, I had no very particular liking for it – that I begged he allow Mrs Horne to wear it, as a token of *friendship*! After that evening we never spoke – and altho' she called, I was not 'at home'!

I do believe it was her last affaire de coeur – and when on my last visit she told me who had been her early associates, I felt for her – and did not wonder at any indiscretion on her part – She had lived with one of the Italian *noblesse*, the Countess de Montara – and had marked with *Lady*

Syke's hair, pocket handkerchiefs for Lord Lyndhurst! – She is now the mother of three children and I believe a good wife – and nobody but *the three* any the wiser!

Tuesday   Baxter is gone over to Sherwood – it has been really unbearably hot, for the four last days – Last year about this time it was much the same – yet I did not *feel* it so much I think – What lovely moonlight nights too –

My servant woman is very musically inclined and has scarcely left off singing an hour today, notwithstanding the heat –

I received a note from Isabella – She writes quite amusingly – and says I must have so much to tell her *about* my *pets* – I have more to say *to* them!

How I long to hear from William – yet I cannot avoid fancying he will come out – oh! I do hope so, if en Bachelor!

My birthday was last week – and 4 days after (28th) was the fifth anniversary of that melancholy day on which poor Captain Pollard shot himself!

Wednesday   Late last evening Messrs Stephen and Cameron came in from the settlement – The former brought me a note from dear Marion & one from Margaret likewise – the former, as usual, affectionate – the latter *miffed* about my writing on a small piece of paper! She says I can always find paper for Marion and none for her! Then Isabella says that she has written twice, and I have not answered her once! Oh! dear, I'm in a sea of troubles –

Marion sent me up a note of Mrs Stokes' to shew me how kindly she wrote – True! it is teeming with affection – and how did she act? Why, was not 'at home' to her friend one day, when she called! Oh! these Irish – they are more deceitful, then any other Nation under the sun, I do believe!

She likewise sends me a paper sealed up, and tells me *not* to open it until two whole days after I have answered her note! She says it is to try if I am not above our sex's foible? Dr Mollison used to say that I had 'Man's candour; and little of Woman's Curiosity'!

Friday   Early today we received a letter from Mr Frazer which *should* have come last week – it was to say that Mr A. B. Smith could not cash our bills on England – What we are to do, I don't know – the License not being paid yet! Baxter went down to the settlement immediately to see about it –

Saturday   I rode over to Sherwood this morning, accompanied by Frank

Freeman Esq! I won the poor boy's heart I do believe, saying that he had a nice voice! But it was only the truth –

Captain Briggs was at home, and I was very glad to see him – He received my little parcel – I heard something casually that pleased me very much – I imagined times were changed, and persons too – 'L'humeur se change avec le temps, et le temps avec l'humeur'! – it is mostly a true adage –

Upon going to my trunk yesterday, I found that the lock was spoiled – Some person, & I presume that to be Baxter, had been opening my box to see what it contained, and injured the lock in so doing – Strange thing being so fond of prying! I recollect now, that men have a superlative share of curiosity – for I once gave three books to an old friend of mine, *two* of which he might read – The *third* he could not help opening – and yet I consider him one of the élite of mankind –

I was reading over some of my honorable Irish friend's letters this morning – Miss G. W. I. Hely Hutchinson, certainly was a very aristocratic girl– yet there was a something about her *aspect*, which seemed to make them think her 'more than she appeared' – Her eye had an extraordinary look – neither asleep, nor awake – yet I'm sure some of the glances did grievous bodily harm – I've known them to do so – Her walk was most peculiar – and she dressed so oddly – and wore spectacles! She might have married very well – but has preferred marrying a young surgeon without hardly a penny – so much for love & romance –

Then dear Cressy Douglas William! I've looked over some of *her* affectionate notes – She refused more offers than I did – and one or two rather better – and all for love! William too, to think that he loved another, and to go and marry the woman he has! Cressy was not pretty! but see her when you would, in the drawing room, or in her own room, she was still the same shy elegant girl – She appeared to glide along – I can fancy I see her long golden hair, and her pretty *profile*, as she used to sit at the harp, and play & sing so exquisitely to me! And she is married to a subaltern in an Infantry Regiment – and has one child! –

What happy days we have passed at dear Twyford Abbey! They are days we must *all* of us look back to, for we were young; & altho' some of us had our troubles, they were not griefs bitter griefs that many of us have felt since – Any trial in youth is very severe – for it is our first – but those that come after, are more enduring, I think –

They say you cannot *love* twice! It is folly to say so – The first surprises you, and you feel yielding your *every* best feeling, to the object of it – it certainly is delicious – yet another is perhaps loved *better* – for he must remind you in some trifle or other, of your first love – and I maintain you love more passionately, as you love the *two in One!*

Monday   Baxter is not yet returned – and I am anxious about my letters! This morning we were in the midst of white washing and purifying the room, when Mr McLeod came over – He was looking for a heifer that we sold to Margaret – He came in for about an hour, and was quite surprised to hear that Baxter was in the settlement – I was in my dressing gown this morning, with my hair fastened-up 'Night fashion', which served to amuse Mr McLeod – I don't suppose there was any harm in it –

I don't think there are any private marks in this journal – W.I.W.L! (English) –

Isabella, in her note says, 'I do believe we shall have Margaret married soon! And the *Fair* gentleman may think himself well off, with such a clever girl!' Mr P. Stephen laughed at her *not* going to Port Phillip now! he did not know the real reason until I told him –

I was very cross with Ada yesterday evening for not following me on horseback, so I gave her two or three good raps – soon after I became penitent, as I always do with her, and upon looking at her, and stroking her, I found a needle half way in her shoulder – and a tick! I cried with vexation, at my being cross to her! Isabella says she loves Scamp – (so do I, one!) but I'm sure cannot love him as I do Ada –

Mr McLeod was asking me if I thought there would be any harm in riding (I mean his sisters) with Mrs & Miss Stephen – I said, & I think, 'not the slightest' – I am sure that the way in which Mrs Stephen is living at Dr Carlyle's, is perfectly correct – I would vouch for it – then what is there against her?

I heard, that some years ago, she travelled on the Continent with a Dr Douglas! I know not how true it is – but she adheres to the Profession! As to the daughter, I pity her extremely – She is a very nice person I'm told – and every care has been taken of her education –

How well I remember being told by a person whose opinions I value 'I wish you knew my dear Mother, she would make such a good girl of you' – Yes! this is a great blessing! a good mother! Mine was very worldly, poor soul! hers was a very strange life – From living in the greatest seclusion she was married to my Father – who was constantly associating with

Royalty – on dit, Mama's beauty made a passing impression on the Duke of Cumberland – when Papa was on the Earl of Chatham's staff – No wonder then, that her head was turned with flattery & adulation – She was not fond of Papa either – and only had on account of his birth et cetera –

She *did* love George's father tho' – with all a Woman's fondness – This she shewed unhappily to her unfortunate boy – I remember she used to remain shut up in her own room for three days every year, on the anniversary of Mr Sinclair's death – How I have seen her kneel by George's bed, and *pray* – May God bless her! She never did, or could love me – *Few* can – but then they love me intensely – I mean nobody as well, as me – I am vain of this!

It is thundering very much tonight – strange how I like it! It reminds me of my own disposition – so rebellious it sounds! Well! I'll get me to bed –

12th Tuesday   Baxter returned this afternoon, accompanied by Mr C. Ducat – I told the latter that I had intended not speaking to him again, as he had passed by so very often without paying me a visit – He said he was told I was very angry with him – & did not wish to see him! – Who could have told him such a thing? I'll find out – I rather expect my right hand neighbour –

Baxter could not get the bills cashed – I don't know what is to be done about the money for the License –

Margaret writes me that Miss Stephen is *so pretty* – and what she would call a sweet girl! And she is determined to bring her out! She does not know many things that I do about this young person – altho' I never heard a syllable against her character – and believe it to be pure – but she *and* Margaret are both anxious to get married – I'm told she has a handsome little nephew with eyes as black as his *Papa's*! The mother, poor unhappy girl, is now in charge for stealing from Mrs Bates –

15th Friday   Mr Salwey was to have been here last night – but has not made his appearance as yet – Mr Freer is down – I dislike this person – He is so coarse in his manner – and made such a pretty speech of me –

I was excessively tired last night, and could scarcely keep awake long enough to think of times gone by, which I make a *rule* of doing – Eh! bien! – I went to sleep, and dreamed – Oh! what I would have given anything in the world to come true – part of it, was what has happened, and part what I almost wished – It was but a dream –

 This passenger on a Robertson and Company Coach is wearing a sensible bonnet to keep off the sun. It looks so much like the sunbonnets worn at the time by pioneer women on the American prairies. Place and date unknown.

16th Saturday   Yesterday I had a visit from Messrs Montgomerie and P. Stephen – I always am very glad to see the latter – and the former I like because he reminds me of Mr Massie, having seen them so often together –

It was arranged that I should go to the Plains, get my horse shod, and return home with Mr Stephen today – Accordingly I started with Baxter this morning – got as far as Mr Allen's – had a good wetting – and it continued raining so much that I returned by myself to my own hut! I'm always so glad to see this place – I love it – I've twice refused to go to the settlement now – and yet I cannot give myself any *credit* for it – as there is a halo round this spot, which endears it to me –

We were at tea yesterday when three of the Police came and remained all night – and this morning, I was going in about 5 o'clock to see Cocky when I spied them all fast asleep – 'They lay like Policemen taking their rest, with their blankets snug around them' – I like to see even the *horses* that went up to N. England with us!

Mr Stephen asked me if I were not going to the settlement at Christmas? I wanted to know *what* inducement there was for me to go? He said that everybody was going – and after making him enumerate their names, I found that *all* would be there – Last Christmas I was contented, but now I know nobody to say to me 'Now, Now, grumble, you *must* not'! The Dutch say that the *Head* is Masculine; the *Heart* feminine! 'The head, like a man, seeks its hapiness in possessing; the heart, like a woman, is happy only when it can communicate what it possesses'!

'Man, the head, endeavours to *meditate* on God, and halts in his presumptuous efforts; Woman, the heart, *feels* God, and this feeling gives her Peace & happiness'!

This is an excellent idea, for who can feel as a woman, but one?

Certainly I begin to *think*, that I must be very unnatural in not loving children! I wonder if all who profess to do so, do so really? It is absurd in me to say I like them, because I *do not* – but I can love a child for its parent's sake – Now for instance, Maria Davies' – and Emily Davis and I'm sure I should love William's – my own too, if –

If I had only not galloped too much at a Rochester Ball, and over fatigued myself, I should have had one nine years old! and how many more, goodness knows! I tremble at the idea of seeing the poor little souls brought up in this Country – and nothing to educate them – No! I'm far, far better, as I *am* – for this I thank God – I often think, that were I acting wrongly in God's sight, in having chosen the *path I have, He* would trouble my conscience with it – Feeling, Inclination, Conscience, all say 'No' –

My life appears a complete 'Romance' – my old friend Mr Hinsley used to say, 'There is far too much Romance in your *eye* to marry yet!' the other day Baxter said that my face would be well enough, if my eyes had not the expression they had – it must be a strange one –

I have lately had leisure & opportunity to wander a good deal alone in the bush about here – and have made quite a nice collection of Native flower seeds – the creepers are beautiful – and the Jassamine too is very pretty – but there is one small white flower surpasses them all – it is so *simply* beautiful –

I am very fond of flowers – Mrs Freeman said one day in her strange way, 'We should love flowers and children; they are so *fresh* from God!' This phrase I'm convinced was borrowed, for the idea is too good for one of her own – This person is always teaching or rather *trying* to teach me 'Contentment' –

Maria was telling me a most excellent anecdote, and altho' it is against myself, it entertains me so much – Some person was saying they liked *my* manners – Mrs Freeman said, 'They are passable' – The gentleman smiled – and Maria said 'But my Papa says that my Aunt is so well connected and has always associated with *Nobility*!' 'My dear girl,' said Mrs Freeman, 'I have seen more *Nobility* (Mobility?) in one *week* than your Aunt ever did in her whole *life*! Why, I have frequently *stood by their Carriages on Drawing room days, and seen hundreds of Noblemen with their Families*!' Oh! this is exquisite! She certainly has the advantage of me, for I never did *stand* by their carriages, nor even saw hundreds of Noblemen! The idea is so truly literal, and original –

I was reading *Chamber's Edinburgh Journal* today, when my eye fell on a piece of poetry which I read many years ago, and which then made a great impression on my mind – altho' at the time I was far from thinking *I* should ever pay the 'desert' a visit – I recollect keeping it to show Mr Dry – and he admired it too – It is written by a Mr I. Pringle, of Cape Town –

> Afar in the desert I love to ride,
> With the silent Bush-boy alone by my side.
> When the sorrows of life the soul o'ercast,
> And, sick of the present, I turn to the past;
> And the eye is suffused with regretful tears,

From the fond recollections of former years;
And the shadows of things that have long since fled
Flit over the brain like ghosts of the dead –
Bright visions of glory, that vanished too soon –
Day dreams that departed ere Man's noon –
Attachments by fate, or Falsehood reft –
Companions of early days lost or left –
And my Native Land! whose magical name
Thrills to my heart like Electric flame;
The home of my children; the haunts of my prime;
All the passions and scenes of that rapturous time,
When the feelings were young, and the world was new,
Like the fresh bow'rs of Paradise op'ning to view.
All – all now forsaken, forgotten, or gone –
And I – a lone Exile – remembered of none –
My high aims abandon'd – and good acts undone –
Weary of all that is under the sun –
With that sadness of heart which no stranger may scan,
I fly to the desert afar from Man!

And here – while the Night winds sound and sigh,
And the stars burn bright in the Midnight sky,
As I sit apart by the Cavern'd stone,
Like Elijah at Horeb's cave alone,
And feel as a Moth in the Mighty hand,
That spreads the Heavens and heaved the land –
A 'still small voice' comes thro' the wild,
(Like a Father consoling his fretful child),
Which banishes bitterness, wrath, and fear –
Saying 'Man is distant, but God is near!'

How often riding in the bush, have I said these two last lines to myself – I like them so much –

As Baxter & I were riding down to Allen's, Cocky put his foot on a stump and fell over with his rider – Baxter at first thought his leg was broken, but [it] was only twisted slightly – his spur had pressed into the horse's side, and rather hurt it – poor little fellow! I never knew him to stumble before – even now 'twas not his fault entirely –

17th Sunday   I have been very ill all day from getting a wetting yesterday – strange too! for I never catch cold hardly –

Mr McLeod came over in the afternoon and remained rather late – I was advising him to marry – Mr Salwey was at the Plains, and went on to the settlement with Baxter – Mr P. Stephen likewise – I am sorry for the latter as I wished to see him particularly –

Mr McLeod tells me that he has applied, or tendered for the contract up here – I hope he may get it, as it will clear him of debt –

Surely I shall have some letters by this post! Well, I must say Good Night to my journal –

I'm quite in the Blues – the pain in my stomach has amounted to agony at times today, and laudanum even has been unable to abate it – nous verrons –

18th Monday   I continue so much in pain, that I sent to ask Mr McLeod if he would bleed me – He came over, and did so – better than I ever was blooded before – He remained for some time watching me so kindly, and fanning the flies off my face – I told him of what I heard he had said about me – it originated in Mrs Johnson's chattering propensities – and I suppose in some *tender* moment, was imparted by her lovely daughter, Mary, to Mr McLeod –

I hear there is to be a large dinner party at the Lake on Christmas day – I wish I could afford to entertain, as I might then perhaps be a little remembered by some acquaintances – I begin to think, however, that those who cannot love me in adversity, will be scarcely worthy of mine in prosperity – The former certainly shows us *who* really have affection for us –

Mary Ann Weymouth is still home in the settlement with Mr Steele – it is a good thing she remains quietly with *one* – she has a child; it is very sickly I hear –

31st Sunday   I am just recovering from a very serious illness – so much so, that for two days I considered I was never to rise from my bed again! I had but *one* enquiry for me – and that from Mrs Ducat – Captain & Miss Briggs went to the Plains, and did not even call on their way to see me –

Margaret started on Christmas-day and came in early the following morning – She is going to remain with me some time –

It appears that if Major Innes becomes Insolvent, Baxter is responsible for the £310 – for Captn Briggs' cattle – so last week, he went to see Captn Briggs & told him he should brand his cattle for the Major – he said he would, and Mr Salwey (who was there) said 'If you consent to this, it is all right, and the cattle can be with you, as before'! However, he has thought fit to let Mr Freer have 10 Cows & calves – so that *now* it would not be possible to find cattle sufficient to pay the sum required – It is the most dishonorable thing to do – and I never could have imagined his doing it – but after *all* I have seen, I will never give credit to any man for truth, or generosity –

Today is the last day of another year! Oh! how I recall all the *old* years – what happiness I have felt in them – What dear friends I have made – and lost! Alas! it were a blessing for me if I had bathed in the stream of forgetfulness – for Memory harrows my very soul – and when I *really* commence *thinking*, I find that all the benefit I have experienced from Religion, is nevertheless set aside, and I am still a Rebel to my Saviour, my God!

Oh! that I had been born with less feeling! I had then passed thro' the world much more contentedly – I should not have heeded the coolness of friends – which *now* breaks my heart almost –

How dear Harriet & William are thinking of me today & I know well, that *they* wish me with them – I often think I am ungrateful to God for giving & retaining to me such good friends – but I know I am very sinful – and I will strive to think more of a future world than this! Yet when I was dying, as I thought, the other day, I felt not the *slightest* fear or wish to remain in this 'Vale of tears' – on the contrary, I felt happy at leaving so much misery behind me – I was going to send away my journal to the other three Vols. and my last words should have been in *it* –

With the old year, I hope I may lose some of my *old* habits & follies – not all tho' – for I would not part with those for which I have been, and am loved – May the Almighty bless and protect all those I love – and grant that I may grow more 'after his own heart' –

Yesabba

31st December 1843

1st January 1844

Monday   Margaret was the first to wish me a *happy New Year*! I am determined on not grumbling this year, *if* I can avoid it – and so I trust myself, that it may be happy!

I have begun it by doing all that I most dislike, on purpose to try and improve my temper – for they tell me, I'm altered for the worse in this respect – Oh! who would not [be] in my case?

3rd Wednesday   Baxter and Mr Salwey rode over to Sherwood – and returned to dinner – and Mr Stephen did not leave until after that meal –

I made a strange bet with him – He, and Mr Salwey have taken this station – and we shall leave in about a month – so I shall go by land with Baxter to Port Fairy – Mr Stephen has bet me his own Portrait against Baxter's, that I *don't* go by land –

I have today written what I wish were unsaid – it is always thus – when you do anything in a flurried way – but I shall see that which ensues –

There is some fun expected up the River today, as Messrs Hitchcock & Jobling, and Major Innes were having their *runs* decided –

I am so tired that I must say Good-Night to my journal –

7th Sunday On Thursday Baxter had intended going to the settlement – but it commenced raining, and we had a delightful quantity of rain – Accordingly on Friday he started early, and was to go the whole way –

Mr McLeod is evidently smitten, I think, with Isabella – he told me so the other day – and I asked him since then how his love affair was progressing? He said 'Oh! so I made you believe it – the idea of my telling *you*, of all people!' –

Now that I'm about to leave this, I love all the various little nooks & corners – I wonder whether I shall ever see them again? or whether I shall ever be thought of by those who visit, or rather did visit Yesabba? –

What a hollow sound appears in Friendship! & what persons calling themselves *friends* we meet with – really in general, if we could only *think* a little, what is there to attach us to this life? Very, very little indeed –

I sat up so late last night, finishing a dress, & reading – it was *morning* before I fell asleep – I so often dream the same thing – I appear to be in a beautiful house, well furnished – but chiefly composed of bed rooms – in one of these, are four large beds – always occupied by pretty women – I then go some way off the first room, to another which has but *one* bed – and a beautiful woman in it – opposite to this is a bath room – and the same ugly old woman, shows me first into the bath, and then into a handsomely furnished bed room – which she tells me is *mine* – I then begin to undress, and she retires – but I all of a sudden seem to wonder *where* I am, and why? I then throw myself on a couch opposite to my bed; and while there I hear a voice lamenting so much to find *me* there – at the same time using the most passionate entreaties for me to return *home* – I look up and see – I then know *why* I am there – ('A man cannot be too dissipated in some ways, before marriage'!!) The house is one of Vice, and I am one of its votaries! And so finishes my 'dream' – May it always remain one!

Altho' I did once say 'If we ever meet again, it will be miserably' –

We were highly entertained by Mrs Freeman's description of her visit to the Scotch Carpenters – She says they gave her such a reception! The next day after she was here, our servants said they wished to leave – the man because there was too much to do & Baxter had attempted to *seduce his wife* – This was very delightful to me to hear – I told the woman that she must have mistaken him – She said 'It is not at all likely Ma'am – the Master offered me cattle, if I would sell my soul to the d–l!'

I have pretended total ignorance on the subject – as I *knew* it was true, by his being so frightened at the man's speaking out loud about it; and repeatedly telling him not to talk so loudly – At the time this occurred, I was in my bed, hardly expecting to live –

It amuses me very much to see Margaret, while I am writing this, trying to peep into it at every opportunity – Whenever I go out of the room, she is into my room in an instant – what she expects to find there, I don't know!

Mr P. Stephen brought me some nice peaches from Wollowbie Hill – I have never been there but once – not so Baxter – his love affair there with the black woman is repeated as a fine joke –

Agnes is not yet returned from the Naanbucca where she is staying with Mrs Scott – the latter is very ill off indeed!

It is most insufferably hot this afternoon, really it makes one feel quite ill –

I did not say to Maria how much I felt their not coming to see me on Christmas Eve, when they passed to the Plains – I thought it was of little consequence – and so made her the present I had intended –

Mr McLeod was saying that if Major Innes got the better of Mr Hitchcock in the settling of the run, that he thought *he* could recover his from Mr Cameron – as it was illegally given to him – That he saw no use of there being a Commissioner, for he had not visited the stations for many months, and he hoped it might soon be done away with! I suppose *to* him, he is all sweetness!

Ada has had puppies, and I had them all drowned – she is in a sad way about them –

It was laughable to see the *tired coolness* that appeared the other day here – I saw so plainly what the real state of the case was!

I have a bet of a riding whip, with Margaret about Miss Stephen & Mr Salwey – She says they will be married before next January – I say

'Not' – Baxter is gone to settle all his debts in the settlement – and then we have nothing to do but get ready for a start – I need not have gone until he was at Port Fairy – but I in the first place, wish to see the country between this & Melbourne – in the next, it is too expensive to go by sea, and I should not go at all – and I wish to *see* the Station before I go home – besides I shall see all my poor horses & dogs taken care of on the road – A bush trip *may* recruit me too – then again, I care little what becomes of me!

8th Monday   We have both been working away today, in spite of the heat – In the evening we rode over to Dandingalon – Messrs Freer and Dent were there but I did not go to the house –

There is a sad story afloat about a poor girl named Blair – She is *said to be* in the family way – and the other Parent is the clerk of the Church – It is a shocking thing – for she was always so well behaved – and the horrible man will not marry her – now that he has gained what he desired – Oh! man! Where is generosity in your composition? People will say 'But he is of the "lower order"' – Man is the same from the highest to the lowest! His are the feelings of a Sensualist – and so that he only obtains that which he wishes for, he cares not what ruin he may have been the cause of –

Mr Purves went down the other day to Mr Arkroyd's in a terrible way – and said that the evening before *two gentlemen* had been prowling about his house after his servant Mary Ann Blair – and that he had determined upon his honor, to say publicly, who the two were, the very next time he heard them – Now altho' 'dissipation may be allowed in single men', still I think that some delicacy too may be used at the same time – I know the *two*, and I will let them get a hint of the matter – I'm glad I shall not hear any more of these, to me, painful tales – I shall be away from them all soon –

Margaret took such a large Centipede off my neck this evening – she was more frightened than I was about it – All is nothing now – to me –

13th Saturday   Baxter is gone to the Plains this morning, so I write a little more here –

On Thursday we rode up in the afternoon to Major Kemp's, where we found all in such a sad state of dirt – The hut looked disgustingly dirty – the children too – Mrs Kemp came out after some time dressed very smartly – It appears that she has since said that she wondered at persons paying such untimely visits – and that altho' in the bush, they remembered who they were!! Oh! Pride –

We have twice ridden over to Sherwood, and not seen its owner – but I will go again – for *I'm* determined too –

Messrs Salwey and Stephen were here yesterday on their way to the Commissioner's about their cattle – The former was 'squiff' – and the latter had shaved off his whiskers, and made himself a perfect fright – I had an answer about the journal – it was a very cavalier one – N'importe!

Marion is to be married in June, I believe – to Mr Mordaunt McLean – She is an excellent soul! but is fretting herself very much about religious matters! She thinks herself not half as good on these points as she should be – I don't like religious discussions, but I love her so well, that I am writing to her on them – as she wishes it – I wish I could love God half what I *wish* – but worldly passions & feelings will intervene – and then I find I am only 'Mammon'!

I have been copying some pretty waltzes – yet of what avail will they be, for I shall have no piano – Cowen will take this one from Captain Briggs, at £20 – The pearls & brooches are gone up to Sydney to be valued – and then I shall take the latter –

I fear very much that I have not the power of entertaining – for Margaret is most decidedly tired of this Elysium retreat – and sighs for more gaiety – I wonder if she could pass her life, as I have? Few women could –

The answer about my journal, was so ill judged! not a line – If my friend thinks it right, I *suppose* it is – but really I can see neither common politeness, or the smallest feeling on his side –

Friday   Mr McLeod came over last night, and he, Margaret & I started early for the settlement – We reached the Plains in very good time – changed horses, and on again we went – About 12 o'clock, I arrived at Yarloowa – They were as usual, glad to see me – They are a delightful family certainly – Annie is looking very poorly – The poor little soul has been spitting blood for some time – and becomes so terribly alarmed about herself, that they fear remarking whether she is looking ill or not –

Captain Jobling had been all day in the settlement, and did not return until evening –

Saturday   Mr McLeod came to the Point for me this morning – and I got into *town* pretty early – The girls were all on the lookout for me–Marion is looking very well – with such a beautiful colour – Jessie is much thinner, and improved by it –

In the evening Miss Hunter, Miss A. Paterson – and some gentlemen came in – amongst others, Mr Massie – It is the first time that I have seen him *in public* for 9 months – and shall I say it? It would not pain me much if I never did so again!

Illness may alter a person – and *time* many! but I never beheld a person *as* altered as my friend – He looks very well – & his eyes are as expressive as ever to other people – but nine months have made a change in his cold, cold heart –

At first I thought he did not intend speaking at all to me – for he merely gave me a formal bow – I had been told he was smitten with Miss Paterson – and was astonished to see how far the flirtation had gone–

I said to Marion 'If Mr Massie cannot remember me, I shall not remind him by speaking' – Accordingly until he thought fit to come up to me, I remained silent to him – He then said he was sorry I was going to leave – and looked exceedingly so, as he caught Miss Hunter's eye, and laughed!

Mr Salwey was flirting with Margaret – it's too bad – She is so fond of him – I cannot fancy a person falling in love with such a man – He & Mr Massie are both regular 'dog–Vanes'! They change with every *breath* – both taken by a pretty face – It would not be worth the *pleasure* of loving – to waste its sweetness on two such men – They are both good companions tho' – and the latter I would never tire of –

It commenced raining this afternoon, and looks extemely like a continuance – so that I shall be unable to return home on Monday –

Friday   The steamer has been off here, for two days, but the surf has been too high, for any boat to go to her –

Yesterday a boat with two men in her, was very nearly taken over the bar – it was frightful to see the poor creatures hurrying on to destruction – Eternity seemed within their reach – oh! who would have tried to turn aside, unless those terrified at the idea of death –

We have seen Messrs Massie & Montgomerie every day – The former positively condescends to shake hands with me; and addresses two or three words to me! Mr P. Stephen ('toujours le même', should be his motto!) has been in several times – Yesterday evening he accompanied us for a drive on the 'Lake' road – It does me good to see his bright face –

27th Saturday   In the evening a walk was proposed; and to my extreme horror, I found myself *linked* to W. N. Gray Esq – We went as far as Mr Salwey's to see his two young puppies – and the whole way Mr Gray was trying to make himself understood in the English language! I never in my life, heard any person express himself so badly –

This day week after all the people had left, and I had retired to my room – I sat musing on 'times gone by' – and altho' I certainly felt glad to have seen my soi-disant friend again, still *Nature* would feel sorry at the reception I had met with – so different from what I had any right to anticipate – Surely in justice Mr M. should have explained *why* he was so rude, as not even to speak to me!

All my thinking ended in wishing I had met with a good husband, and then all my heartaches would have been spared in a great measure – I cried myself nearly into hysterics, & was so far insensible as to say to Marion when she came to bed 'Is that you – ?' She asked me if I were awake, and I pretended not to hear her – She then touched me, and said that she could not bear to hear me sob so terribly – We remained awake a long time – she was telling me all her plans for the future – may they all be as bright & lasting as I wish them! Nobody knows of her engagement but Margaret, her Mama, & myself –

She advises me strongly not to go to Port Phillip – Only one person *could* have prevented me, & that one takes no more interest in me now – I knew so well it was mere Passion – but thought at least I had not been mistaken in a *true* & *sincere* friend – All my dreams are passed! I. C. said 'I'm to have the other journal, am I not?' No – he has not deigned to ask for it, until then most certainly not – at least, so far, this book will accompany the others – but until I am *asked* for it, it shall remain sealed –

(12 o'clock)   All are gone! and I am going too, – to bed – Mrs Richardson, Messrs Massie, Montgomerie, Salwey & P. Stephen were here this evening – I danced the first Quadrille with I. C. and spoke in the Verandah to him, for a minute or two – but he was so eager to go into the drawing room, that I could not say half what I wished – It is the last time I will ever speak to him –

I then danced with Mr P. Stephen – He told me a very bad piece of news – that Mr Baxter had failed – it will involve us sadly, I fear – This, and other things made me feel wretched – I was sitting in the Verandah with Marion, when Mrs Richardson came up; and just behind her Percy Stephen – I was amused very much by Mrs Richardson saying, 'How

 Like Annie Baxter, this woman is accompanied by a greyhound, an unexpected dog for bush life. She seems to be the same woman in the photograph on page 66. Place and date unknown.

much attention Mr Massie pays Miss Paterson; only look at them now!'
Before I could turn round, Mr Stephen touched my shoulder and said
'Don't mind her! I've made you miserable telling you that news' –

I first assured him I was often in low spirits, *without* hearing bad news –
and turned and looked at the pair in the corner – Mrs Richardson was
right in this instance – and I was quite astonished, that in about an hour
after, Mr Massie left his belle amie, to stand an instant by my side – We
neither spoke – and no wonder – Just before he left he shook hands – for
the last time, in this country – or any other – and *I* have found out, that
there is but *one* man I ever met, truly worthy of my love – Thus ends the
Comedy, or Tragedy – for it has been both to me –

Isabella & Annie are both sleeping in the room with me – the former
says she wishes I would put away *that odious book* (this one) and tell her
what I shall do with myself in Port Phillip – I *could* tell her – but won't –

29th Monday   I this morning said Addio to my friends in Port Macquarie,
and started for the Plains in Mr Marsh's gig – with his two horses, and
the old Grey tied to their heads – so that we had three abreast – We jour-
nied on famously – Mr McLeod shaking the vehicle as *little* as he could –

Baxter did not expect me – He is looking very ill – While I've been
away, he has been having *Dr Madden* to quack him – He says he can scarcely
walk with rheumatism –

The woman I left here is gone – She came up when I returned and told
me some long story about her Master & she having words – so that I'm
my own femme de chambre again –

I only dreamt my 'dream' once in the settlement – it makes me quite
miserable dreaming it so often –

Ada was so glad to see me – I do love her – all my pets look well, notwithstanding the rain –

30th Tuesday   Mrs McLeod wishes me to remain with them, & not go to
Port Fairy – but I cannot be dependent on any one – If I could *work* in
any way, all well – but to remain even for a few months, a burthen on any
one, I could not –

Every place about looks so pretty – every little nook has its charm to me
now – But however painful it may be to separate from, & give up for ever,
what is lovely and attractive in natural scenery; it is altogether nothing
when compared to the breaking up of those living attachments which have
become a part of Nature – This is most true – and I shall find that

'Friendship is Love, without his Wings'!

On the 28th after undressing, I gave Margaret my old gown – I'll never wear it again! and to dear Marion, a pretty buff châle – the last time I wore the latter dress it was at a large dance at Mrs Wardell's, in Sydney – A great many Naval Officers were there, amongst the number Mr H. Elliott, of the *Conway* – He knew Baxter very well, but not me – I was talking with Marion, when Mr Elliott said to Baxter 'I would like to know that pretty woman Waltzing with Miss Marion – who is she?' Baxter waited until we came near them, and then said 'Annie, here is a young friend of mine wishes to be introduced to you – Mr Elliott – my Wife'! Poor boy, he looked aghast – but quickly recovered his usual *spirit*, and I found myself talking with a very good partner –

His cousin another evening, at Government House asked Mrs Hazard whilst talking with Baxter, 'Who that singular looking woman was, with *Cain's brand* on her forehead?'

I've been trimming my grass borders for the last time – I wonder who will do it after I'm gone?

6th Tuesday   Today Messrs McLeod & Duff came up from the settlement – The former brought me an English letter, which has been some time in the Sydney Post Office – I wrote last week to Mr Gordon asking him to send me any letters there might be and I received a very polite note in return & a long letter from my darling William, Harriet and my Uncle – They were all at Harriet's, staying some time – She says they only *want me* there! – Just at this time she writes (June) I was out in this Wilderness, enduring tortures! – But I'm happy to think & know, that they are so – Harriet desires to be kindly remembered to Massie – so I've sent her message –

Baxter cut all the names out of the books given me by Richard Dry – however, I've written them in again – I shall get *my* name written in a book that was given to me –

That unfortunate man Knatchball, is to be hanged for murder, on Tuesday next – It would really appear that he was tired of his existence, to go so deliberately and kill a woman –

We have bought Mr Salwey's gig – and when Mr Stephen takes the cattle, we have little to do at dear Yesabba –

7th Wednesday   William's 31st Birthday – May our good Almighty preserve him to see many more – How I do idolize him – it is almost sinful! I never did meet with such a man in my life – By the by tho', he says in his letter, that to be wild and a roué, is only *natural* – He appears to coincide with another person I once knew! –

8th Thursday   My wedding day! Many a bitter day have I seen since that event took place – Mr Benjamin dined here yesterday – He and the Major's family don't appear to agree very well in their Politics – but his chief wish appears to be to try and annoy the said family as much as he possibly can – I told him it was anything but *Christian*-like – and oh! horrors! I never until now thought that he being a *Jew*, it became strictly personal – I loaded him with peaches & cucumbers for his children – What a capital Aunt I shall make – ruin all my nephews & nieces – and of course get the thanks of Parents, Uncles etc for making them pets!

This evening Mr P. Stephen came – He did look so sleepy and squiff – Naughty fellow! I'm afraid he gives way a *little* to dissipation of various sorts – He's young yet – and single – He did not forget my roses tho' – notwithstanding his being elevated – I told him he might go to sleep on the sofa, and I would not take any *gloves* – He said he would not mind losing them –

Mr Montgomerie called a few days ago – I was packing up a trunk for the settlement – & had taken off my dress, and put on my dressing gown – it was so warm – but I soon made my entrée –

The Blacks are all here – Barney too – my favorite Black – They are stealing corn in real earnest from Mr McLeod's, and our Pig-station –

11th Sunday   Such very unpleasant weather! it rains one minute, and is fine the next –

Baxter is going nearly mad about his cattle! He fidgets my life nearly out about them – I have made a bet with Mr Stephen – He is to have Baxter's picture that is here, if we don't get to Port Phillip over land – and I'm to have his, if we do – I would like to have his handsome, saucy face!

He told me that he was sure I. C. did not care for Miss P. – 'Indeed,' said he, 'I think he does not *care* one atom more for *any* one person, than another' – This rather entertained me – He very often talks of *his* favorite – and complains of other persons abusing him for being partial – at all events, *I* cannot complain of the latter lately –

This evening I rode 'Gratis' up to Dungee – accompanied by Mr Stephen – He says he shall often think of these *first* rides over his run, when he is coming home tired at night, after a day's hard work –

The cattle were counted, and given over today to Mr Stephen –

I ought to tell Baxter of his brother's Failure, but I cannot – he is so irritable – and really ill – How frequently I pity him! when I think that altho' I do everything a wife, or servant could do for man; still there is a *way* of doing it – When I ask him how he is, it is not as *I* would ask anybody I loved –

How differently, different persons are affected by any pleasure, or pain – Mrs Jobling, kind, good, and religious as she is; when she receives an English letter, frets herself terribly about it, until indeed, she is quite ill –

Isabella *devours* hers almost, and reads it aloud as she goes on –

Mrs Kemp – it puts in high glee for several days, and she says, she does not mind all her work! as to myself – oh! how does it affect me? Why I wish for one person to communicate the news – and I don't *now* grumble, as I did – at being so far from happiness – for I deserve all, all that I endure –

Baxter says I take less care of myself than ever – Yes! I do indeed – While I thought I was cared for, I did take some slight care of my health – but when I saw it was not the case; it has altered even my heart –

I fancied when in the settlement, that nothing could make me *feel* for any person in misery – my *soul* felt hardened – but I found on seeing the two poor men drowning, (as we supposed –) I had still a tear for a fellow creature in distress!

14th Wednesday   Baxter went to the settlement today –

The Blacks have been very troublesome for some days – they rob the corn most terribly – I gave the men some caps for their guns, and advised them to shoot quietly! – I shall be taken up for manslaughter – or aiding it – 'Same thing!' as Miss Fattorini says –

Thursday   Such a wretched day – raining nearly the whole day – I sat working, and not minding the weather – and have finished a pretty pair of cuffs for myself – the first work of the sort, I ever did for myself –

The fire and Ada, have kept me up very late – it is long past 12 o'clock – I'm afraid of having my old dream again tonight – for last night, it continued so long – and it makes me miserable – Oh! I must never be so low, as that comes to, surely? – I should never *doubt*! –

16th Friday   Such weather! really tantalizing – one minute the sun shines in all his glory, the next – nothing but rain & gloom to be seen – It is a beautiful idea calling the sun 'He', and the Moon 'She' – the latter merely a reflection of the former! –

I've been very industrious today – the Blacks are all come back – Tommy has been telling the men in the kitchen, that the Commissioner is a *better man* than Mr Gray! – (Whoever doubted it?) and a great deal in his favor –

18th Sunday   I should [have liked] Harriet to have seen me with my companion Tommy yesterday evening – I sat down to the Piano at dusk, (which I always do when by myself,) and was amusing myself when I turned round to the open window, and spied Tommy, in an attitude of great attention – I asked him to walk in, and sit by the fire which he did –

He told me that the Commissioner played on the Flute *sometimes*, not *always*! That Mr d'Niban was a nice gentleman, tall as Mr Bell at Yarrowal – and that *he* took horses down from Mr Townsend's to bring the Messrs Massie up, when first they arrived in this Colony – that Mr Massie always stayed at Mr Bodgell's – and he didn't know who made Black fellows songs! Here was news of various kinds –

Mrs McLeod was talking to me the other day, and amongst other things she said 'Do you still continue separated from Mr Baxter at Night?' Strange thing, that people cannot fancy my doing so! I only answered 'I slept with Mr Baxter for the last time in this World, next May, will be 4 years' – and now I think that I shall adhere to my resolution –

The peach trees are so loaded, that they are breaking down – and the fruit on some of them is very tolerable –

19th Monday   I am very far from well – and am rather suffering – Dr Carlyle recommends me to undergo an examination – but this is strangely at variance with my wish, that I would rather prefer going on as I am – I suppose it cannot last *very* long – altho' he says it may for years – They think to frighten me by saying I *shall*, or rather *have* a Cancer – They little know me! I do not fear death – altho' I have been wicked enough to covet it frequently –

22nd February   Baxter was in a perfect fury, at my having met with Mr Massie again – & asked me if I had spoken to him? – Of course, I told the truth – I'm not ashamed of having such an acquaintance, altho' it does not appear to be the same in his opinion of me –

He was quite as furious as ever – I told him that I *would* speak to Mr Massie whenever I should meet him – and that William would account to Baxter for my actions – He was perfectly dismayed when I said I hoped to see my brother out, in a short time – He had never dreamed I was in earnest, when I said I had written home –

24th Saturday   I had a long note from Isabella – she is in hopes that I have changed my mind about going to Port Phillip – No! I am going – Mr McLeod thought to frighten me, by telling me of three Bushrangers being out, on the road – Meeting them will be a novelty – so that they don't take my horses – and then, I really think I should *fight* for them –

Upwards of 70 Blacks were here today – It appears they had been fighting some others over at Yarroowa – and had been Victorious – It was a remarkably pretty sight to see them coming into the paddock – with their spears, shields etc – and as they entered the gate, they filed off in two ranks – these were the separate tribes –

They then ran up together into a circle, and danced & yelled – It was quite an exciting scene to an old *Soldier*! They then sat down – and after remaining a short time, off they all went to the Plains, to fight again!

27th Tuesday   I have been so very hard at work, making new dresses – Messrs P. Stephen & Herring came up this evening and I have passed such a happy evening – as the old gentleman went to bed –

I never should have *imagined* what I was told this evening – strange tho' that it is the *first* time I ever knew myself to feel sorry at anybody's loving me – Poor boy – and he told me so unconsciously too – After saying that he loved Mr Salwey better than any one he had ever known, he soon after told me that that was after me – That his Mother & sister were quite secondary to me –

I was really vexed with myself for having said that had I been single & a few years younger, I should have taken advantage of leap year, and proposed to him – and finished by saying 'but I suppose you would have rejected my suit!' 'Not if you had been old & ugly; I could never have rejected your heart & mind!' He did not mean this as a compliment, altho' to me, from *such* a boy, it was a great one –

29th Thursday   Mr Stephen left soon after breakfast – and I have said 'Good-bye' to him, the first down here – One of the last I would wish to say it to –

4th Monday   Poor Mama's birthday – Would to God I could recall her memory with all the true affection that a child should! but I have been so estranged from her – and now that she is gone, altho' I forgive her all, that she ever did to me, still it is not with a wish to have had her with me longer, that I think of her –

Mary Ann Reid tells me that she saw *G. W.* lately – that 'he is not one bit altered! Just as handsome, and exactly as much of the roué – so much so, that his Mother & sisters would not live with him!' – Telle est la vie! – Had we been married, he might have been reclaimed, and I happier – as it is, we are both lost –

There has been a tremendous affair at Wollowbie Hill! Mr C. Curr was sent away one morning without his breakfast – however, he was nothing daunted, and now that Mr McLean is in N. England, he is visiting again at the house – and people *do* say, that an elopement is very likely to be the termination! Poor unfortunate girl, what will then become of her; drinking too, as she does – Mr Curr has not sufficient refinement to make up to any woman, for the very great sacrifice and sin they have committed –

I have been so busy – and have everything put away – I try so much to prevent myself thinking of leaving this dear old place – I would not mind if I were going home – but to have to undergo all the privations & fatigues of a new Station, I certainly do feel it rather hard on me; especially as I am in really ill health – Mary Ann says she wishes I were at home, as she then would have a confidante to whom she could tell all her troubles, without any fear of meeting with satire – I can always sympathize with a person, let them be high or low – yet *I* never tell a woe of my own to a female – it is a strange thing but I don't like Women –

This will be nearly the last time I shall write in my journal – and it will be left, to be *looked at*! –

I was saying that I need not keep out my hat, as I supposed I could not spare much time to ride at Melbourne; and besides my habit was so bad – 'You'll have something else to do besides riding about there!' said my amiable sposo – We shall see! I rather think I *shall* find time for riding – and that I shall be more trouble to him there than here – for I shall see all my old friends, and I will try and see what he will do, when he finds me befriended – I told him a few days ago, when he was abusing Mr Massie & I, that he had better wait, and tell that all to William – He was perfectly amazed to think that I had written home – as he never thought I would do so – Well! I've endured misery enough in this Colony, God knows – altho' it might have been the same in some respects in any country in the World – It is a most providential thing that we don't know what *is* to be, or we should always be pining –

5th Tuesday   My last day at Yesabba – how very often I shall wish myself

back here again in my bark hut –

I have finished my packing – and this evening I rode over to Sherwood to say adieu to the folks there –

The night is exquisitely bright – and everything in the garden looks so pretty – I suppose I shall never see the place again – Well! let me hope that the change may be for the better – I have passed many happy hours here; and God knows many wretched ones too!

They tell me that I'm mad to leave this to go to Port Fairy! – Perhaps I am – but what, oh, what can I do?

To this question, Annie found no answer. She was a 'Settler' who never settled. After Yesabba came Yambuck, Hobart Town, England, Ireland, France, the Portland district of western Victoria, Melbourne, – then back to England, on to New Zealand, back to Melbourne, and finally to a small farm at South Yan Yean, where she died in 1905.

She had private reasons to feel unsettled. Affectionate ties to her brother and sister dissolved during bitter wrangles over inheritance. In 1855 she learned to her horror that Baxter had killed himself: 'Poor soul! I forgot all his ill-treatment immediately, & only pitied him dying alone & neglected: and he was buried the *following* day to the *one* on which he died! how dreadful – ' Living in Cork at the time, she waited impatiently to hear from Australia 'some definite news relative to Mr Baxter's affairs – and I feel unsettled!' As one might have expected, the news she eventually heard was of a tangled mess. Sorting it out by mail proved too difficult, and at the beginning of 1857 she sailed to Melbourne, spurred on no doubt by an Australian correspondent who was 'very sanguine as to my having some little fortune out of the wreck in which Mr Baxter left his affairs.' She might have ended financially secure in England, with a small cottage and a modest income. Instead, she embraced the precarious life by taking on a new husband, a new station, and – within a couple of years – the new experience of total bankruptcy.

Never again does the journal record moments of peace or security. That was for the elusive future. In Melbourne, Annie wrote: 'If I could only get come copying to do, I should be glad; but I am unable to pay the money to go and look for it, even. Let us hope for ''better days''; and as long as my own and my dear husband's health remain good, I must be contented.' Her husband, Robert Dawbin, remained 'dear' even when he returned to England and did not write, much less send the promised ticket for her to join him. She scraped along as best she could, living frugally in Melbourne boarding houses, and in 1865 was again aboard ship for the return voyage to England.

Her entries have become spotty by this time, and there is now a complete break until, three years later, she embarks on her next sea voyage, this time to Otago, New Zealand, 'my husband having the appointment to taking out salmon ova to New Zealand.' There are no more notebooks to record how they got along on this newest venture, but if Robert Dawbin had been any more successful than before, Annie probably would not have gone to live in various places around Melbourne. The final picture is tinged with melancholy.

Turning back to the journal, however, is to be reminded that Annie's life held much more than melancholy. Six years after leaving the Macleay, she was longing 'for *one* hour of Yesabba and its old & *pure* misery – yet happiness!' Bush life had suited Annie, and she knew it. On board ship for her first return to England, she saw clearly what Australia had meant to her: 'seventeen years nearly, I've been an exile from my own Country: I've made some most valued friends; such in fact, as I may never meet again. Then again, I've been so petted in the Bush, & my wild ways have not only been tolerated but actually admired – and I've been loved for my very faults – ' To readers of her journal, she will remain so.

EXPECTATIONS SADLY BLIGHTED

1840–51

Penelope Selby was ecstatic about the move to Australia. She had the greatest confidence that here indeed was the land of opportunity where money and the good things of life would come to those who worked. They did not come to the Selbys. In her letters, Mrs Selby chronicles ten years of disappointed expectations, although to the very end she lived in hope of capturing that ever elusive fortune which might take her back to England with a horse to ride alongside the aristocrats in Hyde Park.

Throughout her disappointments, a strong Protestant faith helped her to look at the ups and downs of fortune as matters of God's will. Over the years her sense of divinely guided destiny altered to fit her changed circumstances. An early confidence that 'it was ordained for the best that we come here', turned into the subdued resignation of 'we are in the hands of a Higher Power and must put our faith in Him.'

Australia also gave her a purely secular way of understanding success and failure. It taught her about economics. Her lessons, as practical as they were detailed, began with the fluctuating prices she could get for butter she was churning on the family's farm along the banks of the Yarra River north of Melbourne. Soon Penelope Selby was connecting the prices for her butter with the market prices in general, and was beginning to send home her account of the depression of the early 1840's, which was dealing such devastating blows to the six-year-old town of Melbourne and its less than five thousand inhabitants. Unsophisticated though she was about theories of capitalistic systems, she did recognize that 'political economy', as she called it, might explain the plummeting prices of butter which finally would drive the Selbys off the farm where they had dreamed of a good life.

Hard work never got the Selbys far. Australia belied its reputation as the land which rewarded those who worked it. Confidence in the power of individual effort had been misplaced and without that sort of confidence neither the Selbys nor other emigrants would have ventured into the bush. Perhaps the failure on the Yarra was just a fluke, the sign of unusual times, and somewhere else they might do better, somewhere else the promises of the work ethic might come true.

This is the way Penelope Selby continued to think until the last weeks of her life. In the 'day and night dreams' of her imagination, she kept 'looking forward to what will be', her hopes pinned on a future which would make worthwhile the austere and exhausting present. Even after seven years of largely unrewarded labour, she was expanding her dreams to include her six yet unmarried sisters, promising them unreservedly that if they would abandon the 'slavery' of their struggling school and sail to Australia, they would find 'good situations as governesses until married.' 'You might live like a queen on your income,' she assured them blithely, stating as certainty what really belonged to that fantasy land where sisters can build castles in air for governess-queens.

Caution, the careful measuring of prospects, remained alien to Mrs Selby in spite of her disappointments. Having come so far and staked so much on the pioneer life, she held fast to the myth of Australia as the land of opportunity for everyone, – merchant, squatter, 'the poor industrious mechanic or labourer and his wife and family.' Her sentiments were most comfortable as gesture and rhetoric, however. In the flesh, she showed a marked aversion to people lower down the social scale who were also trying to make the most of their chances. Rarely budging from clichés learned in the stratified society of England, she chastized the lower orders for laziness and greed and a generally self-indulgent lack of discipline. Any servant who came her way, any itinerant farmworker or other labourer, was likely to be described with an arrogant lack of sympathy. Aboriginees were to her 'a most disgusting set' whose nakedness threatened the decorum fundamental to civilized behaviour.

She did not see herself as prejudiced, of course. In a letter describing her sister's first confinement, she complained to her mother about having to return home earlier than desirable because her servant was in the advanced stages of her own first pregnancy and 'had only staid to oblige me an extra month that I might leave home comfortably.' This servant had at last sent word that she was unable to carry on the work any longer, and the mistress would be needed to run the household. To Mrs Selby, the childbearing of sister and servant were utterly different matters. After saying of her sister's child, 'Surely never baby was so much admired

Though the poultry-yard was often the woman's domain, she rarely chose to be photographed there. This shot is also uncharacteristic in its informality, the mother actually kneeling in the dirt. She may very well have made those elaborate bonnets for the children and herself. Is the woman who stands in black, proper and aloof, the governess?

before,' she unselfconsciously switched language, tone, and assumptions, to offer a judgement upon her servant: 'She is a good girl but I wish she was not going to be bothered with a piccaninny.' Prejudices of race and class unite in that one word, 'piccaninny', and since this is quite likely the 'Irish woman lately arrived' of the preceding letter, one can presumably add nationality to the list of slurs. Ironically, the mother of the bothersome piccaninny and the mother of the much admired baby shared the same name . . . Mary.

Australia was expected to release Penelope Selby from the shackles of keeping up appearances and yet still allow her to exercise her sense of class superiority. Although never a democrat in her sympathies, she did grow a little less rigid. The change started as soon as her feet left English soil and she got into a boat taking people out to the ship at Gravesend. As Mrs Selby looked at the other passengers, her mind busily distributed them into their proper places on board the ship. She made a crucial mistake about one woman, Mrs Dawson, who was to become her closest friend outside her own family:

> I guessed that as [Mrs Dawson] was at the best end of the boat, she was not a steerage [passenger] but felt certain they were intermediate – what was my astonishment to find the next day that they had one of the beautiful stern cabins and I am sure they are disposed to make themselves very friendly – how wrong it is to judge of persons' stations by their dress.

This rebuke proved well-deserved. Mrs Dawson was open and generous, and as her new friend soon discovered, 'understands all about a farm,' and 'the famous Mungo Park was her own uncle – if we can manage so that we are neighbours when we get to Port Phillip I shall be so glad.' They did manage, and Penelope Selby had every reason to be glad, for the next ten years would sadly blight her expectations and sap her energy, and she would need the deep friendship of this high-spirited Scotswoman to whom she paid warm tribute throughout these letters home.

'Warm' seems the single most appropriate word to use in characterizing Penelope Selby. Limited though her circle of sympathy might be, she spoke in a voice of unfailing love when writing of those friends and family within its circumference. She and her husband George worked steadily together under strained conditions, and their closeness is an abiding presence in the letters. Of Prid and Willie, the two little boys who came with their parents from England, she always wrote with amusement and affection. Of the stillborn children – seven in all – her words conjure up a spectre of pain which did not end when the body healed.

Station on the Yarra Yarra
26th December 1840

My dear Grandfather & Grandma,

We are very comfortably settled about twenty five miles from Melbourne on a station, not in partnership with but on the same place with Mr & Mrs Dawson. George has now 45 head of cattle which he expects in ten years will have increased to 880 head which at the present worth will be about £6000. Meanwhile we hope soon to pay all our expenses by our dairy; the expense of living here being very small, ten pounds a year for a licence being all the rent and taxes. We have as much firing as we like to cut, we have a garden with plenty of vegetables, and poultry and pigs. Persons in the country have been getting six shillings a dozen for their eggs, but I do not expect they will be so high when I have any to sell. Provisions are very fluctuating in price, when we arrived the 4 lb loaf was three shillings, now it is only one, so you may be sure we have laid in a good stock of flour.

This is generally called a very fine climate but give me home as yet. To be sure you have a great deal of bad weather that we are spared, but it is very hot here now, and very changeable, the thermometer at this time is 104 in the shade, I leave you to judge what it must be in the sun. As for insects they are more numerous than you can imagine, the flies bite terribly and being a new comer have feasted on me.

The children have not had a day's illness since their arrival, they do not mind the heat, you may be sure they are not burdened with many clothes. Prid is becoming an expert judge of cattle and grows very fast, so like his father. As for Willie, if ever there was a brag he is one, and it would fill a volume to tell you what he is going to do when he grows up a man. Amongst other things they are both going to take me to London Bridge in a ship to see you all.

Mary wrote me an account of your removal and robbery. I trust you have no more frights and that you now find your new abode more comfortable than the old one; more airy I am sure it must be. I do not think I could live in London now, the air is so fresh here, we have plenty of wind and when it rains it comes down in torrents. I [will] tell you in a few words what I think of this place. Any one, like ourselves, willing to work (for I could not get a woman servant to come here for any wages) and put up with a few inconveniences and discomforts, let them come; but to the poor industrious mechanic or labourer and his wife and family the advantage is beyond description and I would not hesitate to say none would regret leaving England. Unfortunately there are too many here that will always be poor, for they will perhaps only work two or three days in the week and spend all they get in drink. A person in want of food is a thing not known. I saw no beggar while I was in Melbourne and Captain Howey who has lived there these nine months was only asked for alms once and that was a tipsy woman who wanted a shilling to get something to drink.

Now my dear Grandfather and Grandma that I have come to the end of my paper, I must wish you a happy new year and though so far separated from you be sure I do not think of you the less. It was ordained for the best that we came here. I have no doubt it [will] turn out so. We are sure of making a comfortable independence for ourselves and being able to put our children in the way of doing so too. How much better it is than staying at home with no prospect but that of Bankruptcy and poverty staring us in the face.

Your affectionate Grandaughter,
P. Selby

Station on the Yarra Yarra
26th January 1841

My dear Mary and Kate,
The last letter I dispatched was to my brothers about three weeks since. I complained to them of the Postmaster at Melbourne having extracted numbers of 'Master Humphrie's Clock'. I must have accused him wrongfully for we have received two packages last week containing three numbers for which you must thank whoever sent them – I have not read any yet but have no doubt they will be worthy Boz.

And now Miss Polly after telling you how glad I was to hear that you were all well may I request to know why and for what reason you have discontinued your journal. Perhaps you think I have begun to lose my interest in the affairs of your home – alas for me if you think that. You little know me. I feel that if I were here twenty years I should still look upon the place I left as my home and look forward to the time of visiting it again if the friends I most love are spared – but I am not a Scotch-woman, consequently I cannot say with Mrs Dawson that I would wish to return if all my relatives were no more, merely to see my own country.

I do not know if it is worth writing so often, for I am barren of news for how can I possibly have any when I have not been more than a quarter of a mile from my home since I went in November to call on Mrs Anderson my next neighbour, who was unwell and is now dead. We occasionally see gentlemen passing to the next station and bullock drivers who tell very wonderful stories which I do not always believe.

I am truly sorry to hear the bad accounts of Mr Batkin, not that either George or I are much surprised at them for how could he expect to get on in such a concern without money? I do not suppose matters would have been so bad if George had been still there to furrage about and take all the anxiety on his own shoulders – but how much better it is that we are here and though I am still at times, and will always be, a great grumbler and find fault alternatively with the climate and the heat and the smoke from the wood fire, and the pigs (of which we have three as long-nosed lean ill-favoured things as could be met with in any Irish cabin) and sundry other things, yet in the midst of my grumblings I always feel thankful we are here, and would willingly put up with all and much more for the comfortable feeling of independence we enjoy – in Foster Lane I always had to keep up a sort of appearance, while here I care not who comes, how rich they may be or what style they live in. If rich now they were probably poor when they came here and we may be as well off as them in a few years. I would not advise or even wish – far from it – my dear Father and Mother and all of you to come here now, but if we had come in a body ten years ago you would all have been differently off in worldy matters, and I can answer for it both Father and Mother after the first month or so would have liked the country and the life much, and Father would not now have to fag so many hours, but it is but right to suppose that all is for the best and if you want in some things you make up in others.

You must tell my dear Mother and she must keep it a *dead secret* that I shall miss her and our mutual friend Mr Wallace sadly some time next August when if all goes right I shall increase her stock of grandchildren and my own of trouble – I would not have thought of such a thing had you or Kate thought proper to get married and begin, but as you do not seem to have any inclination that way I cannot bear that my Mother should have so many children and only two grandchildren. How I shall get the affair over time only can show, but I have no doubt I shall manage as well as my neighbours. I have serious thoughts of doing as the cows do here, just separate myself from the family three or four days and then return with my calf bellowing at my side. I am very well at present, quite different to what I was at home in the same circumstances, and am sure of a kind friend in Mrs Dawson who is almost as pleased as if it were herself – I wish it had been her, but she is such a fidget that I tell her she never will have one much as she desires it.

You always want to know a great deal about the boys but what can I say more than they are very good ones, just like country children, so shy that if they see a stranger they hold down their heads and run away. Willie's little pet, Esther, is so tame that they have it put in the bale and milked and all sorts of fun, and the little thing is so fond of them that if it has not been home for a week or fortnight, when it does come, it *runs* to them away from the other cattle directly. I made Prid's mouth water with your account of the fruit and he is sure you might pack some up and send here. He thought a little and then said if they have plenty of fruit, Mama, they have not corn and as much nice milk as they can drink –

George is now milking six cows, and if we can get a boy I intend to send fresh butter to Melbourne as soon as ever the weather is a degree cooler, I expect to get 2/6 a lb for it, and if I could only make a dozen pounds per week it would more than pay all our expenses. George would start very early in the morning with it on horseback to Melbourne and return the same day. We must have assistance of some kind, for George has to be out every other day minding the cows and he has so many other things to do that his time is rather too valuable for that.

My life here seems made up of day and night dreams. I seem never satisfied with the present but am always looking forward to what will be, so it will be to the end of our lives and were it not for that future where we may all hope to meet if not again on this earth, we should be miserable indeed.

Would you like to know my dress just now, 4 o'clock pm, the thermometer 98 in the shade (last week one day it was 107)? It consists of shoes, stockings, shift and cotton gown – Mrs Dawson leaves out the stockings but the flies bite my legs. Three hours from this time I shall be glad to put on all my petticoats and make a good fire.

I have not tasted kangaroo yet, but I have a piece a man brought in my safe now, and intend to broil a piece for breakfast tomorrow – Mrs Dawson had some this morning and said it was delicious. There is an animal here they call the Kangaroo rat, about the size of a rabbit, feet like the Kangaroo and head like a rat. They are very nice and eat much the same as rabbit. We called them Bush rabbit, not liking the idea of eating a rat, but the nicest wild animal I have tasted here is the oppossom. It is larger and has a finer flavour than the rat – you can only shoot them at night for they creep into the hollow trees during the day and come out at dark to feed on grass and the leaves of trees. The most delicious bird is the bronze winged pigeon, larger than our own wild pigeon, much the same colour but the wings a beautiful bronze. They are very scarce, as indeed all birds are on this run. We eat black magpies, cockatoos and paroquets all in their turn as we can get them, always a change from the salt meat.

You will think I am pretty well occupied when I tell you I have not yet looked at 'Master Humphrie's Clock'. One comfort, time does not hang heavily on my hands. I am always up at six, sometimes five and go to my bed about half past nine.

Good bye for the present, my dearest sisters,

Penelope Selby

Station on the Yarra
5th July 1841

My dear Sisters,
Since we last wrote we have begun to earn a little by our butter. We are making about 20 lbs a week which we send into Melbourne salted once a month, for which we get 2 shillings per pound for as much as we can send for a year. Thanks to Mrs Dawson I have become a first rate dairy woman and can cure meat, make butter, cheese, fatten calves or pigs equal to Aunt Goddard herself and when I tell you that we have had no man the last month and George has had to be away every alternate day with the cows, that I have all the baking, washing and in fact everything to do and that I am now within a month of my confinement you will allow that we have no time for dress or play.

Indeed, could you see George when he comes in from milking in the stockyard these cold damp mornings covered with filth, I do not know whether you would laugh or cry. A scavenger in the City of London after a heavy frost and a thaw is clean to him, but he puts up with it all and says he would not exchange his present dirty work for his old life of gentility at home.

You will know before this that you are to have a new nephew or niece about the beginning of next month. I was afraid I should be obliged to go to Melbourne upon the occasion but to my great joy I think I shall be able to manage here. A very respectable middle-aged woman who acted as servant to Mrs Howey is coming to stay with me the end of this week for as long as I like. She has had 5 children of her own and great experience that way. George asked her as a favour to come and expected she would and he was prepared to give a pound a week. To his surprise and satisfaction she said would he consider eight shillings too much, which is quite as little as I could hire a raw Irish girl for. Previous to this George has endeavoured to get a man and his wife but they all have infants or young children which they seem to expect should be paid for by an increase of wages, and when you do get a woman, not one out of twenty will be of service to you.

With respect to the gentleman who is to take my old friend Mr Wallace's place, nothing is settled. We are told that there are plenty about Melbourne not in practice who are glad for a moderate sum to go into the country a week or two upon such occasions – George has advertized in the Melbourne papers his want of such a person, and he goes to Melbourne the end of the week to see the result of his application and then I hope all will be settled and he will be able to get a man into the bargain. For myself I must tell you that I am not like the person I was at home on such occasions. I am quite well and though I must confess generally very tired when night comes, have scarcely an ache or pain. I have Mrs Dawson's authority, who knows everything, for telling you that it is *sure* to be a little girl, very good tempered and the image of my sister Mary. Time only can show and the ship that conveys this to you may likely also contain a letter to contradict it all.

Melbourne the place is so overloaded with goods of every description that they are dayly sold by auction for less than they cost at home. Merchants are constantly failing and you may get any interest for money. The worthy Melbournites are now feeling the effects of their speculations. Glad am I that we embarked on no business in that good town. Did George live there, I might buy goods of every description for what you may call 'an old song' by auction, but the retail shopkeepers keep up their prices just the same, so that persons in the country do not reap the advantage – as a specimen you cannot buy a raisin under 9d the pound at any grocer's. George got a box at an auction for 3d and hundreds were sold for 2d. Now, they could not have been bought for that and we shall ere long feel the effects in the high prices, for of course shippers will not send goods next year when they lost so much this.

The boys are quite well. Our new neighbour, Mrs Gardiner, who only lives nine miles off has asked Prid to come and stay with her a few weeks. She was spending three days with Mrs Dawson when of course I saw a great deal of her. She is a very nice person, not young, has been married twenty years but has no family. They have a beautiful station with plenty of servants and a house and garden like a country cottage at home. Mrs Dawson rode on horseback to see them but I was obliged to decline. She was delighted with the place. They are most attentive and take to Melbourne and bring back all that we require by their drays.

Give my love to all,

Penelope Selby

Yarra River
21st November 1842

My dear Sisters,

It is long since I wrote to you. You must not wonder if I have not much heart to write frequently when I have nothing new to tell you, unless it should be that things in the business line are in a most wretched state in this country – almost every merchant in Melbourne is failing or has done so – and numbers of squatters likewise, amongst others the grocer who had contracted to take our butter, which will be a serious loss to us, for we got 1/10 a pound for it and now that it is broken we will not be able to sell it for more than 1/- indeed many persons have got only 10d lately, so much has everything come down in price, but when things are at the worst, people say they are sure to mend and there is nothing like hoping for the best, but it really is provoking when one thinks that they will have a few pounds at the end of the year to be worse than nothing. But enough of the dismals, not that we are downhearted, for we are better off than hundreds and will hold up our heads and come home with a fortune yet.

I have been a great rover lately. My dear friend, Mrs Dawson, has a very nice little girl. You may be sure I had been rather nervous some time previously, it being her first child and she so delicate, and the Doctor so many miles to come, and I had never been at a like exhibition before, but we managed admirably. Mrs Dawson was very ill but never dangerously so, and has recovered very well though still weak – I am quite an oracle with regard to baby, for both Mr & Mrs Dawson are so anxious and frightened that it will not live, that they are almost for sending for me every time it cries, but I would not wish for a healthier or nicer babe and you must trust me for not sparing my lectures to Mrs Dawson on the necessity of her not suffering herself to become over particular about it, and I will tell her that if crying would kill a child, neither my worthy self or my son William would grace this country with our presence now. How often do I wish that you knew Mrs Dawson. She is the funniest creature I ever knew and can make a joke of everything. How often I think of the comfort I have experienced in having found such a friend. Now you will wonder if I manage to walk so often to see her. No indeed. I have a beautiful little mare which carries me so nicely and in time I hope to become a first rate rider, not that I am yet quite so bold as a lion, but wait until you see me riding in Hyde Park and joining the followers of her Majesty with George beside me – perhaps then I may sometimes allow you to try a canter too!

I have serious thoughts of paying Mrs Howey a visit in Melbourne shortly. George is quite determined I should go. It seems he was so happy while I was with Mrs Dawson that he wants to be his own master again! I really care very little about the matter myself and am of course quite at a loss for the fashions. It will be of little use my cutting and altering here as I have neither seen a person or gown of a newer cut than when I left London and the ladies here are so very smartly dressed in the worthy town of Melbourne. I well remember when I was staying there having a good laugh at the old-fashioned figures that I saw who had evidently come to town after a few years rustication in the Bush, so I must not complain if I am paid off in my own coin.

The country is looking beautiful now. We have not had dry weather enough yet to scorch the grass and have passed through the very wettest winter ever known here. The Yarra has twice risen to such a height that many families have been completely washed out of their houses and [it] has done a great deal of damage to crops. I hope I shall never have such

Civilised behaviour would not be lost while there were pots of tea and an occasion for indulging in dress and manners. Date and place unknown.

another for dirt. We could not go out of our door for months without being ankle deep and as the whole family were constantly in and out, the house was never better than a pig sty, and when clean it is such a nice little place that I often wish you could see it. Sometimes I really like the place and the life so much, and think if you were here you would like it too; at others, when I am not in the best of temper, I wish the country had never been discovered and think how much more comfortable you are at home.

If you have had patience to get this length you will say 'what an interesting subject self is; I wish my sister would tell me some news' – Indeed, we have none. We seldom have visitors and even the blacks have been away for some time. Of course there is plenty of gossip and tittle tattle going on about our neighbours, but as they are unknown to you, you won't care to hear it, but it is wonderful how everything connected with every person, what they say and what they do, flies like wildfire through this place, and when I perchance see any of my neighbours, what wonderful tales we have to hear and relate. And by the time that the story reaches another hundred miles, it becomes so improved that you would not know it for the plain unvarnished piece of goods it was when it left you.

The boys are well and hearty. They are getting on slowly with their booklearning, and many of your town bred boys would eclipse them, but give them a chopping axe and a tree as big round as themselves and as high as the church steeple, and then see which would beat at chopping it down and then into lengths for firewood. Prid is as strong as a horse now, Willie more robust than I ever expected to see him. He has a fine memory and can read or repeat anything without trouble to himself, but has such a very quick indistinct way of speaking that no person can understand him, just like John used to be. Prid is a very slow coach but you can understand all he says, for he speaks very well.

We have a great many pet calves but one especially is so fat behind that I say she always puts me in mind of my sister Mary. Is not it strange but I never look at her but I think of you, and Mrs Dawson has a little dog that always puts me in mind of cousin Mary Giles, and whenever I look at [them] a thousand things of by gone days come across my memory. In one minute I have passed through thoughts and scenes that would take me hours to relate.

Our establishment is now reduced to one boy, but George has two men hired to put up two miles of fence to form a paddock which will contain about fifteen hundred acres of land in which he can keep the horses and any of the cattle who are apt to stray. This river Yarra should have been called the Serpentine, it has so many bends, and this is a bend, and just the fence across one side. You would think it not a very small place to turn the horses in that you are likely to want every day, but here it is reckoned quite handy, for if you are two or three hours before you can hit upon their lordships you are sure they are there, and that they have not been able to follow the inclination that they often have for visiting their neighbours several miles off.

I can but ill express what I feel for you all and the pleasure it would give me once more to be seated round your cheerful fireside, but as my lot in life is cast here I can only assure you all my dearest Father Mother Brothers and Sisters my Grandparents that I am and always will be

ever attached and affectionate,

P. Selby

Yarra River
3rd February 1843

My very dear Sisters,

It is long since I wrote to you but having nothing either new or pleasant to communicate has made me lazy. I fancy I hear you say 'I wish Pen would tell us something about the country,' – Alas, I can say little good of it, for just now it is looking very barren, the grass is all either burnt with the sun or the fires and we are anxiously looking for rain.

I have had Captain and Mrs Howey with their daughter staying with me the last week, and as it always happens in this country, George's horses – that is, his mare, my mare and a foal – most mysteriously disappeared out of the paddock the day before their arrival, and he has not found them yet, so that the whole of his time has been taken up seeking them and we ladies could not have any rides, but it is always the case here if you want to do anything or go anywhere. Either the horses or cows cannot be found, and you are obliged to stay at home. The most provoking part of this business is that George has been at great expense enclosing a paddock for these beasts and thought himself so secure and we had them at the door late the night before we lost them.

Everybody in the very worthy town of Melbourne either has or is likely to fail, and the distress they say is very great. The settlers too are nearly as badly off. As a specimen, one settler has a fine run and about 400 head of first rate cattle. [He] put them up to auction and was only offered 22 shillings the head, with the Station and all the improvements to be given in. For cows no better George paid thirteen pounds when he came here. They say that they who can weather the storm will do well and I have no fear that we shall be able to do so. Still, we feel it though we may not be so likely to be uprooted as the proud oak. We only now get 13d for the butter and that we would not have had if George had not made a contract for the year, and I do not think that commodity will ever be higher, for all the large stock holders that scorned making butter when they could get 2/- the pound for it, now that it is half the price are establishing large dairies. If you should chance to meet Miss Martineaux, you may mention this to her, and as she is a great writer on political economy, she may write a book upon the subject.

Our establishment is very much reduced. We have only ourselves and cousin George, who has not suited himself with anything yet, so he is staying with us instead of a boy, and milks the cows and tends them through the day just as the boy did. He is a real good tempered lad. I often say to him 'how are the mighty fallen', and he only laughs, and I am glad he has the sense to put pride in his pocket.

The boys are growing fast and are very useful to me. They have been staying a week with Mrs Dawson and almost as soon as they returned told us with great glee that Mrs Dawson and they had dug a long time near where her little baby was found, and at last they came to one which looked just like a chrysalis wrapped in a piece of brown paper, but that in six months it would be big enough when they would dig it up again and bring it to me – she is a funny body and though she may have the chance to dig out one, it will not be before the middle of September.

With our best and lasting loves to all around your fireside,

I remain,
your affectionate
P. Selby

Port Fairy
6th November 1844

My dear Mary & Kate,
This is my dear Mother's birthday. She will surely be fifty-two. I cannot

fancy her any older than when we left five years ago. How quickly time passes and yet it does seem long, long to me since I saw you all. Well is it that the future is hidden, for were it not so we should not have left England with such hopes for after days. What were we not to do in five years – and see the result. We have both grown older and poorer but still with hope and willingness to try for better times.

I wrote about a month ago an account of our settlement here upon a very fine station, but unfortunately not ours. Mr Dawson is the owner of it, but George has the privilege of keeping his cattle on it for one or two years if he pleases free of expense, and he thinks we shall be better off than fighting on with a dairy now butter is so low, as it takes more than the profits to pay wages, besides spoiling the growth of the calves.

Mr Dawson does not live here. He is going to commence melting down at the port. He is putting up buildings upon a large scale, and I hope he will succeed. There was a misunderstanding between him and George with regard to this station but it is amicably arranged, and although we have not the half of the station as we supposed we should, it will be better for us in the present state of the finances to be relieved from the expenses. Mr and Mrs Dawson have always shewn themselves sincere friends to us, and I should have been sorry for anything to break the friendship. Mrs D. is now on a visit to me and after being sometime alone you may be sure it is a great treat to talk over our respective troubles.

My old friend the Yarra Yarra has overflowed beyond the calculation or remembrance of any persons here and done great damage. Entire houses have been washed away. The blacks still say as they said the last flood, 'This is only piccaninny – big one coming.' My affection for the Yarra is still great, and this run not being George's I never shall feel at home here as I hoped to do were we owners of a really good station such as this is.

If my last letter is duly received, you will know that I have again had a still born child. It came at the seventh month, the 12th of September. I had been very unwell the month previous and was truly thankful when all was over. I was very ill for some time after and I think so when I wrote, but am now recovering very well though I fear I shall never be so strong as I have been. I need not repeat the particulars as I filled my last sheet with them, but I fervently hope I shall have no more. If ever such a thing should be likely, I shall be obliged to have medical advice all the time as constant bloodletting they say will be my only safety and that of course must weaken me much.

When in Melbourne I saw a gentleman who knew the Palmers well. He did not give a very favourable account of their circumstances. Poor Mrs Palmer like so many others has had her expectations sadly blighted. They are very ill off. Frederick, who was troubled with epileptic fits, fell into a river and was drowned. The other boys are variously dispersed, none doing well. The daughters are very nice girls and he speaks highly of Mrs P. but said that Mr P. was sadly given to drink, a bad thing for the family, but I recollect my Mother suspected him to be guilty of that failing.

Mrs Dawson is sitting beside me and she sends her kind love. I wish you knew her. I never met a woman with such a heart and so sensitive for the troubles of others. She is a universal favorite. She has been living in the town of Port Fairy called Belfast but prefers the Bush. She finds no one like me, so she says, but I don't believe her. I much fear this air will be too keen for her, and she will not take the rest which the doctor says is the only thing to prolong her life. I must confess I have a great fear for her and feel convinced that some of the violent attacks of pain she has will carry her off but dare not tell her so.

Some day perhaps we shall get a batch of likenesses from Chester; it is quite as well you never came here, though the best off now are steady young men who came when we did without any money to lose. They received such high wages that they could save the greater part. A great many persons here have become insane and it is said to be in consequences of the reverses and great shock their expectations have received.

Prid is the image of his father in face, figure and walk. I must make him write a letter soon. He gets on the best with figures, and though not at school is really not bad at his books. He will soon know all I can teach him and is constantly longing for books.

Am I to believe my letters are such a treat? I get quite stupid at writing and if you can make sense of the epistles and decipher the words it is more than I sometimes can myself – this is not the life for intellectual improvement and few children reared in the colony have hitherto had more than a Charity boy's education at home, with the addition of being taught to swear, smoke and ride. The first, some children of those that consider themselves snobs are adepts at. I never heard my boys utter a bad word, but they are fortunately uncontaminated. How they would be injured by bad example remains to be proved.

With lasting love to all assembled at our cottage fireside,
I remain
my dear sisters,
P. Selby

I begin now to get nervous before opening letters, death has been busy with so many friends at home that I always fear the loss of nearer and dearer ones. Every time we remove our hut is worse. I often wonder what you would think of this one.

Melting Establishment
Port Fairy
1st March 1845

My dear Mary,
You will perceive that I am a truant from home. George has been the last month in Melbourne and he would not leave me alone in the Bush, so we placed our moveables under the charge of Mr Mitchell and I am here with the boys to stay until George's return.

My memory will not tell me if I have written you since we heard of our beloved [cousin] Mary's death. The box arrived here last week containing dear Mary's clothes, shirts for the boys and a gown from my dear Mother which I am now writing in. It is a capital fit. I am struck with my own stock, which is still good, and with poor Mary's I shall have enough to last my life. My dress is all presents, Kate's bonnet has been most useful and is quite good yet.

I suppose you will expect to hear something of the town here called Belfast, such a town, a few scattered houses close to the sea, but it is a rising place and will doubtless improve. Mr Dawson's establishment about three miles from the township is the Lion just now and has cost more money in the erection than all the buildings in the town together. He commenced 'boiling down', as it is called, a fortnight since. He has two immense vats which together will contain three hundred sheep or twenty bullocks, which are cut into pieces and placed inside. A steampipe is inserted in the top and all the fine meat goes to waste and the tallow is kept. It is a fine thing for this district, and I have no fear but it will do well, for before, the settlers could not dispose of their surplus stock.

Such a houseful there has been since I came, for every person inspects the place and then they must come in, in the easy way of the country, and take what is going. Mrs Dawson has been allowing her tongue to ramble about me. The consequence is all the people of the town have been most civil, they – that is the ladies – are mostly colonial and quite different to the home. We – that is, the particular ones from the old country – we see so much want of delicacy and respect for themselves, and children here are sadly brought up. As a specimen, Mrs Cox's son, his father quite a gentleman and rich, has a pony of his own to ride where he pleases, associates with all the bullock drivers and worst characters of the place, will go to the public house and call for anything he likes, and use such language as would shock you to hear from a man, and he is just six years old, his younger brother aged four quite as bad, and I could instance many that have come under my limited observations quite as bad.

The natives here are a most disgusting set. We have plenty here carrying away the offal, and I am not surprised at the want of what we consider proper delicacy of feeling when all classes are constantly coming in contact with men and women in a state of complete nudity. I must say I have felt my own cheeks burn when I have seen ladies in company with gentlemen talking and laughing with savages in that state, and know that I am considered most fastidious. I hope my boys will not get contaminated. They are good as yet, and are thought so very quiet.

Upon the whole, your visit to the North must have been pleasing and satisfactory and in reading your accounts of the persons you saw and places you visited, all past events appeared like a dream to me, and I could have fancied myself there once again. We were young and fresh when dear Mary left me on Belford hill to run to meet her beloved sister. The moon was just rising magnificently and from that day I have never seen the full moon rising among the trees without thinking of that night sixteen years ago. What has happened since? Dear Mary sleeps in her quiet grave and I am an old woman – but the less upon that subject the better, as you are creeping on I suspect. My Mother would have the advantage of me now – has she lost her front teeth yet? – for one of mine is gone.

The boys are quite well but the sea air does not agree so well with them as the Bush. Poor Willie was crying with toothache the greater part of the last two nights. He has had two drawn since he came down but I must have Dr Ritchie for the other two, which Willie dreads much. The M. D. is a great bungler. Fortunately they are his first teeth, but I have little hopes of the next.

Willie's Sunday suit is the one you sent for Prid, very small for him.

Prid has waist coat and jacket I made out of his Father's old surtout, a capital fit. You cannot think what an expert tailor I have become, and all the hats the boys or their Father have worn I have made from old sugar bags. George sometimes thinks I can do everything and expects accordingly. I shall knit the boys some socks this next winter, or at least try. I often wish I could help you with some of your needlework. I have plenty of spare time now, for we have no dairy and I have only George and the boys to do for. Indeed I could not work as I have done but am pretty well now and hope [I] shall manage to keep out of trouble for the future. Often when I have been lonely have I thought of my little girl, I have had so much spare time, but God's will be done and I never wish for another trial.

Sunday 3rd. I have just written a few lines to my Father. There was no service in the church today, a miserable room but a very good Scotch Minister, with less of the bigot in him than any of his class I have met. He gave George some useful school books for the boys which I thought was kind of him and I was much in want of them, and had we the means I do not know where we could send them. They will soon know all I can teach them.

Give my love to all my family and kind friends,
your affectionate sister,
Penelope Selby

[The father of Penelope Selby died on 15 January 1845]

Kangatong
27th August 1846

My dearest Mother,
Your last letters were dated February, wishing us to return, but our lot is cast at least for the present here and were we to return we should be in a worse position than when we left. Besides, I trust the worst is past. We could live here now upon the increase of the cattle, in your country it would not pay house rent. Had we a station now we might be saving money as dairy produce is again paying well, but the country is so much taken up that I fear there is little chance of procuring one so George thinks of turning farmer but we are still unsettled yet as he will not be able to get

this land, if he does, until the beginning of next year.

I wish my mind was easy about you all. Mary does not seem to be getting so many scholars as I could wish. Dear Mother, I cannot tell you how constantly you are all in my sleeping and waking thoughts. The forms of the departed ones are always more vivid to me when asleep than the living; doubtless they are the same to you. Well, I for one would not want my nightly visions for a trifle.

I am glad you like Mrs Slate although one part of Mary's last letter grieved and astonished me, that relating to the Dawsons. I suspected that his friends would not be so free with their cash as he supposed and frequently said as much as I could do to that effect to Mrs D. but to no purpose and when they lately received a bill for one hundred pounds they were consequently disappointed. Still I think Mrs Slate ought not to have said to any of you, almost strangers, what she did, and I hope you will not repeat in your turn anything I may say about the D. Family, for it is necessary to bear in mind that all persons are not as sincere or little given to make mischief as yourselves. I am really sorry for Mrs Dawson. She would give her last penny to another, and she fancies all are like herself, and I am convinced this expectation of money from home has done and is doing them a great deal of harm, for they spend a great deal uselessly and though there are plenty of milking cows on the run and butter and cheese are realising good prices, they are not yet milking any.

Mrs Dawson is still very unwell. Indeed I fear she will never be better. I am sure hers is a life of suffering, and yet she clings to it. A change to her must be for the better.

So poor Mr Aspland is released at last, he was long ill. I saw a notice of his death in two different London papers and cut one out. The boys read aloud one of his sermons every Sunday night, which brings you all to my recollection. Mrs Dawson says that Mrs Slate's father and mother were Unitarians, what she is, and that the Dawson family are also. She says that Mr D. here is one, but I think he is an Anything Arian.

An old Irish woman gave me a lesson in stocking knitting, so now I can knit [the boys'] socks and can consequently make everything they want but boots. My eyes are not nearly so young as they were, I cannot read at candlelight or work much, consequently I knit or plait.

If I return with a fortune and reside near London some part of Hackney will be the place but I do not think I should like your forms and fashions and coal fires, and would long to be in the Bush again.

 This mother in Victoria has set out her paths and gardens much as she might around a cottage in her homeland. A hut which would otherwise look makeshift and temporary takes on a settled appearance. c. 1899.

The boys are quite well. Prid is riding to Mrs LeMann's to borrow some sugar and George is seeking the bullocks to send the dray to the port for stores. The weather has been very wet, and the roads are so bad it has been put off as long as possible. Mrs D. has borrowed my sugar while it lasted. Pleasant, is it not? This is one of the comforts of the Bush.

Do you know, they are talking of railroads here. I wonder where the passengers will come from.

Lasting love from us all,

I remain
your affectionate daughter,
Penelope Selby.

What fearful accounts there are of Ireland. I trust the worst is over now and that the potatoes will be sound this year. This free trade will surely benefit you among the rest. I have taken great interest in politics lately. We get the *Examiner* and another English paper from Mr LeMann.

Farnham, Port Fairy
31st October 1847

My dear sisters,

Since writing we have received [a letter] from Susan. Tell her how pleased I was to see her writing and to find she is so contented with her lot. I wrote to all my sisters at once, so she must not think I forget her or any of you from my always addressing my epistles to the oldest of my six unmarried sisters. Is there one of them who would think it worth while to come to Australia with a husband if they had the chance? If they were all here they would soon get off, but marriage is a greater lottery here than at home.

Little did I think when we left home that we would be no better off after seven years working than we were when we left, but it is better to be born lucky than rich. We must try on and see what an apprenticeship at farming will do.

Your last was a very satisfactory letter. What pleasure it gives me to know you are comfortable and your school increasing. Many hours have I thought of you all during the time of scarcity and wished you in this land of plenty and waste. If the government does not send some emigrants, I don't know what will become of us. From fifty to fifty-five pounds a year is now wages for a man and wife with two or more children, all of which are to be found in what they choose to eat and waste. The men are so particular now they will not submit to be kept on rations, but must have all they like and work as little as possible. Nearly all the men about this part are old Vandemonian convicts and a notable set they are, but I trust their days of extortion and impudence are nearly over.

Did I ever mention that Mr LeMann was going to visit his family at home? He intends leaving about Christmas and will be away about two years. We will give him letters and ask him to go to see you. I know you will be pleased to see one who has been so kind to us and who is really worthy. He is very quiet and unaffected but well informed and well to do in the world. I do not know if he wants a wife, but she will be a lucky girl who gets him.

William has been most anxious to write to his Aunt Esther and has a letter nearly finished but I must send this without telling as I do not think it worth while to make you pay postage for him when he can send it by Mr LeMann.

We have had a disagreeable winter but hope to be quite snug by next. We are having the fence put up now. Our farm is a mile long and one-third of a mile wide. Our neighbor does the half of the fence. We shall then be able to keep our bullocks without trouble. As it is they have to be constantly watched, which comes very hard on the boys. Almost every person in the colony has been laid up with influenza. Never was any disease so prevalent as it has been. Our men have had it and I was in hopes we were going to escape but Willie is very bad today and my throat feels sore, so I suppose it will go the rounds. My poor Mrs Dawson has been very ill all the winter. I fear she will not hold out much longer, but God only knows. How much I have missed her, it is not likely I shall meet her like.

We have a very nice neighbour about half a mile off, Mrs Urquhart. Indeed, this is a more civilized place, and I shall have to furbish up my silk gowns etc that are precisely in the same condition as when I left home, but I am rather at a non plus for I saw in the paper that the sleeves are worn full (I do hate the tight ones). Now mine are large with a vengeance, I wish I had you or some *fashionable* to give me a shape.

November 21st   This letter has been lying long but I have had no opportunity of posting it. Besides, we have been bad with influenza previously mentioned. I have had nothing like it since we left home. The boys, particularly Prid, was very ill but I am thankful we are all better now.

Willie has finished his letter and makes so much work that I must put it in though I am ashamed of the mistakes, but it is entirely his own. Prid has been the last week staying with Mrs Dawson and come home quite well but has brought a sad account of [the Dawson's daughter] poor Isabella. She has turned so weak she cannot walk. I am very unhappy about her. She is a sweet child. Mr D. had been to consult a doctor but I don't know what he thinks of her. I am going to try to go up to see her this week. Poor Mrs D. has her share of the troubles of this life. I think the high spirited and merry often have the greatest portion of them.

Our garden is looking well. We shall have peas and new potatoes by Christmas. I wish I could send you some. I have a fine lot of young ducks. The boys are very keen to have some on Xmas day, but too many good things won't do. I begin to think with all its troubles this is a better country than yours, no fear of famine, all we want is people to eat. If you were all here on this snug little farm you would think it holiday time, fine grass, you could live in the open air if you chose but the sun is rather hot.

Your very affectionate sister,

Penelope Selby

Farnham Survey
15th December 1848

My dearest Mother,

I would have written you before this but have been very unwell for many weeks. Thank God I have been once more spared although as usual my baby was dead. I was really a pityable object for some time but have recovered very well. I am now undergoing an ordeal of calomel and my mouth is very sore in consequence, but if my health is improved by it I will not mind that. I have really been favoured with kind neighbors ever since I left home, indeed you may now know what a neighbor is, for persons that I came here a perfect stranger amongst have been as kind to me as my nearest relations could be. It is strange that my most intimate friend here is a Scotch woman, and the only English family near us I shall never become very sociable with. The lady gives herself too many airs. I perhaps judge her harshly, not having seen her but once. It is from hearsay I speak.

Our crops are working well. We have had the wettest and coldest spring ever known here. The melon plants are but just in leaf. Last year they covered yards of ground and melons formed at this time. The hay making will commence immediately after Christmas, then the harvest time. There is great fear men will still be scarce spite of the number of immigrants who have come in but I hope not.

Prid came home for his holidays last week. He has grown a great boy. We were anxious to send them both to school after Christmas but don't know how to manage it. Their board is so expensive; indeed it is a constant struggle for the 'filthy lucre' as my friend Mrs Dawson calls it, though we are certainly in a more promising condition than we were three years ago.

Did I thank you for the worsted you sent through Mrs Slate? Indeed, my dear Mother, we can supply our wants and I am quite sure you have far more calls upon your purse than you can well manage to supply. Do not fear I shall forget you without these remembrances. The most of my wearing apparel consists in gifts from one friend or other. I am writing in the gingham gown Susan sent and a very nice one it is too.

You must all have been in a state of great excitement with the Irish rebellion and revolutions on the continent. We are better off here, no want of necessaries of life or even the luxuries, and working people's children ought to grow up strong and able for they are never stinted as the poor are with you, but have as much good bread and meat as they can eat, and yet half of the parents think that no advantage and forget they left starvation to come here. Oh they are a saucy race. It often vexes me to think how I strive to save as much as possible to see the servants wasting your food and if you say a word to them you are told they do not wish to stay, they are quite willing to go. The women here are far worse to manage than the men.

I left off this yesterday to call on a neighbor where I met a Londoner who has lately arrived here with his family. It did me good to hear him praise the country, such meat, such bread, and so on, and all so cheap. He says we ought to be the happiest people under the sun with no tax gatherers around with book and pen to take your money, but he will find annoyances and plenty too even in this happy land.

How often I think of your little [motherless granddaughter] Clara. If I had her here I would love her very much. I quite agree with your mode of feeding. I always intended to adopt the same plan had I had a living child. My last was a very fine boy although little more than seven months. What a lot of boys we should have had about us had they all lived.

I owe all my sisters a great many letters, but I consider that one does for all. Oh what happiness it gives us to hear you are all so happy and I have no fear they will all yet get good husbands, or if they do not, it will be for their own good. Better none than a bad one.

Love from all,
your always affectionate daughter,
Penelope Selby

Newlands, Port Fairy
20th October 1849

My dear sisters,

[Sister] Sarah has been most fortunate in her experience of governessing. I suppose in another year her boys will be too big for her management and she will have to transfer it to a husband. You, Mary and Kate, do not seem likely to fix on one for your calves. By this time it will be decided whether either of you have been plucky enough to become Mrs LeMann, for I cannot think if you had the chance you would refuse him. I do not think there is any magnet at Bath except his family, and I know he much wanted a wife but would not have a fine lady one. He fortunately for himself – and his wife too – knows the Bush here too well to risk his happiness with one who would not be contented.

Mrs Dawson had a letter from him mentioning he had been to see you. He was quite astonished at my dear Mother's youthful appearance. I will not flatter you by repeating what he said of you. Mrs Dawson is in high spirits. She thinks already she has one of you for a neighbor. For myself I am not so sanguine. I have too long held the first rank in Mrs D's estimation to wish to be superseded by a younger sister. Still I am willing to waive all selfish considerations and would receive either with open arms, but it is nonsense this, for before this time the die will be cast, and though both George and I have occasionally built a few castles, we have not allowed them to be any more than air. When I think of the way you have to slave at school – and embroidery and old age will overtake us all – how much better you would be here with a good husband and home even though you do leave many near and dear to you behind.

Did I tell you I had taken a little girl six years old to live with me? She was motherless and I was to have thirty pounds a year. She was just three months here and both George and I were becoming fond of her when she was attacked with water on the brain and died after a week's illness. I cannot tell you how I missed her, and I was going to do so many things with the money.

This has been a bad year for farmers. Wheat has been so low that we have been unable to have many comforts we intended. Still, George does not despair and we are creeping on, not racing. I hope it may not be a short race. I do not know what farmers would have done had emigration not commenced. As it is wages are still high in this part, the immigrants not liking to come so far from Melbourne.

Prideaux has left school and William taken his place. He is very thin and delicate. Unfortunately for himself he is too watery headed and lately teased so that the boys at school lead him rather a hard life. I cannot think who he takes his crying propensities from, but do you remember if I ever disliked teasing?

Our garden is looking well now. In another year we shall have plenty of fruit. I am trying to get a few flowers too. I have very little to write about. Year after year passes much in the same way here. I leave home but seldom, see very few strangers. This has been the wettest winter ever known, consequently the roads are quite impassable. They talk now of spending half the purchase money for land in making roads, and much needed, for you can have no idea of the difficulty of travelling in the bad weather. I went into Belfast about three months ago and about six miles of the way it was as much as my mare could do to get her feet out of the mud. It was above her knees, rather different from your railroads! Even now that summer has almost come, George has ten bullocks, and as much as they can do to drag a light load of wheat through part of our farm. Fortunately it is not so bad all the way to the mill.

We have nearly seventy acres cleared now and a most expensive job it has been, a great many of the farmers saying it cannot pay and there is such a demand for them you can always find parties to buy. Time will show if we do better than our neighbors. From my two years experience of the country, had I my choice it should be a good cattle station as the least risk and expense with the surest profit.

Be assured my dear Mother brothers and sisters that though we are far from you, we do not forget you, but will love you as long as life is given us and though we may not meet here, may we hereafter is the sincere prayer of

Your ever affectionate sister,

Penelope Selby

Newlands, Port Fairy
23rd December 1849

My dearest Mother,

We received a letter from Mr LeMann about a fortnight since containing the very best news to us we have had since we came to the country. I need not tell you it related to my dear sister and the prospect of seeing her here at no distant period. I cannot express to you the unbounded joy and happiness it gave both George and me, for although we had built many a castle on the subject we were afraid they would be merely castles in the air, and indeed I have partly resided in that very light element since. I know she will grieve at parting from you but hers will be much sooner removed than yours.

With regard to any imaginary privations you may fancy she will have to endure, you may make your mind quite easy. Port Phillip, is a different country to what it was ten years ago and the Bush a different place to live in. You now see houses and furniture there that would not shame a town and as good living as they have in Northumberland, very different from what I had to put up with. Besides, is she not coming to friends who know her through me and will be ready to welcome her as soon as she sets foot in Australia, to say nothing of those she will have for her husband's sake who is universally respected and is every way worthy of such a wife?

Mr Dawson was here yesterday, he had got a letter from LeMann. Mary had, he said, won the hearts of all his family. He wrote in capital spirits and was most anxious for Mr Dawson and George to have everything nice, but we all laid our heads together and determined upon putting up no building until they both should see the place. As we could not agree where the house should be, our plan is that they should come here first. Of course it will take Mary and I a long time to talk over the events of ten years, quite as long as getting the house ready. Besides if everything is so very comfortable, she will think we have been exaggerating all this time.

If Mary arrives safely here, I shall begin to think there is a good time coming and we will get on by degrees. I am thankful to say my health is

better now than it has been for many years. My friends tell me I am growing young, but I shall never be strong. My only fear now is of anything
happening to dash the cup of happiness from our lips, but we are in the
hands of a Higher Power and must put our faith in Him.

I do not despair now of seeing others of the family here. My sisters
would get good situations as governesses until married and you might live
like a queen on your income. Now what have my sisters to look forward
to at home? Slavery all their lives to keep up an appearance. Kate must
really make a move after her cousins have done so well. She had better
seriously think of the offer I have had for her, but I fear the gentleman
will not wait long. Courtships are always very short in this country, seen
one week and married the next. Another peculiarity of this country is that
men, gentle and simple, are rather fond of beating their wives – a gentleman residing in Belfast killed his the other day. He had not been married
six months.

Our harvest will soon commence. I hope men will be more plentiful
this year. Oh servants are a bother and the newly arrived ones the worst,
for they have their heads filled with such absurd notions before they leave
home. I have an Irish woman lately arrived who can do nothing but boil a
potato, but she grumbles at everything and wishes herself back in Ireland
where she had *cream* in her tea.

>Your always affectionate daughter,

>Penelope Selby.

>Newlands
>1st November 1850

My dear Mother,
I promised Mary when I left her yesterday, I would write to you and tell
you all about the down lying and your little Australian [granddaughter]. I
went to Woodlands ten days before the event occurred as I was anxious to
be on the spot and was becoming rather tired, but we managed very well.
Poor thing, she had a long labour, very much like I was with Prid. She
first complained on Monday afternoon, so I dispatched Mr Hood about
four o'clock to Belfast. He returned with Dr Hurne about twelve at night.
She did not become very bad until about three the next day, and baby was
born soon after twelve at night. The watch was where I could see it, and I
was watching every minute that it should be over on the Tuesday but it

was a quarter of an hour too late. She was sorely tried towards the last and quite lost heart, but there was never the slightest danger, only she never thought 'it would be so bad'.

I laughed when baby was born and told her it was truly 'the mountain bringing forth the mouse,' such a little thing but very strong and healthy and growing so rapidly. The Dr said Mary was the strongest woman he had been with many a long year. Indeed she had not had a days ailment during her pregnancy, which is saying a great deal, though I was glad to see she was losing flesh. Indeed dear Mother when I consider her age and fat, I cannot tell you how thankful I feel to the Almighty that she is so well, and the baby spared to her. All the time she was ill it was the baby feared for, and she feels repaid for what she suffered. I don't know whether Father or Mother are most taken up with it. Surely never baby was so much admired before.

I have been going by the name Mrs Gamp. Mr Hood says that I don't look fat and comfortable enough. He thought I ought to be lying in bed and Mary going about, as she was much more the figure experience told him nurses should be. Mary has recovered very well. She will be an excellent nurse, but unfortunately her supplies are rather sore, cracked. I do not know that we could have avoided it, however in a few days I trust they will be all right as they were much better.

I must question if she would have found a man – could she have had her choice of all she ever knew – so thoroughly devoted to her as Henry is. She said 'he was not much of a lover' but he makes up for it now, and would certainly spoil her had she not too much good sense. Indeed she ought to be a happy woman and I am sure she is, though she does abuse the country. I of course take the opposite side and praise it and tell her when she has been here ten years she will do so too spite of all the petty annoyances, the difficulty of getting servants being still about the greatest.

I was vexed at having to leave Mary so soon, but my servant who had been with me eight months and was just married when she came, sent me word she was not able to do the work anymore, so I had no choice as she had only staid to oblige me an extra month that I might leave home comfortably. She is a good girl but I wish she was not going to be bothered with a piccaninny. The worst is I don't know where to look for another and I have my neighbors in the same predicament. Wages are as high as ever and very few men or women either are good for anything.

George and I got wedding favours in the shape of Gloves and cards the other day from Mr Osborne, so tell Kate it will be of no use her coming out for him. I hope Kate won't break her heart. I don't know why she should, it is merely from what Mary says I express that hope. I do not know what she may have written to her of the gentleman and his abilities but this much – she intends to threaten him with an action, breach of promise of marriage – of course made through her. I hope she won't call me as a witness, for I really cannot recollect much about it. I only know that he was certain in his own mind that Mrs LeMann would bring out a single sister and he was determined to have her for a wife if he could. However, I am almost as pleased as it is. I wish she were as well to do in the world as he is, but he has a queer temper.

I have not said a word of my own household. They are very well, going on much the same as ever, always striving with little good. However I hope the time for rest will come.

I remain,
Your affectionate daughter,
Penelope Selby

Newlands
21st January 1851

Dear Kate,

Mary came here for a little change with baby a few weeks before Xmas. She wanted it for she had got one of her low fits on her and was not, as fancied, very strong. She was wonderfully benefited by it and writes me word that everything at home now wears a different aspect. I never saw a baby thrive as hers does. She is a sweet little thing and would be very handsome had she a better nose. Oh dear, that nose will stick to the Earles! I never thought Mary would be such fidget with a baby. Indeed there is a pair of them and Henry spoils her – Mary I mean.

We are in the middle of harvest, the wheat spoiling for want of men, who are very scarce. What we have are earning 10s or 12s a day with beer and spirits and the best of living. George has a splendid crop and I think he will get a good price as there has been very poor ones in every other district but the Port Fairy.

It was reported that the Bishop was putting up prayers and exhorting the people to be careful for fear of famine in Sydney – and with these men

I have in the Kitchen! Each has a lump of beautiful bread after every meal – I suppose they think it ill manners to eat up all they cut. The waste makes me angry. If you said a word they would talk of the feed at the different places and won't go where it is *rough*. Fortunately there is less used here than at some they do not like, but I have the scraps cooked up a second time which they are very fond of, in fact any *mess*. Of course they don't suspect it is the bits they leave.

Believe me always,
Your affectionate sister,
Penelope Selby

17th August 1851

My dear Mother,

I know you will not mind my commencing this letter with self, and telling you that through God's blessing I am once more in a fair way of being strong again. You will certainly have received letters intimating that I was expecting to be confined about the end of last month, and also in consequence of my health being so much improved, my friends had great hopes that my baby would be born alive, and so it proved, but indeed only to make the disappointment greater, for my dear boy breathed a few hours, long enough to make my heart yearn towards him and to be deceived into hoping that he might be spared to us. I was not told at the time that although a remarkably fine grown child, he had an enlarged liver, so that it was better that he was taken soon than that he should have lived even a few months, for the Dr told me that it was a very uncommon thing for an infant ever to outgrow or recover. I did not think I should have felt so sorry, having become accustomed to the loss and not even this time allowing myself to be sanguine, but it makes a great difference when you have heard a feeble cry and have them with you in bed.

I am wearying terribly to see my dear Mary and her little Kate, and am trying to persuade myself and George that I shall be able to go up in a few days. He shakes his head, for it is a long way, and the roads here are such as you cannot imagine. However, when the will is strong it goes a great way. Mary was very anxious to come down but the journey would have been almost impossible for her with the baby so I promised I would see her

 What connects this group at Rourke's Bridge, a farm on the Yarra thirty-six miles northeast of Melbourne? Two of the men seem to position themselves apart, as though consciously aloof. A third stands near a Chinese mother and her daughters, but a little in front. The women – Chinese, Aboriginal, and white – are separate figures, associated only with children. Date unknown.

almost before she could expect me.

This country is in a state of great excitement in consequence of the gold discovered. One person, a Dr Ken, got a lump the largest ever was found, weighing more than a hundred pounds. It is being discovered now close to Melbourne and within a few miles of our old station on the Yarra. I have not the least doubt it must have gold on it as it is precisely the same kind of country. Indeed there is no telling where the discoveries will end. Meanwhile, labour has risen enormously, and it is said this crop of wheat will rot in the ground for want of men to reap. Woe to the country if such prove the case, for it will take all their gold next year to get bread. At present it is very high with a prospect of being still higher, and we poor farmers are beginning to hold up our heads.

I thought of you this morning when I was on a little hill at the end of the farm and saw the wheat looking so green and beautiful in the clear sunshine and such a pretty view beyond. All this that a few years ago was thick timber. Indeed everything looks well to a person that has been almost chained to one spot for many months.

Another cause of excitement at present is the elections which are to take place next month. Our landlord, Mr Rutledge, is one of the candidates. George promised of course to vote for him and moreover he really believes he will make the best member for this district. He has so much interest in it. Henry [LeMann] votes for his opponent Mr Manifold, who is a Squatter, and these squatters wish to have all the country to do as they please with, but I think when it comes to be better known how few their numbers are they will not be able to carry things with quite so high a hand.

George and the boys are quite well, Prid growing very fast, almost as tall as his Father, and so like him. Willie is very little but I suppose will spring up in time. What should I have done if I had had my eight boys about me? The one girl would have had plenty of work shirt making. I should have been obliged to send them home in a body to seek wives. I must just hope the two I have combine the good qualities of all, for indeed they are good boys. I could hardly expect all would have become equally so, and I ought to be most thankful to the Almighty if he spares them to me.

You will have a mob of grandchildren soon. If my Prid had been a girl you would likely have had a great grandchild shortly. Many girls marry in this country between 15 and 16 and are broken, worn-out looking creatures at five-and-twenty.

Believe me, dearest Mother,
Your affectionate daughter,

Penelope Selby

A few months later Penelope Selby once again chased away her melancholy thoughts and turned her dreaming mind toward fortune and the future, those two things as enwined now as they had been upon her arrival more than a decade before. Her last surviving letter is not to the family in England, but to her husband George. There is a second significant difference as well. The gold rush had begun, and in Mrs Selby's imagination, the old idea of a fortune to be made by hard work was swiftly vanquished by the new and alluring prospect of 'a fortune to be made for nothing.' Sticking with the work ethic no longer seemed such a smart thing to do, and Penelope Selby changed her values to fit the times:

Newlands
Sunday, 4th December 1851

My dear George,
As Mr Tierney is going to Belfast tomorrow I think I may as well give you a line if it is only to say the people are suffering a relapse. Monaghan and Tierney are starting for Mount Alexander this week. They are sure there is much gold to be got there. I think if you go and there really is a fortune to be made for nothing it will be a pity for you not to try should you have a chance.

I hope you arrived safely in Melbourne and found Henry well. Tierney has to deliver his wheat in Warrnambool for 4/6 so I fear we have a blue lookout. I shall be glad to see you back. The time appears so long but if you bring a fortune I shall not mind.

I am,
dear George,
your affectionate wife,

Penelope Selby

The lookout for Penelope Selby was blue indeed, the gold rush irrelevant. Two weeks after writing this letter she died. The woman who had come to the bush from a London suburb and proudly learned to ride a mare so that she could visit Mrs Dawson more easily, who had amused herself with fantasies of following the queen on rides through Hyde Park, died suddenly on 19 December 1851 after falling from a new horse which ran away.

Somehow the death was fitting, if death ever is. Mrs Selby had worked hard at learning the skills she needed to do well in the Australian bush. When things went wrong, she tried to accept her lot with a stoicism bolstered by religion. Through all her sorrows, through the horrifying experience of repeatedly carrying children who were born dead – with not one single live birth during all her years in Australia except for the baby who lived only long enough to be held – she never gave way to despair. Her spirit was indomitable, but the letters are a sobering reminder that however admirable an 'indomitable' spirit may seem from afar, the pioneer women themselves paid a high price for our later admiration.

LADIES AND MUSHROOMS

1867–72

Louisa Geoghegan was sympathetic to rural Australia. Being a governess on a remote Victorian property did not send her reeling into despondency. Under the circumstances, she counted herself lucky. At least her employer was of the proper sort, whereas 'in this district, for three gentlemen there are six mushrooms, I suppose you would call them'. Why they should be called 'mushrooms' remains obscure. Because they lacked elegance and were positively thick? Because they thrived in manure? Whatever earned them their nickname, there is no question about what was wrong with them. 'Mushrooms' were the bush's *nouveaux riches*, who 'pay largely but expect rather queer things – viz that the Governess should light the Schoolroom fire & similar things. They have been accustomed themselves to manual exertions & don't understand not keeping it up.'

Clearly, the homes of mushrooms were not suitable places for ladies, and the English governesses sent out by the Female Middle-Class Emigration Society clung tenaciously to the portrait of themselves as ladies. The Emigration Society which arranged their passage, and often lent them money for it, was established to help the indigent gentlewomen whom Victorian England preferred to send away rather than find places for at home. Not that its first honorary secretary, Maria S. Rye, would have put it this way. In rhetoric with a decidedly feminist ring, she asked, 'Are women to perish simply because they are women?' How in the world were they to earn their livings in an England where '810 women applied for one situation of £15 per annum; still later, (only ten days ago,) 250 women applied for another vacancy worth only £12 a year; (the daughters of many professional men being among the numbers)'. At the same time 'the latest and safest colonial reports' record a total 'deficiency' of 155,636 women in the Australian colonies and New Zealand. The solution is straightforward: there must be a redress of the imbalance 'by some further extension of emigration, by the steady departure from these shores of our superfluous workers, and by an influx into the colonies of a body of women infinitely superior by birth, by education, and by taste, to the hordes of wild uneducated creatures we have hitherto sent abroad'.

Perhaps these words stirred the hearts of Miss Rye's audience at the 1861 Social Science Congress in Dublin. Behind their fervour, however, is something looking suspiciously like a failure of imagination. Surely Miss Rye never for a moment stopped to conjure up particulars, to question what sort of life a low-paid governess might be letting herself in for, if she felt 'infinitely superior' to the people she both worked for and lived with.

Fortunately for Louisa Geoghegan, Miss Rye was exaggerating. The Hines family who employed her were far from being 'wild uneducated creatures' and she did not need to feel superiorly aloof from them. That was probably a great help. Her letters from the very beginning are shaped by a willingness to throw her lot in with this family. She could accept life on the Neuarpur station as something harsh and uncomfortably restrictive for everyone there. She did not see herself as specially singled out for suffering.

Neuarpur – Apsley
Victoria
19th February 1867

My dear Miss Lewin,
On arriving at Melbourne I sent you an *Argus* containing an account of the voyage made by the *Swiftside* which was a very pleasant & favourable one though a little longer than was expected being exactly 12 weeks. I hope you received the *Argus* else you will think it very strange never having heard anything of me. We only remained in Melbourne from Friday to Tuesday. My brother was there waiting for me.

On Christmas Day we began our journey up the Country – went by rail to Ballarat. There Mr Hines' brother-in-law met us, we made all one party & were 12 in number. We drove up about 260 miles – used to start very early in the morning, rest in the heat of the day & make another start in the evening – the weather was very hot, more so than has been felt for the last 4 years. We had all kinds of adventures in the shape of kicking horses & broken poles but we reached Benyeo (the residence of Mr McLeod –

An unidentified woman crosses a bridge over the Ovens River in northern Victoria, date unknown.

brother-in-law to Mr Hines) on the following Sunday – It is 14 miles distant from this place –

Mrs Hines & I were over here for a day or two – made all right for the children to come – but when we returned to Benyeo for them, Mrs Hines took measles & from that day which was not a week after we reached Benyeo up to the present there has been nothing but sickness. Just as Mrs H. was over the worst of measles the eldest girl was taken ill the day after her 12th birthday. She was affected very strangely & tho' a Doctor was sent for at once it was 48 hours before one arrived. Then Bessie was dangerously ill with inflammation of the lungs – about 10 days after she was first attacked measles came out on her slightly – the Doctors (for now there were two) thought she might now get better but her strength was all gone & she gradually sank & died at Benyeo last Saturday, exactly the day month of her birthday when she appeared in her usual health.

Her death has cast a great gloom on everything. She was a gentle companionable intellectual child liked by everyone who knew her – the second girl misses her sadly – Bessie was laid beside a brother in a small burying place adjoining the garden on Sunday & on Monday we all came over here for good – Every one at Benyeo who had not had measles before had them during the six weeks we were there – 15 cases in all. Fortunately I had had them & was able to look after some of the invalids.

I like the people I have met in Australia much better than I like what I have yet seen of the country but it is too soon to judge – I have experienced nothing but kindness from Mr & Mrs H. all through but particularly lately. We have done nothing yet with lessons – they brought out a beautiful piano, the only thing poor Mrs Hines now cares about – she idolized her eldest child. As soon as I receive any money I will remit it to you. Please give my kind compliments to Miss Rye,

hoping she & you are well I remain dear Miss Lewin

Very truly yours,

L. Geoghegan

Neuarpur – Apsley
Victoria
18th October 1867

My dear Miss Lewin,
I am very glad I came to Australia, but I cannot say I like it very much. It

is such an out of the world place and so monotonous, but as far as kind treatment goes I could not meet with nor desire kinder – with no one in this neighbourhood have I seen the social distinctions made with Governesses that there is at home – I have very little work here in comparison with London – I do not think £80 per annum here as much as £60 at home, dress is very expensive and the people are dressy – You will be glad to hear that my pupil has made great progress in all her studies but particularly in music, which pleases Mrs Hines very much. They brought out a very nice piano.

In fact 'Bush life' is a strange mixture of roughing and refinement. In this district are two distinct sets, one gentry, and one *would-be* gentry – there are more of the latter. In the former I think an unfinished unladylike Governess would be unwelcome. Literature is much more brought forward here, in the general way, than at home because there are no new daily topics – the standing one is sheep – in which ladies take no part – of course.

Accept my kind regards
and believe me truly yours
Louisa Agnes Geoghegan

Neuarpur – Apsley
Victoria
17th May 1868

My dear Miss Lewin,
I am now so reconciled to Australia that I was surprised to see by your letter I had apparently been disappointed at first. At times I feel it is rather dull work never to go beyond the garden or Croquet ground but then I remember I can rake or hoe in the garden as I please & freedom to please oneself more than compensates for monotony. Occasionally we have a good deal of riding, & I have a nice horse for my own use – then if Mr Hines is busy we are sometimes weeks without going outside the gates.

Latterly there has been a great deal of gaiety for this place – one public Ball & two private ones – one of the private ones here. The style is to dance till daylight, because it is impossible to ride or drive in the dark, so those who must go, dance until it is light enough to start & the rest take thankfully anything they can get in the shape of a bed – when it comes to provide for thirty you cannot be very particular.

I felt the heat much more this summer than last – but then it was more continued, & unusually severe – this part is nearly as hot as Adelaide – I hope this Xmas to be able to take a trip to my brother & sister. Travelling there is very very expensive & last year I felt economical –

I remain dear Miss Lewin

Very truly yours

L. A. Geoghegan

Neuarpur – Apsley

Victoria

12th August 1868

Dear Miss Lewin,

I am so glad that my gratitude has caused you pleasure – but it did not half acknowledge what I feel or the benefit you have done me – I cannot tell you anything about the wants of Melbourne – except that I see in the Melbourne Newspapers accounts of a Society for '*Educated people* in Indigent Circumstances', their applications to the Society published etc, & teachers of both sexes figure largely in the list.

In this district (colonial term) for three gentlemen there are six mushrooms, I suppose you would call them. The former I have heard say would like thoroughly good lady Governess from Home if they had any one there conscientiously to select them – the mushroom class pay largely but expect rather queer things – viz that the Governess should light the Schoolroom fire & similar things. They have been accustomed themselves to manual exertions & dont understand not keeping it up. In my short experience, I have known of two cases where *ladies* got with these people & very soon had to separate.

It is a totally different life from what it is at home. In *nearly* every instance you are looked on as the Intellectual Member of the Establishment. You are the constant companion & associate of the Lady – considered, I might say indulged, in every way – & your only difficulty is to civilize the children, which you are supposed to do through example as they are uncontrolled to a degree, & the parents object to anything else. I believe in Adelaide salaries are much lower than in Victoria.

I think with you that capable women have a better chance here than at

A young governess holds her cup with studied propriety as she joins the Packham family for afternoon tea on their Western Australia property at Tammin in 1895. The mother, seated stiffly behind the table, looks like a woman determined not to surrender her gentility in the bush.

home – but I think a few of a good class not *long* accustomed to home scrubbing & drudgery would be a better importation than a larger number of the common run of Governesses – I think it a mistake unless very strong minded to come out here without having some relatives in the Colony – no out-door variety – no change of face or scene – so that the feeling of monotony & exile is apt to take forcible possession of you, unless you know you have a resource to shake it off. My thoughts on the subject may be very imperfect ones for I have never given it deliberate consideration.

I remain dear Miss Lewin
Very truly yours
L. A. Geoghegan

Neuarpur
Victoria
10th August 1870

Dear Miss Lewin,

I must begin by telling you about myself, but I will try and be as short as possible. I have gone on steadily here for three years and a half, and have managed to scrape together money to buy a piano and otherwise enable me to go live with my brother in Sale, Gipps Land, and enter into partnership with my sister who already has a pretty good school.

I do not leave Mrs Hines until Xmas. She is sending home for a Governess, or rather she is getting me to do so for her, as she knew no one whom she could depend on. Mrs Hines will not pay the passage for any one, and as I do not think there are many Governesses willing or able to embark the necessary sum, I have mentioned you as helping through your Society deserving persons in such a dilemma. You will perhaps wonder that when Mrs Hines had so much difficulty in the matter, she should send home – but she came to this decision from her observation of Governesses in this district who have come from Melbourne, and as a class they are not much to be admired.

Mrs Hines and Mr Hines and the children are very much to be liked, but no convent life could be more monotonous than life here is. The routine is teaching from 8 o'clock to dinner at 1 o'clock, again from 2 to 3 o'clock after which you are your own Mistress, but your resources are limited solely to intellectual amusements. Walking, owing to the heat and wet, is only possible a short time through the year & then you must be brave enough to go by yourself, for here they think it laborious. Driving is inconvenient, there being no roads only tracks, & as Mr Hines is now his own overseer he seldom has time to take us out riding as he used to do & a book, the piano, & fancy and plain work occupy you until bed time. No one comes & there is no place to go to. I have never been unhappy here, and though I am sorry to part from Mrs Hines I am not sorry to leave the Bush. Believe me

Always yours gratefully

Louisa Agnes Geoghegan

Louisa Geoghegan was a remarkably adaptable woman. From England she had travelled directly to a remote area of Victoria on the southern edge of the Little Desert, quite close to the South Australian border. She knew no one in the entire region. The expense of travelling made her brother in Melbourne virtually inaccessible, however consoling it was to know he was there. She had to be, as she implies, strong-minded. She was. The governess who replaced her seems different. Miss Oliver's description of getting to Neuarpur and of life there has an hysterical edge absent from Miss Geoghegan's letters. The comparison makes interesting reading. One woman felt part of the life of the place; the other felt very much a stranger in a strange land.

Neuarpur – Horsham
Victoria
2nd October 1871

My dear Miss Lewin,

I did not write immediately on arrival thinking it better to give myself time to form an opinion of Colonial or rather bush-life. I started for my 300 miles up the country. Such *travelling*, in a vehicle one can only call a covered cart, across miles of uncultivated flat country, diversified only by ugly dark pine trees, heath, & swamps; not a person to be seen; every 20 or 30 miles a station or small township. In my opinion it is very disagreeable for a lady alone, travelling in this style, especially in a country where society is so mixed, & it is impossible to say who may be your fellow-passengers.

I have now had nearly six months experience & without hesitation I can say it is not a life I should like to try long, notwithstanding the nice kind people I am with. There are perhaps few families as intellectual & well educated as this, at all events not in Victoria. Still, had I known the very isolated life I was to lead, I do not think I should have been induced to come out. This is not the only drawback. One could cheerfully bear it two or three years if there were any advantage to be gained in the end, but I must candidly confess from what I have heard & seen, there is no better chance of getting on out here than at home. The expenses are far greater & the salaries not in proportion. Consequently, £100 is not more than £60 in England, that is taking travelling expenses into consideration.

The bush life is a perfect exile. There are about three visitable families near. If a Governess has friends in Melbourne it is something like £20 if she takes a holiday. The transportation of luggage is fearful. Only small portmanteaus are allowed & if there be anything extra, it is heavily charged.

I am perhaps putting things in their worst light but Home ideas of this Country are very false. The greatest amusement we have is riding, but even too much of that becomes monotonous, with no object in view. As to scenery, there is none. It is certainly the ugliest country I have ever seen, reminding one of the N. of France.

I only wonder the sheep thrive on such poor land. Of course mutton forms the principal dish. The living is simple enough. There are times when we cannot get butter. I have not yet experienced the hot weather. The winter is over now. Altho' not the cold of home, still I think I felt it quite as much. Perhaps this was owing to the house being only of one storey, and the rooms all leading into the garden, so that it is almost like living in the open air.

The garden is looking nice, but nothing to equal the flowers at home. The soil is bad, & the heat with hot winds dry up every thing. All I can say is that I do not like Australia & would rather be in England, or on the Continent with £50, than here.

With kind regards,

Believe me

Sincerely yours,

M. A. Oliver

Miss Oliver was not alone in wishing she had never come. Many governesses were, very simply, shocked by Australia. Cries of confusion and resentment can be heard today in their letters copied into the Emigration Society's books by some neat and diligent hand. Women complain of being duped. Everything had sounded so regular, so easy. 'Go and we will look after you', they were told. The London office made its routine sound foolproof:

> The Society has established regular correspondents at most of the colonial ports. As soon as a party leaves England, notice of their departure is sent by the Overland Mail to the correspondent at the port to which the emigrants are bound; a list of their names and qualifications, together with copies of the testimonials of each applicant, are sent at the same time; and as the notice is received six weeks before the emigrants arrive, there is time to make preparations for their reception, and even to seek for situations.

All well and good – but an illusion. In no real sense did the Society's organizing network extend beyond the British Isles. The 'correspondents' at the colonial ports were society people who had lent their names to yet another worthy cause. They did not expect to *work*, as the Melbourne correspondent, Mrs a'Beckett, reminded London in a stiff note:

> 22nd December 1864
>
> My dear Madam,
> I write by this Mail for the purpose of stating that I receive so much annoyance from the fact of the ladies sent out by your Society taking it for granted that I should meet them at the Ship, provide accommodation, or get a situation for them, that I wish it to be distinctly understood that I disclaim all responsibility concerning them – the *utmost* I can promise is to give a letter saying I have heard of them from you & that they have their own testimonials upon which they must trust for engagement.
> I remain, dear Madam,
> Yours faithfully,
> L. J. a'Beckett

Of more lasting importance than such deficiencies in organization were the Society's blithely untrue assurances of immediately available joys at splendid salaries. The women in the London office should have known better than to foster such notions. Time and again they had heard from emigrants the sort of refrain struck by Miss Richardson in 1863: 'Situations are not so plentiful nor Salaries so large as is represented in England & travelling or moving about at all is so dreadfully expensive.' Such comments did not impede the progress of propaganda.

Interestingly, the women were always reluctant to attack the Society itself for misleading them. Bound by middle-class pieties, they did not ask whether the London organizers might be helping themselves more than they were the distressed gentlewomen who were their clients. Politically naive, the emigrants never railed against an exploitative economic system. Often they blamed Australia for their financial difficulties without seeing that its market forces were the same as those which had exiled them from their English homes in the first place. Without a political context, the inability to make money was characteristically seen as a personal failure.

When Ellen Ollard recounts a series of woes so complete that only a previously unknown cousin has stood between her and total collapse, she brands her miseries failure, and in the failure she finds shame. Even her father, who has behaved as though her emigration were death, dissolving promises and obligations, has left her feeling more hurt than angry. She writes to London in anxiety about the loan made to her by the Society for her voyage. She cannot repay it; she doubts that her father will; she fears the guarantors will be pressed. The situation is humiliating. She addresses her letter from the Melbourne Home for governesses, an institution which seems to have been designed to turn away the women who most needed its shelter. It was an oasis of respectability – at a price beyond Ellen Ollard's means.

Melbourne Home, Little Lonsdale Street
4th August 1876

Dear Mrs Sunter,

I am sure you must think me very ungrateful for not having written to you before after all the trouble you took on my behalf, but to speak truly I have been ashamed to write as I have been so very unfortunate since I've been in the Colony; and I have been hoping against hope that I should be more successful by and by and be able to give a pretty good account of myself. I will commence at my arrival here and tell you what I have been doing as far as I can remember.

The voyage was a very pleasant one and I need hardly tell you that I was very sorry when it came to an end, and I found myself for the first time in my life at the mercy of strangers. We anchored in the Bay on Saturday the first of November at about half past one in the afternoon and never while I live shall I forget the feeling of despair that took possession of me when I saw everyone on board talking to their friends who had come out in the Tug Steamer to meet them. Miss Davis (my cabin companion) came out to be married and her intended husband took her away in a little yacht and Mrs Thomas, the only remaining lady, went away in the Steamer with her husband and of course all the gentlemen got away as soon as they could, and I was left to indulge in my grief and to wonder what would become of me in this strange land.

On Monday morning one of the passengers who had been very kind to me during the voyage offered to go to the 'Home' with me and when I got there I found that my Father had not kept his promise of writing to me; and I had only a few shillings in my pocket, not sufficient to pay a week's board and lodging in advance (17/-), which Mrs Roe told me was necessary. I had only one sovereign in my purse when I left England as my Father said he had not got it to give me, having had so many little things to pay for, but he promised to write to me and send me at least £10 so that I should have it on my arrival in Melbourne, and from the day I last saw him till the present time, which will be two years tomorrow, he has never taken the slightest notice of me. Now I consider this most cruel of him as he wished me to come, thinking that I should be sure to be successful, although if you remember when I came to make enquiries of you some twelve months before, he would not sanction it.

When I had been here but a short time I obtained a situation at a place called Boggy Creek near Kyneton, and there I took the measles from the children and the unfeeling woman sent me home when I had only been there five days and I had them very severely. My Cousin kindly had me at her house and nursed me herself. The doctor said that I might have lost my life. I had to have my hair cut short like a boy and it has not grown yet.

After I had got quite well I got another situation through an advertisement which was supposed to be as a companion to a young lady, but when I arrived there I found that there was no servant kept and the man was a travelling hawker and I was required to help his daughter make fancy articles for sale and do all the housework besides, so I did not stay there very long.

After that I went to Wangaratta and when I had been there a little over two months they gave me notice to leave and I think they were in difficulties. After I left there I did not get employment for a very long time and what I should have done without my Cousin I really do not know, for I should have wanted for food and clothes too but for her.

Mrs Roe at the Melbourne Home is one of the most kind and motherly persons I have met, but she is quite powerless to assist anyone who cannot pay their way and the ladies of the Committee have passed a law that nobody shall stay there who cannot pay 17/- weekly in advance, so that really I do not see what benefit is to be derived from being there excepting of course that if one stays there 'tis a guarantee (to the employers) as to their respectability.

From what you told me and judging from the report (the little book, I mean) I quite thought there would be someone to meet me at the vessel and also that some little interest would be taken in you by some of the members of the Committee, but I soon found that I was mistaken. Of course if any one comes to the Home requiring a Governess or Nursery Governess as the case may be, if you are suitable you have a chance of getting the situation; but if you are staying elsewhere and you see the Advertisement you stand just as good a chance of getting it, if you answer it in time.

Now I should very much like to know if you have received the £15. I think that was the sum borrowed. When I left England my Father told me not to trouble myself at all about it, as he intended paying it within a month or two, but as he has not sent me any money or even written to me, I much fear that he must have been in difficulties and I do not think my Uncle or Mr Dalton would be very pleased at having to pay it. I should indeed be very thankful if I had the means of sending it to you, but when I tell you that since I have been in the Colony I have only earned about thirteen pounds you will know that I have not got it to send especially when I had nothing to start with.

I never thought that I should live to be in the unhappy position that I am in now. The very first day that I went to the 'Home' I was told that I should never get on here without music, for the very commonest people have a piano and have their children taught to play it. There are very few respectable situations to be got where music is not required. I was in a nice family in St. Kilda for a time where I used to do all the needlework and attend to the younger children, but I was not very well while there and the lady told me she was sorry to part with me but she required some one who was very strong. She had only been married a month, when I went there, to a widower with a family of five and as she was very delicate I had to leave, so it seems as if misfortune attends me wherever I go.

My Cousin (whom I had never seen till I arrived here) is very good indeed to me and never allows me to want for anything & always gives me a home when I'm out of a situation. Still I cannot help feeling that I've no right to be living upon her & her husband although they are both kind enough to tell me not to worry about it. I had no idea that Melbourne was such a large place as it is or I should never have come to it. The people here are very different to what they are in England. Gold is their God and it does not matter to them how ignorant a person is if they have money, but if they have not they are not considered worthy of notice. My Cousin lives a very quiet life and does not visit any one or receive any visitors so I do not see any chance of getting into society where I might be likely to meet with any nice situation, where I should be kindly treated.

Several people in England promised to give me letters of introduction to friends or acquaintances of theirs out here; but I had no time to go for them & my Father promised to send them & so I have not had them. I wish my Father had sent me to learn a business – millinery or something of the kind. He always used to tell me never to marry for a home & that at his death I was provided for, but now I find that I am entirely at the mercy of the world. Sometimes I think of working my way back to England, I mean with a family, but perhaps I should not find it any easier to get employment there. I know a lady much older than I am who is far worse off, for she has no relatives here and she is now giving her services for board & residence & she has not a penny in the world. 'Tis all very well for people to say 'Take a situation as a housemaid or nursemaid.' Employers require thorough hard working servants who fully understand their duties, & I am sure that I could not do the work they require.

I fear you will consider this a very miserable letter & I am almost ashamed to send one so badly written, for I have left it so many times, but I have not time to write it again as the 'Mail' goes tomorrow. If it is not asking too much of you I should be very glad, if you would kindly write and let me know about the loan.

With kind regards trusting that you are well,
Believe me Dear Mrs Sunter,
Yours very truly
Ellen H. Ollard

Ellen Ollard was a woman without power. She had been dealt all the worst cards – poor health, a father's betrayal, other people's difficulties, the wrong skills for the place. No more letters came from her to the Society. Did she vanish or sink?

We know that Rosa Payne left. This is scarcely surprising. From her first letter histrionic attacks sweep over the countryside condemning whatever seems un-English and (the same thing) un-ladylike. In her defence it might be said that nothing in her background had prepared her for the dry and flat plains of the Wimmera, but to say that is simply to offer a more sympathetic formulation of the first point: the Wimmera was not England and however kind-hearted Mrs Scott may have been she did not have the aura of a genteel English lady. Even at her most positive, Rosa Payne merely put up with bush life. To adapt would be to lower herself, and she chose never to stoop.

Rich Avon, West Avon Plains
by Glenorchy, Victoria
13th August 1869

My dear Miss Lewin,
My impressions of Melbourne & the Colony are *thoroughly* unfavourable. I was not one hour in it when I regretted deeply the step I had taken. Had I possessed the money I would returned in the next ship. I do not use too strong a language when I say no one with the tastes, habits, or feelings of a lady should ever come out to Australia. It may do for mediocre governesses who can put up with roughnesses, or I should rather say, vulgarity of mind & great want of intellect, but I never would advise a lady to try it. I hate Australia and the Australians. I shall be with them but never of them. I would ràther have £15 per annum in London than £50 here.

Australia is by no means the Eldorado it is supposed to be or perhaps once was. There is a vast amount of wretchedness & poverty in the Country & men of talent & ability find it most difficult to obtain employment. Even I, lately come to the Colony, know instances. How much more then for a Governess.

As to the Town of Melbourne it is beyond anything abominable in every respect. I was more than thankful & glad to leave it. I was quite sorry to find by a letter I had lately from Mrs Roe, another lady Governess was coming out in the *Highflyer*. I think it is a great pity. There has not been one Governess to whom I have spoken on the subject, but has not told me they deeply regretted ever coming out, & who would return to England could they afford it & so very very many have gone back hating place & people. You have no idea of it.

I am quite satisfied with my present abode, I leave the word 'happiness' out of the question. I only feel as if all the brightness had gone out of my life. I am very sorry I did not think of India, or Rio, unprejudiced, & unbiassedly. With no feeling of actual home sickness do I write, only weary disappointment. Now that I am here I should be ashamed to return without feeling I had made some effort for good. On all sides do I hear sad tales of the struggle for our daily bread, the last few years & seasons have been so bad. There is of course much wealth, in some instances, but it is confined to the few. I would recommend no one, unless indeed servants, to emigrate to Australia.

The climate is trying also, so many sudden changes. This winter has been very severe. You will say perhaps I am writing very one sidedly. Not so, I am & have been most fortunate in getting my present situation, & have *by no means* seen or felt the worst side of the picture but I hear a great deal & cannot help judging accordingly. One thing I do know. I never never shall like or be happy in Australia, & would leave it tomorrow if I could.

I just try not to think, or else I would die, but there are times when I must think, & I am weary of life, & everything, & everyone. Mrs Scott, the lady in whose family I am, said to me on hearing I was writing Home 'Tell your friends Miss Payne we are both, Mr Scott & myself, much pleased with you, you are so attentive to the children, & so bright!' She does not know my heart is nearly breaking sometimes. I knew they were satisfied with me, & I am with them.

Dear Miss Lewin this is a different letter perhaps from what you expected from me, but I cannot write otherwise, it would be untruthful. Will you write to me? How much I wish you would. It would give me such pleasure of happiness.

Yours very sincerely,
Rosa Payne

Rich Avon, West Avon Plains
by Glenorchy, Victoria
25th March 1870

My dear Miss Lewin,

I am now satisfied. I must have written my letter to you in great bitterness of spirit & in utter disgust too of the colony. Now I shall endeavour to modify & moderate my feelings & give you a juster & unprejudiced view of things. My lines are now cast in pleasant places. Strange as it may seem to you, it just feels here as though it were my groove in life. The Scotts are pleasant, educated, kindly people. My duties are not laborious & what they are I like greatly.

In Bush life there is a great charm. Lonely perhaps some people would find it. I never have done so. I have seen more of life, of the springs of action in people, their ways, and peculiarities, than I ever did in my life before & I have travelled & seen *much*. Perhaps it is because there is less reserve, less stiffness, less of the conventionalities of life. I like it. I am very happy with all this. I feel I am in the Colony simply not of the people, or with them, beyond our own household.

I had the pleasure of staying at Mrs Somerville Learmonth's about six weeks ago. She is very nice & I liked her greatly. So like home is she. She regretted not having seen you & spoke so highly of Miss Rye. At the same time she quite agreed with me that it is a mistake sending Governesses out to Australia. There are quite sufficient to suit the requirements of the Colony and in so many cases utter misery to the ladies who do come out. I have heard some sad strange tales since I came out. I never would advise a sister of my own to act as I have done, particularly now the Colony seems to have reached a culminating point of difficulty & embarrassment. There is nothing doing in business. This is quite universal. Many settlers – (Squatters) have failed. Many have abandoned their run. If rain does not come soon, I don't know what will be done, for the sheep are dying so for want of food. Literally there is not one blade of grass.

You ask me why do I *hate* Australia & Australians. I expressed myself rather strongly then. Now I shall just say I do not like place or people, nor *never* shall but as I have made it my home I shall put up with it & all its shortcomings. Place & people with few exceptions are verily the antipodes of home, selfish mortally and so unsympathizing. I think I have said all I have to & I wonder what you will say on reading this production.

 None of the governesses sent out by the Female Middle-Class Emigration Society worked at a grand establishment such as this one with its cook, housemaid, and parlourmaid. Would the loneliness have been less, would snobbishness have kept the women apart? Date and place of photograph unknown.

Thanking you once more for your kind letter & hoping when you have leisure you will sometimes bestow a thought on me, I remain dear Miss Lewin,

Yours very sincerely

Rosa Payne

Rich Avon, West Avon Plains
by Glenorchy, Victoria
18th May 1871

My dear Miss Lewin,

You may possibly be surprised at hearing from me again but the fact is, that do my very best, I cannot like the Colony or people. More and more do I dislike both & am exceedingly unhappy & heartily weary of it. I have been in my present situation ever since my arrival which will be two years next month and during that time have had more to contend with than I ever before had in my Governess experience.

Mrs Scott & I never have got on well, be the fault where it may. One thing, she has not one feeling like a lady, altho' one ostensibly, & I cannot conscientiously approve of children having their own way in all things. It has been and is a very difficult situation to fill. I should long ere this have left it but the difficulty of obtaining another situation in this country is extreme and remuneration not adequate to the disadvantages! I tried in many quarters and made many an inquiry about another situation but to all my applications there was the invariable reply, any number of applicants on the same errand & no chance of their being supplied, nothing to be got.

Into the details of a Bush life I shall not enter much, its advantages & disadvantages. Of the former the principal is one does not spend too much money which is desirable as things are very dear in this Country. Of the latter the place feels like a prison to me, only without the ignominy. No books, no society, *nothing improving*. Everything retrograde – conversation, scandal & gossip, things I hate & have never been accustomed to. You may say perhaps I am overdrawing the picture because I am prejudiced against. Not so. I would not wilfully or willingly do it. It is the case.

Now I am quite determined to return home (I have saved sufficiently for the purpose) and want to ask you could you assist me in obtaining a situation in England, on my landing. I would rather have £25 there, than £100 here. My own cannot help me. They find it quite enough to do to aid themselves. I must bear my own burdens, but it would be no burden were I out of this land. Can you, & if so will you, help me in this? I would not care how much I had to do, preferring an active life to my present desultory one.

I know all you would say of the overpopulation, & number of applicants for situations, but in extenuation for returning home my plea is I so dislike the Country & everything in connection with it I am satisfied I shall not regret taking a step homeward. I doubt if I am suited for the climate or people or an Australian life at all. I should very much like to be in or near London, having an intense admiration, if not love, for the Metropolis of the world.

I remain
Yours very sincerely
Rosa Payne

Melbourne Home
Little Lonsdale Street Melbourne
June 1872

My dear Miss Lewin,
At the risk of again incurring your anger I write once more to you. When this reaches you, I shall have sailed (D.V.) for England, and I do not think even you would blame me under the circumstances, did you know what life in Australia for a Governess is – its sense of intense loneliness and unprotectedness – utter friendlessness. All whom I have met in the same position reiterate what I write. I have saved sufficient money to take me back 2nd Class, would have had more, but sent money home. I would most willingly go as a Nursery Governess, children or teaching is no trouble to me – I do teach French & Music. I enclose you a testimonial from Mrs Scott. It is a favourable one, & without boasting, she could not have done less, but my life there was a difficult one in every respect.

How deeply grieved have I been in having left England, the intense selfishness of all classes, the great want of intellect, & in so many cases the utter want of truth, straightforwardness & frankness is most trying. The great expenses of everything, travelling especially, often hundreds of miles by Coach, constitution & purse suffer alike.

Will my appeal be in vain this time, or will you still say you will not help me? I am so unhappy, for my family are very poor, & I am wretched out here alone. Granted that I should have weighed all this before leaving home, still I could not foresee much that has occurred, & I was sanguine thinking that I could battle against everything. If you would kindly help me! and you have so much influence! May I ask if it were possible for me to obtain employment in London, in the City, I dont care where. It has always been to me such a wonderful place.

I have been since I left the Scotts in a School in Tasmania, into the detail of which I need not enter, the Principal (lady) as is usual with Bush ladies, no mind or thought, and in consequence is fast losing her Pupils. Hoping you will kindly think me over & not too severely.

I remain
Yours sincerely
Rosa Payne

Rosa Payne returns to England; Lousia Geoghegan marries a Victorian squatter. Bush life does not account for the difference in their fates. Temperament does – and values. If the Bush was to be home, an emigrant gentlewoman needed to believe that there was more to life than gentility.

Ann Williams and Lucy Jones
TRAVELLING THROUGH A STRANGE LAND

1882 and 1883

'A conglomeration of wonder and hope' – so Lucy Jones signs the letter she has written for her family and friends in the home she has left behind. This 'home' is not England: it is the little stone village of Goolwa, on the South Australian coast. For the Jones family, as for so many others, the journey's end did not come with the landing of an emigrant boat. Settlers moved around in pursuit of that same promise of economic prosperity which had lured them to the southern continent in the first place. The women who went to the Bush rarely stayed in one spot. Annie Baxter left Yesabba on an overland trek across New South Wales and down through Victoria to the Port Fairy district where Penelope Selby had already arrived on her westward journey of subdued dreams after the farm on the Yarra had failed. Such overland treks were rarely as dangerous for women as the long voyage out from England, and yet the two journeys had much in common.

Whether by sea or land, women left people they cared for, and the written word was their one solace for the loss of daily contact. This is why emigrants kept diaries on board ship, and why on the road Lucy Jones and Ann Williams resolutely made their daily entries, even if they had to write on a stockyard rail or a 'grubbox'. They had promised to let the folks at home know how they got along, and their diaries are a record of the love they affirmed regardless of distance. At least the women trekking across land could with reason believe that the separation was not forever, while emigrants like Mrs Selby could pin their hopes only on a reunion after death, when space would be no more.

Private impulses, silent and unrecognized, may have added their encouragement to the travelling writers. Journeys break the shape of ordinary life, and diaries can go some way towards filling the common craving for order. Daily events fixed on a page make it possible to go back any time later and say, 'Yes, that happened there, at that time, I wrote it down just so.' Diaries allay the fear that the past may slide away into uncertainty, leaving the self less solid as it becomes confused about experience. The same fear may lie behind the widespread use of 'diaries' today, although instead of recording the past, these books are entrusted with appointments and obligations of the future which the mind, left to its own devices, might lose hold of. Lucy Jones and Ann Williams may well have been reassuring *themselves*, as well as the people for whom their diaries were written.

If so, they appear successful, for self-esteem shines through these accounts. The two young women had reason to be proud of the way they handled the difficulties of the road. They expected to find themselves tested, and they did. Their competence and stamina pleased them, even though as Ann Williams said after picking up the pieces from her accident, 'It would have been better if it had not have happened at all.' Unlike Annie Baxter, they wrote about their trials and tribulations with no literary flourish. The whimsy of Annie's letters to Henrietta would have puzzled these earnest young diarists who do not think in terms of 'doing rustic', or of writing about their travels as the adventures of a gypsy caravan. Indeed, such pretendings might well be morally suspect from their point of view. Would it be honest to pretty up a story for its entertainment value? Would it be right to withhold the bleak side of things from people who were counting on a true report? Lucy Jones and Ann Williams were too unselfconscious to think of such things. Their writing reflects a narrowly-bounded world centred on family values. When Ann Williams met people she liked, the language of her approval was characteristically domestic: 'they seemed like very nice homly people.'

The simple and straightforward responses of Ann Williams are embodied in a prose almost childishly naive. Spelling follows sound as often as it does the dictionary. The unheard 'e' in 'homely' remains unseen as well. Sentences, too, are shaped by sound rather than rules. They neither begin with capital letters nor come to an end with a full stop, and yet the prose is seldom difficult to read because she has a much better ear for the language than textbooks alone can teach. A personal speaking voice comes through, matching what she feels with what happens to her.

That combination is by no means easy to achieve. From the moment pen touches paper, language inevitably begins to filter experience, and among the contemporaries of Mrs Williams were many educated women whose language gushed with sentimental phrases and pretentious pieties, especially when they were writing with an eye to publication. Here is Rosa

 This shot has an unusually intimate quality about it, with a man lounging at his ease, and none of the figures looking directly into the camera. People, place, and date unknown.

Campbell Praed, for instance, trying to make the Australian landscape exciting for the readers of her autobiography, *My Australian Girlhood*, published in London in 1902 after she had a well-established reputation as a novelist:

> Words fail for painting the loneliness of the Australian bush. Mile after mile of primeval forest; interminable vistas of melancholy gum-trees; ravines, along the sides of which the long-bladed grass grows rankly; level, untimbered plains alternating with undulating tracts of pasture, here and there, broken by steep gully, stony ridge, or dried-up creek . . . who can see the land in its hoariness, and the convulsions that have torn it, and the curious mammals that are upon it, and upon no other land, and the gum-trees of such weird conformation unlike all other trees that are − who can see things and ponder over them, without pondering too and greatly wondering over the story of the lost Atlantis and of Lemuria that was before, and over the rebuke of the priests of Sais, and the legends and the myths which have come down through the mists of many ages!

This extravagant prose is 'educated', and if today we would also label it 'bad', the judgement reflects our aversion to particular excesses no longer popular. These excesses date the prose as typically nineteenth-century. In contrast, the language of Ann Williams, with its spare directness and laconic tone, seems familiar to a modern ear, and that raises an interesting point about the mixed blessings of education. Mrs Campbell Praed's 'educated' prose sounds contrived and foreign and far-away, its fantasies of Atlantis and Lemuria now silly and indeed rather obscure, while the grammatical faults of Ann Williams do not interfere with her ability to make readers a hundred years later imagine quite precisely what her journey was like. Education does not always aid expression, although it often does a good job of indoctrinating people with the vocabulary of their day, the jargon and references which will in a short time make their prose almost unreadable.

In the simplicity of Ann Williams' diary a woman we never knew comes to life in her time and place. She is travelling from beyond Queanbeyan, in the area where Canberra now is, down to the coastal area around Moruya, New South Wales. Although Sam, a friend or relative, is with them for the first few days, Ann and her husband Tom travel alone with their little son Albert through most of the three-week journey. Alone, that is, except for their animals. Tom Williams is taking a bullock-team to the timber-cutting region in search of work at a sawmill. The Williams also have horses with them, and on a wagon they are carrying all their household goods. Like the emigrants lured across the sea by a promise of a land with plenty of work, the Williams are on the road in pursuit of a job.

1st Day Started on Friday 6th Oct 1882 beautifull day Dick Shumock came by going fishing and of course wanted to know if we was off came on to Booths when Sam went in and got me a nice bleu Necktie and Baby some lollies came by a lot of men working on the hill when we got to the top we had to load some wood for night got to the camp had tea fixed our tent Sam and Tom took the Bullocks away to the river I made the bed and put Albert to bed he went to bed early it is a miserable camp to night so windy and no grass much we let the cat out of her box when we stopped and I have not seen her since so I suppose she has cleared out

2nd Day Saturday Morning Saw the commet this Morning and it is beautifull I never saw anything like it it rises about 4 oclock in the Morning we had a very good bed in [the] cart last night but it is hardley big enough for three but it will do Albert slept well all night

got to Queanbeyan went to town got Baby a Horse with a long mane for Sids present had dinner made a start heard very bad accounts of the grass along the road got up the big Hill met a Carrier asked about the grass he said that there was good grass at Bungendore I hope so for we are very nearly disheartened got to the Molonglo River Camped found not a bit of grass all a sheep run I expect that the Bullocks wont stop my face is very bad and has been ever since I started I am writing by lamplight on the grubbox little Albert is asleep he sleeps nearly all day

3rd Day Sunday Morning Oct 8th Tom and Sam has been after the Horses Since Sunrise and has not come back yet so I have gave Albert his breakfast and done all that I can my face is a good deal better today I do hope that we will soon get some rain the cat is quiet at Home we let her go as soon as we stop of a night and she stays by the fire all night

4th Day came through Bungendore to day and camped at the Back of the Church of England Parsonage going to try to get the Bullocks in a paddock for a day or two to give them a spell for I dont think that there is any feed this side of Braidwood it is like rain to day and the wind is blowing the leaves of my Book over so that it is a job to write we had some very

nice rain   it came up a pretty sharp Thunder storm with plenty of Wind
Thunder and lightning but we had some very nice rain throught the night
and morning   our tent is not proof against a strong beating rain for it
beat in at the side that was next the storm but I hung a blanket up and
that stopped it

5th Day   Yoked up about 11 Oclock   saw Ted Rolf and Johny Ryan
They sent their cattle away to the Coast   nearly all the people about
Bungendore sent their Cattle away and I think that they would have done
better to have kept them at home for out of what they sent away they are
only getting about half of them back   we are camped to night just over the
deep Creek past Charley Moss's and can see the Lake like a mist on a
plain   the Bullocks are awfull discontented   they will not stop unless in a
paddock   we had a good place for them last night but we have not got
much grass to night   the Travelling Cattle camped there last night   I
think that we will be tired before we reach our journeys end unless the
grass gets better after we leave Braidwood   Albert is such a good little
fellow   he sleeps nearly all day in the cart and as soon as we stop at night
after he has a run about he gets his supper and off to bed again and sleeps
all night   The Bullocks are going to be a bother to stop to night and as
Tom has been up nearly every night since we left home I told him that
I would stop up till twelve to night and stop them going down the lane
so you see that I am not very frightened in a strange place

6th Day   started this Morning   beautifull day   came to Long Swamp
Creek for dinner   after dinner came on to the Doughboy Creek, worst
camp we have had since we left   it is getting worse instead of better   if it
was not for Cabbageing a bit of grass the bullocks would all soon be dead

7th Day   dreadfull hot day to day   looked like rain last night but has all
gone off with the Sea Breeze clouds   we have not yoked up yet for we are
only going to go a short distance to day and in to Braidwood tomorrow
this would be a pretty place to camp if there was grass but it is overstocked
with sheep so there is not much   We was down at the Creek just now   it
is so nice and cool and shady with green Wattle trees, Albert has got his
old complaint again and is very cross

8th Day   started early this Morning   just as we was yoking up by came
the Gold escort with 2 policemen with it and 2 on Horseback   had dinner
at the six mile flat   came on again   met a Man that Tom knew   came by

a Public House   he gave me a drink of lemonade   it was a Man by the Name of Harris   but after to night we will be in a strange land to me and I hope a better one than this for you think that it is bad over your way but I can [not] compare Braidwood to anything but the very heat of Summer time when everything is burnt up so that you can judge what state the country is in over this side   we had to buy Hay for the Bullocks to night   it has been dreadfull hot to day and looked like Thunder

9th Day   This morning when we woke it was a thick fog   we got the Bullocks for we had them in a yard all night but Tom was walking all morning after the Horses and them not far away but they had no bell on and he could not see them   while I was waiting for him to come with them there was a woman sent me a cup of new milk for Baby and an egg so that was not so bad

we got yoked up and started and came through Braidwood and I think that it is a very nice town   I was in one shop and it is so nice   a great big shop   such a lot of shop men   we came on then till dinner time   I dont know the name of the place that we stopped for dinner but it was not very far out of Braidwood

started   came to Jembaicumbere   it is a nice place   a nice level country but it has been all dug up and it looks so funny now that the grass has grown all over the hols and what was dug up out of them   there is Streams of water running in all directions, what was there races for gold washing   there is much good grass now for we have got out of the sheep country   you see nothing now but cattle and Horses   after we pass what they call Jembaicumbere we begin to see tall Trees what they [call] the Ribbon gum and deep gullies and we will soon be in the wild country   a little further on is the Araluen Mountain   I thought that we was at it last Night for I thought that we was in a pretty wild country but it is 4 miles further on

I must tell you that I got a great fright to night   I asked Tom where I would light the fire and he told me against a log close to the road and against where I lit it was a big gum Tree and it had such a lot of Bark hanging from it that when I lit the fire it caught the Bark and up the tree it went right up nearly to the Top and run on about the ground and I had such a job to keep it out of Hassels paddock   Tom was away watering the Bullocks at what is called Bells Creek and I was very glad when he came back for if the wind had been coming towards the waggon it must have got alight so that I will be more careful in future when I light the fire in the Mountains where there is so much Bark and leaves to burn

10th Day, Sunday   the further we go it seems to get Hotter for to day is just like what it is at Christmas   The Locusts are singing and the Lizzards are running in all directions and when Tom was after the Horses this Morning he saw a snake   I went to a creek down in a deep gully for some water   I expected to see some but I didnt see any   it is such a long miserable Sunday   we went for a walk after dinner and I saw a big snake   Tom tried to kill it but it got under a log   came back and I never saw such strange weather as it is with us   I doubt if it is the same up your way but it all got foggie and dark and just like rain but it all goes off in the morning and is as hot as ever   They say that it is a sure sign of a draught but I suppose they must have something to say

11th Day   we lost our poor cat this Morning just after we started   we was going over some rough mettle and she jumped down off of the waggon and away in the scrub and we could not see her again   I was so sorry for she was such a nice old thing and would jump up in the waggon or the cart when she saw us preparing for a start in the Morning

we came on a good long way along a cutting running alongside of a creek and I thought that it was the bad piece of road that I had heard them talk about but you can judge of my surprise when Tom stopped and told me that we was at the Top of the Mountain and that we had it to go down yet   so he took all the Bullocks off but four and put the rest behind and tied the two Horses up behind the cart and then we began the decent   it is good road cut in the Mountain but it is so very narrow that if anything was to happen [to] the Harness you would be sure to meet with an accident for as high as you can see on one side is the Mountain above and as far below you can see the top of trees and such beautifull creepers climbing up the stems of the Trees

there is one creeper in particular that I saw if we only had it up our way we would be glad to have it growing in our gardens   it has a nice green leaf and is smothered in big branches of flowers   I hardly know what flower to compare them to   they are not very unlike Orange blossoms but not quiet so white as they are

I have not seen any Maruya side of Araluen   you keep winding down the Mountain and after you come a bit down you see Araluen like a little dot amongst green trees   the houses dont look to be any size when you first see it   I was coming down a good bit behind Tom when the Mail passed us and the Mailman told me that the grey filly had her leg over the Halter so that if he had not have told me I would have been in a bit of a mess, most likely broke the cart where she was tied   you can judge the steepness of the Hill when Tom used to have to stop and put water on the Brake and it used to fiz and smoke with haveing to have it on so much but it is a good road with anything els but a Team and the Corners are so sharp that you can hardly turn with a waggon but we got down all right and had our dinner at the bottom   then we started and went up the town and camped in an open piece of ground

it is a funny old town for it is enclosed all around with big high Mountains   you cannot see where there is any get out to it at all but they are very kind people in Araluen for there was a man came down and asked us to come up and spend the evening and so we did   they were such nice jolly people   just about the time we was going to camp the school children was coming out of school and Albert was playing on the road so I watched what he would do when they came up to him and so what should he do but lay flat down in the dirt that shy that he would not look at them

it must have been nearly 12 oclock when we went to bed last night there was not a bit of grass so that we had to get the Bullocks some chaff as we could not get them any hay   it was so strange last night for whenever you woke you could hear engine whistles blowing and the Machinery at work for they work the claims night and day and the Cocks was crowing all night   it looked very much like rain to night   I dont know whither it it going to rain but I hope so for things look very bad over this way

12th Day   started this Morning all sign of the rain gone   came through the whole length of Araluen which is about 3 mile long and has only the one street running through it and most of the Houses look as if they have seen better days which I suppose that they have for we was told last night that it had at one time thirty-six Public houses where it has only 4 now

came along till we came to the cutting which is all the [way] from Araluen to Maruya and if I thought that the Mountain was bad yesterday this was ever so much worse for in every two or three hundred yards there would be [a] turn as sharp as your elbo and as it was nearly all up hill pulling we had to have all the Bullocks on and it was such a job to get them round turns   it will let you know how close we was over to day when the two off Wheels run off and was nearly down the cutting   you are all the time working round a Mountain between the Top of it and the River and in most places you cannot see the Top of the Mountain and looking down you see the Bottom of the River such a long way down   as we was going along we saw a lot of men diggin   they had six or seven Horses and carts and they would load the carts and start the Horses off and they would go to where they had to be unloaded where they was washing the dirt [then they would] start them back again and they would come and go without the driver   it looked so curious to see them marching up and down by themselves   we came about nine miles to day and we are camped to night close beside the River that we have been following all day

I do wish that we was at our journys end for I am getting tired especially of this nasty cutting but it is all the way to Moruya like what we passed to day   there are such a lot of houses all along the Bank of the River   we see them as we pass along and all of them with fruit gardens   most of the Trees are peach and they look to have a lot of fruit on them and so green and healthy the trees   there are some such nice trees all out in flower there is a scrubby kind of tree all out in White Blossom   you would think from the distance that it was Elderberry and then there is another tree   it is something like our hickory trees   it is all out in beautifull bloom   and then the sides of the Mountain are all covered with ferns   I would like going along if we had not got the Waggon to take for I am so frightened that we will meet with an accident before we get there as they are such contrary bullocks to drive

13th Day   Started from Camp this Morning   just as we was starting by came a Man driving pigs   we had no grass for the Bullocks but they done very well on cakes and such a road for it is all a cutting and such sharp turns you never seen   I was frightened to drive the cart in some places   we got on very well though   had dinner   started   came through some nice grass land   saw a lot of young calves and cows   started on the cutting again

came to a very sharp turn in the road when over she went right over and over and if it had not been for a tree it would have went down to the river and took the Bullocks with it but it went right over   pulled the off side polar right down on his knees, we had a job to take him out but we got them out and none of them was hurt in the least which was a good job for there was enough damage done but it could have been a great deal worse the things that are hurt the most are the chairs they are destroyed altogether and the poor old Preambulater I am more sorry for it than all the rest the table got all the legs broke off but one but I think that we can get it mended they are broke off right up at the Top the Washstand it got the sidepieces broke off and the Toilet table 2 of the legs off but it only wants a bit of glue The Cheffinere was right on top and it escaped with very little dammage The Tubs Buckets Pot-oven Saucepans all escaped all but Babys and it got broke my Saddle never got a Scratch, The big case was broke to pieces and my old Blue box, the grubbox Babys chair is the only one that is any way whole at all the cradle was broke too The Waggon has only the front crosspeice broke so that on the whole we escaped pretty lucky but it would have been better if it had not have happened at all I dont know how the crockery case got on for I did not inspect it to see but I think that it is pretty right

it was a great job to get the waggon up again but they got another Team of Bullocks and Pulled it up with the two Teams but we did not get any loaded that night for it took us all our time to get the things up on the road and in the Morning we had four men come to help us to load so that we was not long before we had it loaded again – and ready for a start

I was so frightened for I thought that Tom was under the Waggon we was just coming along a very steep cutting where this sharp turn was I was a little bit behind waiting for him to get round this turn I heard him shouting to the Bullocks to stop but they would not he then run round on the off side but it was no use for the leader run right to the edge of the presipeice and they pulled the two Pole Bullocks and the waggon over it would have been a dreadful smash if the Tree had not been there we was busy till dark and just about dark the Mail coach came along and a gentleman got out and came and spoke to me so nice and kind and after he was gone I was told that it was Judge Mcfarland on his road to Moruya we went to bed but not to sleep much I never undressed myself or Albert

14th Day got up and it was a disheartening sight for all along the side of the road all the things was strewed about and we was to the Tops of our boots in dust only just the road and so much traffic on it but we set to work and soon packed it up again one of the Men that was helping us was the Maintainance man so he asked me to come down to his place so that when we was packed up we started and came on to his place had dinner   camped there all the rest of the day   I done some washing   the People was real nice people   they were young married people with one child   poor little Albert when he saw his carriage broke he did cry bitter poor little fellow   I did hate to see him for he thought so much of it – we are in the tick country now but I have not seen any as yet

15th Day   came 9 Mile 1/2 to day through some very ugly places quiet as bad as where we met with the Accident but we got on nicely to day though the Bullocks was very contrary sometimes, saw trees to day such a height that you would not think trees could grow as high   Saw the first iron Bark that I ever saw to day and such beautifull Ferns and what they call the Burranang   it is so pretty and I saw Orange trees growing   where we are camped to night is a Chinamans place   there are dreadfull Bush fires in the Mountains about us and has been this last week   we have been following a River since last Tuesday   they call it the Dooey River   I never heard the name before

   it has eels in it   we was going to try and catch some to night but it is raining   the Way they catch them about here is to take a light and paddle up the river with your Boots off and have a pitchfork and spear them with it   they say that they will come round the light   this is a great place for Bears   you can hear them shouting in all directions of a night and there are lots of snakes for you can see their tracks across the roads making for the River   they say that there are deaf Adders too   I dont want to see any of them gentlemen   you can think that the trees are a good size when it takes 3 Men to fall one Tree down

16th Day   started   looked very much like rain   came about a mile and a half when we came to the foot of the Moruya Mountain   got up all right   It was a long pull up to the Top   there was one very bad turn   I had to go and be off side driver round it but we got round it right   when we came to the top we took all the Bullocks off but four to come down   if it had have been a nice clear day we would have seen the sea and the town of Moruya but it was raining and foggie so that we could not see any distance

   you never seen anything so beautifull as the sides of the Mountain is as you are coming   nothing but one Thick Mass of Green Trees and Vines there was a dead sapling and all up that the vines was just like ivy   so pretty   you cannot see the bottom for green shrubs all out in flower some with flowers and some with fruit   I got some wild rasberries yesterday

 In 1904 the Halfords, with their four daughters, made an heroic trek over some of the continent's most forbiding and arid territory as they travelled from the Murray River in South Australia hundreds of miles west and north to Kalgoorlie in Western Australia. Like Ann Williams and her her husband, they loaded their household belongings onto a wagon pulled by bullocks.

such big ones but I dont like the taste of them a bit   They just grow like the Rasberries in the Gardens only they are ever so much bigger   you never seen such long trees in all your life as there is in that Mountain   we had our dinner at the bottom and I saw a Tree Fern it had leaves about 5 foot long and about 2 foot wide it was so pretty

we came about 2 mile and then camped for the night   it has been rain- ing off and on all day   after we camped we went a walk up in the bush and Tom shot such a pretty parrot it had a purple head, green and yellow back purple and yellow breast and nice long tail   when we got back it was raining a little   we could hear the sea like anything   it was roaring so loud although we was 7 or 8 miles from it

17th Day Sunday got up was raining   Tom put up the Tarpauline like a verandah and we had a very good place but Albert would keep running out in the wet   had our dinner   it cleared up a bit   we went for a walk but it started to rain and we had to come home again and my word it did rain all night as hard as it could come down   it came through our tent and we had to get up and put a blanket up that stopped it from coming through   it want greasing

18th Day   Beautifull Morning   it looks to fine to last   Tom went to some of the Sawmills to see if he could get a job without going all the way down to Wagonya as some of the Bullocks feet were very tender   I went to the Top of a hill with him   I could see Moruya but not very plain so that I cant tell you yet what I think of it   we went a Mile and Albert walked all the way back   his father carried him up on the Mare

got back   put out the Bed Clothes to dry   put Albert to sleep when up comes a Thunderstorm so I had to bustle about and cover things and I did not know what to do for I thought that it might be a very heavy Storm there was people living quiet close to where we was camped so I plucked up courage and went to their place and they made me very welcome so I had some dinner there and stayed awhile and came to the waggon again when another storm came on but I stopped this time   I did not like to go again to be so silly and before it was all over Tom came back and he has got a place at Lynchs at Mago so that we will soon be there now and if we had to go to Wagonya it would take us all the Week   it is not very far from Moruya so that it is not such an out of the way place   it is a Weatherboard house that I have to live in   some one is living in it now but they are leaving in a day or two we have lost the Bullocks to night so that while I am writing this Tom is after them   Albert is in bed   I have put 3 pairs of dry socks on him today so at last I took his boots and socks off and then after running about play-ing a while where should I find him but laying down in a stream of Water with all his cloths on the young Scamp so that I had to put all dry clothes on him   there will soon be good grass here now after all this nice rain

Butter is a shilling a pound here   Oranges are 6 pence dozen   this is a great place for peaches   every house you see here has a lot of peach Trees and loaded with fruit and all looking so green and healthy you will see them growing along side of the road where someone has dropped a stone I suppose

19th Day   Got up   looked like rain but we thought that it was going to be fine so we packed up and yoked up and just as we had everything ready for starting down came the rain again so we waited a bit to see if it cleared up but it did not look like clearing up a bit so we let the Bullocks and Horses go and as we was out of Provisions we put the Mare in the cart and went to Moruya

I thought that Moruya was a nice big town but it isnt   it is not as nice as Queanbeyan to my thinking but it was raining dreadfull hard   perhaps it will look better on a nice fine day

it is nice Country about the town for grass   you will see little paddocks there white with clover blossoms and such nice orange trees   I am tired of eating them and so is Albert   after we got our things we came back   it was raining all the time and rained all night   the flats are running with Water and we cant get out of the cart for getting our feet wet   I hope that it will soon be fine now for I am tired of so much wet

20th Day   came about 6 miles   camped in a wild scrubby place   turned the Bullocks down in a swamp   good feed   a young chap come along and was yarning for about 1 hour or more

21st Day   beautifull fine Morning   I forgot to mention in my yesterdays travels that I saw the big sea but I would not have noticed it if Tom had not have told me that it was it   it looked to me like a flat plain with distant mountains in the back and as I thought white houses but upon viewing it more closely I see that it was white foam on the rocks   but I must go on with my to days travels for it is our last days for a while I suppose

we had our breakfast and was takeing our time for Tom had seen the Bullocks and Horses quiet close and I was just saying that I could laugh at you fellows for I had had no Ticks on me   I had not the words scarcely out of my mouth when I feels something on my leg gives it a scratch and my word it soon let me know what it was   a tick   so I took the scissors and cut him in to   I never had anything to pain me so for a while   I have taken a great lot out of old Spot   I expect that he will soon be dead

now packed up   went for the Bullocks   could only find 6 where the others was we could not make out   Tom looked everywhere I believe   he was 2 hours or more looking for them   when he went up to the others out of the scrub they came with their tails straight up in the air galloping like mad   we had a job to get them yoked up and while he was looking for the Bullocks I fetched the Horses up   Harnessed the Bay Mare   the little filly always follows the others   while they were waiting for the Bullocks to come away marches the filly up the road   I thought that she would soon come back   I did [not] bother for a while but after a while [when] she did not make her appearance I put Albert to bed   I went up the road a piece but I could not go far and leave Babe so I put old Blossom in the cart and trots along to see if I could see her   After I had gone a good way back I sees her walking along the road so I thought that she would stand when she seen the mare coming but the faster I went the faster went she   I tied the Mare up and tried to get round her but she would best me so you may depend that I was pretty wild with her then and mad enough to do anything so I takes the mare out of the cart   I had brought a bridle to lead her back so I jumps on the Bay Mare and gave her a chase for it and I soon got a head of her and caught her and fetched her back

Baby had never stirred and was fast asleep so I harnessed up and went back to the camp again and just as I got there Tom got the Bullocks and if I had not have done that he would have had to go to Moruya for her so we got started at last and came on when we stopped for dinner and we had just got out to have it when we saw a man coming to us and it proved to be Willie Lynch   he was out with his team for a log so he would not hear of us stopping for dinner there   we must come on to the house to get it so we came on till we got there and went and had our dinner   they seemed like very nice homly people   there is the old laidy and Willies Wife and a young girl and I think that there is another girl but she is not at home just now   so we began unpacking our things and putting them straight but they are very much knocked about so that we did not get much done to night

22nd Day   Got up   nice fine morning   Tom started on the chimney   I wish it had a fireplace for it is so miserable cooking outside   Mrs Lynch fetched me down a basin of milk for Baby   he is so fond of a drop of milk in his food   poor old Spot is bad now with the ticks   I expect that he will soon die   they are dreadfull things   they have been known to kill Horses   My travels are done now   I dont think that I have anything els to tell

you must excuse this writing, for sometime I had not much light and no table and after the Accident I had not even the grubbox to write on for it got all smashed up   I dont expect that you will be able to make it all out but I will send it for I promised to

I intended to have sent this last time we went to the Post but it was not quiet ready but I will send it to night for I am going to the Post this Evening   I was there last Wednesday   they call it a town but it is not much of a town   there are two Sawmills and some stores but I dont know how many   there are three churches but I have not found out yet how often there are preaching   I expect that there will be some Post for me for it is five Weeks since I left and I have never heard a Word   We had one paper sent here so I expect that they will all come now

I am going to try tonight to get some fowels   it is a job to get any here   I could get some from Mrs Lynch but they would not stop if I did   we are nearly eat alive with Misquietoes and fleas and there are Native dogs   Mrs Lynch had a hen sitting at the back of our place and they took her last Saturday night   we heard him howling but I did not think that it was a native   it is a terrible scrubby place not a bit like what I thought the Coast was like

Albert is getting so fat and big you wont know him when you see him again   Tom is starting to draw this Morning with his team   the Bullocks has picked up very well

we was at the Ball the other night in Town and it was a grand affair   I left Albert at home with Mrs W. Lynch   we did not want to go but the two girls was going to drive and they wanted our mare so we thought that we would go   I went with them in a Buggie and Tom came with the men

I enjoyed myself very well considering [I] know no one but I am used to that now that I make myself at home with strangers   there was a great lot of people there   it seemed so strange to look round and see no face that you know amongst such a croud

'Strange' – the word rings a refrain. Ann Williams has managed the strangeness of unfamiliar territory and of people she does not know, and yet her pride in coming through all right is tinged with disappointment. After the long journey, after the dry and then the wet, the constant worry about the animals, the bad luck of the accident, to arrive at the end and find a house without even an inside fireplace, set amidst ugly scrub near a settlement with scant claim to be called a town – it was not exactly what she had in mind. Life would be soberingly primitive. Although the original pioneers had come and gone, their successors would find the bush a struggle, even in this by no means remote coastal region. Further north in the Coonamble district of New South Wales, Barbara Baynton was at this same time a young mother, married to a selector, and living in a stark world of bush battlers about whom she would later write her grim and powerful short stories of *Bush Studies*. Hopefully, the Moruya district offered a more gentle existence to Ann Williams.

The prospects for Lucy Jones look worse. Leaving the coastal town of Goolwa, established in the 1850s and by now offering the comforts we think of as civilized, the Jones family made their way over the sandhills beside The Coorong, a shallow, narrow lagoon of salt water running along the South Australian coast for 140 kilometres from the mouth of the Murray River. The Jones were travelling into that region of Victoria which Miss Oliver had described as 'the ugliest country I have ever seen' when she arrived in the neighbouring parish of Neuarpur twelve years earlier. Stunned by the place, she saw nothing in its favour and could only cry plaintively, 'Had I known the very isolated life I was to lead I do not think I should have been induced to come out.' This giving in to misery is something Lucy Jones resisted, although the temptation was there.

She was luckier anyway. She had a family with whom to share the expectations of a better life, and she could participate in the family enterprise without feeling threatened by a loss of status, as the impoverished English gentlewomen so often did when they went into the bush as governesses. Getting her hands dirty was something Lucy Jones took for granted, and she would have been amazed by Louisa Clifton's self-conscious initiation into washing clothes – especially at the belated age of twenty-five! Miss Jones did consider the unladylike state of her hands, but only after a day when she had 'helped dig a small waterhole' and 'chopped down trees and wood'. No wonder she feared her hands would be less than nice for piano playing.

And that mattered to her, for unlike Ann Williams, Lucy Jones saw herself as middle-class, and counted on such things as her musical accomplishments to place her among people of the 'right' sort. Along the road, she might wear out her gloves in driving a cart all day, but in the evening at the inn, she would quickly put her talents to social use and at Mrs Tuff's hotel, three gentlemen who requested permission to hear her play, spent the evening showering her with compliments in return. The very eligible young lady was delighted.

Presumably the older Jones also saw themselves as middle-class, and Lucy was clinging to her status rather than climbing. This would explain the money and effort spent on what looks like sheer folly: dragging along a piano to a desert property where there was not even a hut, much less a house. 'First things first' takes on a new meaning. Lucy's father may well have been one of those English gentlemen who failed to make good in the dreamland of fortunes, but his marriageable daughter was not going to lose the trappings of her class.

Under these circumstances, it is interesting that she should write such markedly uneducated prose, really no better than Ann Williams', although sprinkled with full stops and capital letters. If the parents of Lucy Jones wanted an observably middle-class daughter, why didn't they look more attentively to the matter of her education? The answer may come from Penelope Selby, who apologized for the letter her son wrote to his aunt and complained that 'few children raised in this colony have hitherto had more than a Charity boy's education at home'. With little formal education available, children often acquired fewer writing skills than their parents. Lucy Jones probably played the piano more competently than she wrote sentences, and yet, without falling into the romantic trap of valuing ignorance as innocence, it is possible to say that her natural and unaffected style is strikingly appropriate to the experience she describes.

Booroopki
West Wimmera, Victoria
18th May 1883

My dear Aunts, Uncles, Grandma, Cousins, Nellie Tucker, and Birdie Price This must be passed round to you all.

My Diary

1st Day Started from near Goolwa on a Monday going up a hill dray pin slipped out, dray tipped up with furniture, fowls &c. Took Pa and boys over an hour to prop it up fasten pin and secure with chains, I drove spring cart, two horses. Scenery, trees and sand.

Camped in an old deserted house. Pa and Will got in broken window. Unscrewed door lock. Fine paddock, good well water. Ma and I slept in cart, boys and pa under dray. Too many fleas in old house. Slept in clothes and boots.

2nd Day Rose at moonlight, started sunrise. Cat got out box rode rest of way on bedding in cart sometimes on cart seat Very rough road, horses took bad drinking muddy water, one fell down in dray shafts. Pa took him out, physiced him and whipped him along to keep him warm. Another horse fell down. Camped near fence, physiced all horses. Scenery, gum trees. Bad road. Camped at Mulgundawa opposite hotel. Passed lots of wild turkeys and native companions. Slept as before.

3rd Day Started 6 o'clock a.m. Very cold, ice on water. Coorong on one side. Good road till reached Wellington, then hill of sand above axles, horses on *noses* pulling. Unloaded dray at Jetty, crossed in punt to pretty landing place, willows and tall grass on either side. A long drive. Wellington properly styled 'The Sand Hole' is a small place houses half buried in sand. Stores some yards from road. My gloves fell off, worn out with driving. Hot day, faces and lips nearly blistered. Wrote the above on stockyard rail Wellington while men reloaded dray. Picked up a tramp, gave him 4 miles ride. Camped at fenced paddock, good feed for horses, boys had to take them 3 miles to water. Slept as before.

4th Day No water to wash faces, enough for tea. Road puzzling, perfect circle round dry salt lake, could pick up handsfull of salt. Missed top of lantern Will rode back three miles Chinaman coming same way picked it up gave it to Will. Pa went up a steep sandy hill, sand up to axles, to a cottage. Asked an Irish woman if we were on right road, she replied, 'You great big silly, why didn't yer go to yer left insted of comin' up this 'ere 'ill.' Good road for some time, then a steep sandy hill with stones half a yard above ground. Again good road along Coorong. Fine scenery, green grass, birds of all species swarming on water. Passed flocks of dead and living cattle and sheep. Reached Meningie at sunset, mail steamer arrives at night there. Camped in hotel yard. Ma and I slept in hotel, men in cart. Landlady asked me to play, her husband with the station master and two other young gentlemen spent the evening with us singing and playing, the lady was very fond of my waltz   asked me to play it three times over, did so. I played all accompaniments.

5th Day   Started at sunrise, made another circle round dry salt lake came to banks of Coorong midday. Turkeys, pelicans, swan, fine great geese and other birds on water. Sheoaks, Gums and pretty trees on side of road. Kangaroo dog chased a sheep down, tied him behind cart. Camped under Sheoak tree   poured with rain. Will cooked chops. Slept as usual, but pa watching horses all night. Ma fretted, could not find kerosine or matches for some time.

6th Day   Caught enough water on top of canvas over cart to wash faces in. Started at sunrise. Jack's birthday. Continued by Coorong, scenery the same as before. Dogs chased kangaroo 'no catch him'. Several hares sprang over road. Stopped at Wood's Wells, bought milk. White girl buried there who was murdered by Mileky Martin 20 years ago. Bad road, lots of Teatrees. Passed several dead and living cattle, pigs and sheep. Camped at Salt Creek where Mileky Martin murderer of the white girl lived. Water salt in Creek. Slept as before.

7th Day Sunday   Woke at 3 o'clock a.m. Poured with rain all bedding &c. soaking through, flood all round cart, horses strayed away. Took me till 10 o'clock a.m. to bail water out of cart, found horses $^3/_4$ mile away. Stopped all day in cart. Will cooked chops, pa waited on us in cart. Rained all day, wind blowing, rocking cart like a cradle. Blacks camped near us their dog ran away with our boiled beef out of boiler on fire. Jack's straw hat smashed, table broken with wind. Kept awake all night by wind and rain. 'Cart too muchy rocky'.

8th Day   Started 8 o'clock a.m. Poured with rain, miles of deep sand, miles of road covered with 4 feet of water. Plenty Kangaroos on side of road. Pa told me to drive on to Kingston 32 miles ahead for food, he took one of my horses to ride back and help the boys through the sand. Ma and

I in a fever, sand up to axles   my horse done up   went some miles   came to Coolatoo hotel. Camped, horse's back all raw, Pa came galloping after us for fear we could not get on, glad to see us camping, galloped back for boys who had camped, Tackled up again came 8 miles through heavy sand and water   pitch dark   raining. Ma and I waiting with clenched hands, reached hotel, had tea, slept there, bedding in cart too wet, dried some blankets in hotel. Will's accordeon box smashed, tied it up in one of my dresses.

9th Day   Started at sunrise, rained all day. High wind blowing. Road fearful 9 and 10 miles through deep sand and water, in one place above the axles of the dray in sea sand and stones, to avoid newly metalled road. Dray horses done up, left them in paddock, dray on side of road with all in it, 8 miles from Kingston. All went on in spring cart through a river of rain on road, could not find road but for water shining, pitch dark. Reached Kingston 8 p.m. had tea at Mrs Tuff's hotel   wife of Mr Tuff's brother of Currency Creek. I was playing at Mrs Tuff's request my pieces, when three gentlemen, musical gentlemen, asked her to allow them to come and hear me. She introduced them, one a doctor, a very musical widower, he had one of his thumbs shot off some time ago, he was delighted with my pieces, said 'My dear, keep up your music, the Almighty has endowed you with a wonderful gift, if you only keep it up your fortune is made, I only wish I were younger &c, &c, &c.' Flattery, flattery, Oh the gentlemen! One of the young gentlemen played some quadrilles, the other sang a nice song. Slept in hotel, men in cart.

10th Day   Pa went back for dray. When starting from hotel the Dr gave me a book. Started midday, boggy stony rough road, Sheoaks on either side camped under tree.

11th Day   Started at sunrise   road boggy   sand hills and rough stones, beautiful trees on one side   Lost one of pa's hats. Camped on roadside splendid feed for horses, had to go over a wide deep ditch for wood. Passed several flocks of living and dead animals during day, went through river up to axles. Slept as before.

12th Day   Started after sunrise, lovely day. Road stony and stumps half a yard above the ground. Reached Lucindale 12 o'clock a.m. Pretty little place, nice stone buildings. Road continued boggy sandy and stony. Kangaroos in great numbers, too fleet for dogs to catch. Beautiful trees. Malee, Tasmanian Blue Gum, Red Gum, Honey Suckle Teatree, Sheoak, Stringy

Bark and others, Rosellas and other birds. Lost stirrup off saddle coming through thick scrub. Some of the limbs had to be chopped down to allow us to pass. Camped under tree. One horse bad, physiced her.

13th Day Started after sunrise. Bad stony road through thick scrub then good road. Lake on either side, good grass, native companions feasting in grassy paddocks. Reached Naracoorte about 4 o'clock p.m. Pretty place fine buildings good gardens, fine government buildings with livery stables. Found a horse's bit in thick scrub. Camped at a native well. Little cat rode on my horse's back for a little distance. Poor fowls *bumped* about, glad to have some fresh grass put in cage.

14th Day Sunday Started early, went 10 miles on metal road. Met some young gentlemen *out shooting*. They told Pa we were 8 miles on wrong road, turned back to proper crossing and bad road, one of my horses lame. Pretty trees, several fine stations with fine fruit gardens. Camped under gum tree.

15th Day Started about 10 o'clock a.m. Horses gave us a hunt of five miles for them first. Fearfully rough road rest of way. Reached Binnum, a wretched place with 3 hovels and a station in it about midday. Found our things which had gone by sea all exposed to all weathers, the piano case *bottom upwards* and partly prized open and ma's large sea chest ditto. Clara's and my drawings exposed on top in a box to wet and heat. Camped in paddock, pa went 17 miles for Mr Beard and his bullock waggon to cart our house, could only carry half. Then had to go several miles in dark for chaff for horses. Slept as before.

16th Day Old dumb tramp came along gave pa a paper begging. Pa gave him a shilling, he picked up his swag with the arm the paper *said* was useless, and trudged on. Took Pa and boys till 2 o'clock p.m. to turn piano case right way up and unload trucks, which had our belongings on. Bad road heavy sand stones, &c. Reached Mr Beard's at dusk. Mrs Beard kindly sold us bread and pork.

17th Day Started with Mr Beard's two sons for guides with bullock waggon, about 8 o'clock a.m. Heavy sandy road, thick timber, had to cut some down. Camped near 'Bring Albert' station, a fine place situated on the bank of a fine lake, beautiful fruit garden. Pa rode on to find road. Slept as usual.

18th Day Started sunrise, bad road, pretty trees, lots of birds. Pa went before with axe to cut a road through thick Stringy Bark scrub. Reached our land about noon. Scenery like Currency Creek. Fine dam on Clara's block. Plenty tadpoley water for use. Plenty wood. Spent rest of day rigging up galvanized roofing for hut to put luggage under. Lots of wild birds.

19th Day   Will shot wild duck and rosella. Cooked bread outside. I made a mud fireplace and washed socks in Tadpoley water. Several parties of surveyors and station hands passed here, boiled their tea on the land.

Ma and I still sleep in cart, men under iron huts. Pa went 7 miles to post yesterday   received letters from Uncle Will and Ethel   Uncle's advice came too late, but his letter was welcome. It was the anniversary of Pa and ma's wedding day yesterday. I am kneeling on the men's bedding by a box writing this, ma is cooking outside. The boys gone chopping trees, & pa gone for a sheep for 'muttony'.

We are like a lot of bears let loose in a desert, and will have to go 30 and more miles over fearful roads for provisions. We have kept pretty well excepting colds which Jack and I have. Please tell Burnet the Australian stamps are no use to *Victorians* so I have returned them, excepting two which pa wanted. Now with much love to all I must say farewell.

It is cold, and I must go to sewing, fancy we have had to go for days without washing our faces or hands. Plenty water now. Hoping you are all well now and happy, as we are not *yet* and with love from all to all,

I remain
Your loving relative and friend
Lucy Jones

27th May 1883

My dear relatives and friends,
You will see this epistle was written on the 18th, Pa took it to Booroopki Post Office then to post it. When turning out his coat pocket yesterday 'Lo and behold!' There was this letter, so I opened it to add this.

Will went out shooting a day or two ago, shot at an *old man kangaroo*, wounded him, he turned to *scoff* Will but he hit at him with the *butt* of his gun splintering it in the act, but killing *Mr Kangaroo* with such *vigor* the Australian¹² stamps are no use to Victorians so I have returned them. * Now with much love to *excepting two, which pa wanted. all I must say farewell. Our address heads this epistle. It is cold, and I must go to sewing, fancy we have had to go for days without washing our faces or hands. Plenty water now. Hoping you are all well now and happy, as we are yet and with love from all to all

I remain

Your loving relative and frie[nd]

Lucy Jones.

How this sketch Lucy Jones drew at the end of her letter must have horrified the relatives comfortable in the stone houses of Goolwa. 'Slaving over a hot fire' takes on vivid meaning here, and the word 'hut' is wildly exaggerated.

that a piece of that *brave* creature's head bone entered the woodwork of Will's gun, and remains there. Will mended his gun though it was badly splintered.

Ma manages to cook a damper, pancakes, and meat outside. The piano which pa and Jack brought the other week from Binnum is out in *hail rain &c* only a tarpaulin over it. No room under iron for it. Pa and boys commenced building chimney today. No stone here. The chimney is to be made with Bulloaks and filled with pugg (mud). The Squatter's sons came here yesterday, they seem very nice. We see station folks pass every day, nearly all come up to have a *chat*.

I have been washing today. The clothes are completely *spoilt* [with] *iron-mould* and mildew and some rubbed in holes.

I helped dig a small waterhole yesterday, chopped down several trees and wood, so you can imagine what nice hands I shall have for piano (If it be any good after the *exposure*!) We had a letter from Walt on Thursday, he was well and busy. It seems so *unpleasant*, here we are with our things all tossed together sleeping in [the] cart with rain sometimes soaking our pillows, or ice on water, and piano &c exposed to rain, our clothes all mouldy. We cannot change those we have on either for the water is full of *toads*, and our clean clothes are mouldy in boxes.

I believe the journey through rain has ruined £20 worth of bedding and clothes. When uncle Will comes over he will come by mail and not see the horrid roads. A good thing too! He would be too disgusted to get here. Of course, we came a different way.

Please Nellie tell Fred the boys will write when their busy time is over, they are always saying 'My word, *wont* we have fun when Fred comes over to stay with us by and bye.' Nellie you should see the poor puny looking folks here. Of course I have not seen many. There are two Squatters living not far from here. Mr Hamilton and Mr Broughton. The former has a daughter who plays the piano, *so we heard*. Her two brothers called here yesterday, one is 22. There were 7 young gentlemen here one day.

Must close this with love to all relatives,

I remain,

A conglomeration of *wonder* and *hope*!

Also your wellwisher

'Luce'

Lucy Jones' 'wonder and hope' seems a brave response to the conditions she describes. Her youthful resilience helps. Her mother by this time may have been less cheerful. If she was, she did not encourage her daughter to be gloomy, and in fact the Jones family comes through as a model of co-operative effort. Like the Williams, they worked together to survive. The image of Rosa Payne, stranded all by herself at the Rich Avon station not far to the north, becomes all the more poignant by comparison – and understandable. Who can judge harshly the solitary governess who wanted so desperately to escape from the place where she could only try 'not to think, or else I would die'? Who could expect anyone other than the strong and the protected to survive?

'WE WAS COMING TO BETTER OUR SELVES'

Memories of the 1840s

'My husband was quite nervous,' wrote Sarah Davenport. Small wonder, really. There was his wife arguing with a bunch of Ballarat miners – 'old Vandemonians' amongst them – and threatening to break one of their horse's legs unless the men kept their part of the bargain and took the Davenports along with them to Mount Alexander. Who wouldn't be nervous? Who, that is, except Mrs Davenport. A woman with more pluck would be hard to come by.

'Nervous' is a word Sarah Davenport never applies to herself, and somehow it would not ring true if she did, even though the situations she found herself in were so often disastrous, or near-disastrous, that for a moment the reader may be tempted to ask, 'Did all this actually happen? Didn't some novelist set out to invent a scenario of catastrophes and rogues?' And yet, coming back to the spare prose, listening to the matter-of-fact tone, one realizes that a novelist in search of the sensational would have written more flamboyantly. If the situations are extreme it is because life, not art, kept plunging Mrs Davenport into the fray. She wrote as she lived, concentrating on what happened, on what she needed to do. Just as she had at the time 'battled hard against brooding over my trials', she is in her reminiscences little given to self-reflection. The prose mirrors the personality.

It needs to. Otherwise the sketch (as she calls it) would sound false, the re-shaping of experience by an older self who would not have put things the same way at the time. Mrs Davenport creates the impression of reliving experiences as she recalls them. Gifted with a detailed memory, she is able to conjure up for her readers a world which has much more in common with the harsh and brutalizing London of Hogarth's engravings than with the pleasantly unthreatening Australia drawn by her contemporary S. T. Gill.

Hers is a world of people without access to property, people who never stay long in one place and rarely have much control over what happens to them. It is an insecure world full of uncertainties and reversed expectations, and surviving in it requires a cool head and a determined spirit. This working-class wife had both, and it was just as well she did, because she was burdened not only with young children but also with a sickly and inept gentleman-husband who would turn his hand at nothing less refined than cabinet-making and could not even be relied on to keep the family all together, much less to keep them fed. Without Sarah Davenport, this nervous gentleman would surely have found himself 'bushed'.

Sceth of an emegrants Life in austrailia
from Leiving England in the year of our Lord 1841

as maney pepole leving home for new south wales and Port phillip sent gloing accounts of the country both for good wages and no scarcity of work and the healtheness of the climate my husband having a sister hear [heard reports of the place] her husband was a soldier but he had bought his Discharg and got a publick house in the country and [was] making money fast so the news to us was from them that we shold come out

we had 4 yong chilldren   we sould our house hold furniture gathered up our effects Paid our Dets and got an order to come out by Paying two Pounds each for the 4 chilldren 8 pound   we left manchester for Liverpool October 4 1841 and pased the bord of comishonars on the 6 and whent on the ship, ship urainia, and set sail on the evening of the 7 of october 1841 thair was about two hundred souls on bord the ship named urainia, Omens and smith of Liverpool owaners   we was all in good hopes that we was coming to beeter our selves tho sorry to leve our friends

we had not sailed long before meney was sea sick but not all for some was singin and some roughs was bawling nex my galley   the Poilot had left about half an hour as near as i can think   we seamed to be goin very smothley and some was in bed, others preparing for the night as we had maney famyles with chilldren and meney was sick   my little ones 3 was sick but i had got them in bed and was sit near them to attend on them feeling anny thing but comfortable when sad to tell the vessell struck about half past ten o clock   she struck on the sand bank   i shall never forget it the srikes and screams [of] wemon and chilldren and some of the men was terrified   they did not know what they was doing

1 Sceth of an emigrant[s]
Life in austrailia —
from leiving England
in the year of our Lord 1841
to 1869 as maney pepole seeing
home for new south wales
and Sant philly sent gloing
accounts of the country both
for good wages and no scarcity
of work and the healthyness
of the climate my husban
having a sister hear
her husband was a soldier
but he had bought his
Dischary and got a puble
publick house in the
country and making
money fast so the nuews
to was from them that
us
we shall come
out we had to yong
chille[ren] we soulde our
house hold furniture

With no artistic fanfare, Sarah Davenport launches straight into her 'Sceth of an emegrants life in austrailia'. Only the first half of this painstakingly written account now survives.

i was in an upper birth with my four chilldren my husband ran on deck to see what was the mater i saw him no more till Daylight all the passengers tryed to go on Deck the Captain ordered the hatches to be nailed down but it was no use the vessel kept striking with the waves till 3 o clock, us poor passengers expectain the ship wold break up and i believe had thair been a storm i shold not have been hear to write this it was comparitiveley calm i heard the mate say to the captain we was 6 nots out of the right way that was before we struk

direckley affter the ship did strike the mate offred to take the vessel throu the irish chanel if the captain wold allow him but he wold not and it seems the captain did not understand wat he undertook as soon as Daylight brok the Life boats came and took us off the wreked vessel and landed us at a smal vilage caled hoy Lake and we remained till annother ship was ready the ship brok up on the 14 we had nothing but what we stood up in till the ship broke up and then we got two boxes of the least vaule of som of the passengers must have got some off our other boxes as i saw some of my chilldrens close sold by auction in sydney at a sale room in Georg st i claimed them but my husband wold not allow me to force them to give them up

wile we remain at hoy Lake i went to church the first sunday the minister took for his text st Pauls ship wreck the 27 chapter of acts vers 43 44 and well he laboured to instruct us he seemed to me to be a sincere cristain i have never forgot his kindnes and work of Love among us how he exorted us and strove to comfort us his words has struk my memory in the wild bush like an eacho and i have ever resolved that shold [i] visit my native home i wold go to hoy Lake and see that minister if he is still alive

affter we had [been] at hoy Lake a few Days i whent bak to manchester as my Parents was living and my husband had not a pair of shoose to put on he had taken them off the night we ware wreked and he never got them again he lost 2 pair besides what was paked up i whent to Liverpool and Mr Smith gave me a pas on the railway to manchester it was eigh o clock at night when i got to my parents and a great maney of my old neighbours and friends came to see me and shewed me much kindness but i did not wish to stop in manchester we had broke up our home and lost all in the wrek

i did not wish to begin Life again in old England i wanted to make a fresh start in a new country my husband was a cabinet maker by trad and he used to suffer with the sick headach almost every week   i had to work very hard my self to keep our familey and i found my strenth getting very low   i concluded the best to try a new country

on the 27 of october 1841 we went on bord the Champion of Glasco – eigh hundred tuns burden – and set sail a second time   it was very rouuf in the bay of biskay   after we got through the vessel rolled a good deal

on the 8 of November in the morning about eigh o clock a yong woman was coming down the hatch way with some gruel to her mother and she was pitched off the Lader   i was siting in my birth with my yongest little son on my knee, one year and eigh months old, named Albert   her gruel splashed on his head and down his ear and scalded him so severely that he died on the tenth of November just fourteen days affter we had set sail a second time

this was a more sever tryal than the ship wrek   i cold not cry one tear   i was stund   the yong womans name was Ema Patmore and a good yong [woman] she was, aged about fifteen   she was like myself she cold not cry but in one short month she died and was buried in the sea   sad it was to me

i had what was caled purmature labour and that babe was throne in the sea   i was almost Dumb with grief   i thought my tryals was heavey but i cryed unto God to help me for my chilldrens sake   i had no one to comfort me in all my tryals for my husband seemed indifferend affter the ship wreck   his kindness seemed to be all vanished and [another] spirit might have [taken] position of him   he [would] go on Deck or about [his] own pleasure   i saw [it] and felt it too but [said] nothing   some of [my] ship mates was [very good] to mee and when i [was] able to go about [again i] returned it to them again   i must make myself usefull   i felt happier if i was Doing some good for some of them but i had a sore hart but i battld hard against brooding over my tryals

we had a good comander in Captain John Cockerin a schoth man, and two Dockters, Heuuet was the name of one   i hav forgot the name of the other   they was very kind to the passengers generley [thair was] maney different tempers abord a emmigrant ship   [we] mustred about three hundred souls but i think [we had] as orderley a vouage [as aney] that came out at [that] time for the captain [did] have a system strict and orderley [because] he looked affter it him sellf and if thair was anney complaints brought to him he wold make all inquieres and put the passengers to rights as far as he was able wehen [we] was passing the cape of good hope we had a rather sever storm   it was on the 31 of December and lasted till the 3 of january   one of the wemon was confined on the first of january and i went on deck to get somthing cooked and a wave came and washed me under the Long boat and washed part of the galley away, but i was not much hurt and the poor woman had had nothing warm to eat so i got on some dry cloaths and tryed again and did my best under the curcumstances and made her as comfortabl as i could but a few days after i was taken very ill with a sever cold and i got a sever blow on one of my legs   i thought it wold be nothing but it began to inflame and i was not well [for] some weeks affter we landed   it is a very trying time to be pent up on bord an emigrant ship for 4 months   we was all very glad when 'land a head' was caled out

the next eveining about 8 o clock we cast anchor in Port jackson February 13 1842   just as we saw land Mrs Patmores child infant died and was buried in sydney buring ground   that was two she lost during the voyage, her Daughter Emma and her infant   they was about a ten deaths during our voyage out to sydney

when we landed in sydney thair was not a house or roome under ten shillings per week but the government Provided tents for the Poor Pepol [a] great maney emmigrants coming in so close togather and sydney was but thinley inhabated at that time, that was the cause [of] house rent being so high   wages was about 8 shillings per day but in two months time they was reduced to 5 and work scarce   my husband soon got work but instead of beeter wages [than in England] he got less   he was very Dishartend for he wold not turn his hand to annything els but cabinetmaking

i was very ill for the first three months affter we landed   my left knee inflamed very much and when my knee got beeter my right arm began [to swell] from my finger ends to above my elbo   it was very bad and the muscatos did play up with my face

i suffred very much and got very weak   at last i went to a friend of my Fathers and told him who i was and what i wanted meddical advice as goin to a docktor was out of my Power   i cold get no advice under one pound and i had no pound for my husband did not earn more than 5 shillings per day

he got Dr bland to perscribe for me and got me the medicen and Dr bland brought Dr Cuttle to visit me as he said it proceded from my blood being so poor and my liver was out of order   i soon got beeter under his care so i could go about my house work and do a little sewing but i was still weak

as we cast anchor in sydney harbour one of our docktors burst a blood vessel and died a few days affter and he was buried in surry hill ceme-tary sydney   he was a fine yong man about 28 years of age   one of the Pasangers, a yong man about 25, died a day or two affter we landed   he was coming out as a Farmer bringin his Plow with him and five hundred Pounds in money and he was a free emigrant to this country   he was a single man   his name was Flanagan   who got his money i never heard

he was rather gentlemanley and did not seem to have aney real aquan-tance on bord but as soon as it was known that he was ded two or three wanted to claim his goods   i never heard who got them

Wee was but a few days in the governments tents when i met an old neibour from home   her familey had been in the tents 4 weeks when we landed so we took a two roomed house at fourteen shillings per week   i [and] 3 chilldren and she and [five]   her husband was a tin smith   he seemed to get plenty of work and seemed to get well Paid for it but he spent a great Deal in Drink   the rest of the familey was very good and strivin but they soon left sydney for Adalaid but he still remaind a Drunkard as far as i ever herd   thair names was Atherton

we then got another house near the hay market at a place caled cockle bay   the rent was 15 shillings per week   4 roomes   we let two down stairs for 5 shillings per week so we [had] two uper rooms for 5 shillings per [week] with the risk of geeting the tennants   the first house we had we could count the [stars as] we lay in bed and when it rained we could keep nothing dry but the weather was very warm but it was very uncomfort-able   we was poor   beg i could not but the second house was weather proofe but it was a long way for my husband to go to work but he did not keep in work long, i think about 4 months out of 11 as we onley stopt in sydney 11 months   work got scarcer and wages lower   sydney at the time was badly regulated   i believe most of the Police men was what they caled 'old hands'   they did not like the emigrants

when pepol went to market home fashion they must call at the wine shop a very bad Pracktice [to] allow and when they got a little wine it made them talkative and mery   they wold very likeley get josled and if they resented it they wold very likeley get knocked down and taken to the watch house and thair market basket took from them with thair weeks grocerys and get confined from saturday night to monday morning then fined one shilling but no basket or groceres returned to them

In the foreground a clothesline, a heap of wood, a little boy in a dirty smock – but capturing the centre of attention is a young girl sure of her attractiveness. Somehow amidst this poverty, the rapidly ageing mother has seen to it that her marriageable daughter can have a dress of which she need not be ashamed. Date and place unknown.

i went to buy some groceres one eavening tuasday and goin up George st i met two of these Poliece taken Mrs Patmore to the watch house i stopt and asked the reason a sarjant of the Poliece coming up at the time ask me if i cold identfy her

[four pages of Mrs Davenport's account are missing here]

we may never meet again in this world but i trust i shall see a good number in the beeter land i have seen but two since we left sydney

wile we lived in sydney a lady that lived near us her husband was gon to England to have a boxing match with the champion of that time in London she had four chilldren 3 boys and a girl he did not leve her in very good curcumstances she had a law suit about some Property but one [page] of parchment was mising her yongest son between 4 or 5 years of age had got it and 'planted' it as they call it hidind hear and neither coaching nor threats nor Punnishments wold [persuade] the yong child to tell what he had done with them his Mother spoke to me about it this was on the saturday and the tryal was coming on the next week

she did not know what to do we knew he was affaraid of the blaks i thought about it so i said to his Mother 'when you strip him to wash him let me know i will try a plan' accordingley when he was striped i went in to the kicthen it was a sellar kicthen stone built i tryed to coax him but no, he wold not tell me and [he] clapend his little sides for he was naked [as] much as to [say] 'i will not tell you' i got some blaking and a brush his name was roland

'now rolly, i will black you all over if you do not give your mother that parchment and i will give you to the blaks' he looked at me we was by our selves no he wold not 'hear gose', i begon to blak his boddy [he] did scream 'tell your Mother' said I 'or i will give you to the blaks'

he wold he took a peice of morter out of the wall and pulled out the parchment so yong and yeat so art full fear made him do what nothing els wold his mother won her law suit

my husbands sister came to see us and seemed very kind to us we wrote to them as soon as we landed and told them of our misfortunes they wrote to us very kindley and sent us a five pound note i thought they ware exceding kind but it was years to pay it back they came to see us in august as they was moveing further up the country they had a slab house built for a Publick house as things was getting worse in sydney they said we might do very well in the bush i took all that was said to be tru and soon consented to go up the bush and as a bullock dray was coming from that part we wonse more brok up our home and prepared to go up

when the bullock dray arrived the bullock driver had got other loadding but he recomended another to us and we shold have to Pay him so we wrote to brother in Law of the curcumstances   he said when we got to Yas thair was a bank and he wold send the money to the bank in Yas as we had to go throu that township   the parttys name was harrison that had charg of the bank   the bullock driver agreed to take us to Yas   he said if he got Paid he wold thake us further as brother in Law had promised to meet us part of the road   we started on a journy of four hundred miles under rather uncomfortabl curcumstances   however we stardted January 18 1843

a few of our shipmates went [with] us the first day   we onely went a few miles to what they caled the accomdation paddocks to arange the loding for a regular start   we joged on till we came to a place caled Liverpool and thare we camped near a Publick house   the driver whent into the publick house and stoped in all night   they was a lot of ruffians and he was affraid of being robbed as he worked for him self   the dray and bulock was his own   we made our beds under the dray the tarpouling fourming a rude tent and our beds was on the ground

they was a great deal of bad languag used among them and fighting one among another and they was for pulling poor me from under the dray for thair own brutal purpose   we never spoke to them but we armed our selves my husband with a small axe and me with a carving knife   i felt determined to defend myself   we was in that Position till Daylight   i believe they wold have assallted me but one more humane resisted them   that was one cause of thair fighting   at last i heard them make up a robbery for the next night so they dispersed   at that i hartley thanked god for preserving me from violance

nothing more ocured till we reached Berima and thair we lost one of our bullocks and my husband lost him self endeavouring to find it but meeting someone he got home by sundown after travaling miles in serch of the missing bolock   he was a bad bush man   i offten had to go with him in affter years   we had to start again with out the lost bolock as it could not be found

we traveled very slowley   i think we was about 20 days goin to Yas about one hundred and ninety miles   we arrived in Yas on the saturday and camped about 2 miles out side the township

my husband whent into Yas to the bank expecting to get some money

Mr Harris or Harrison told us my brother in law had an account but he had no orders to give us anny

we was stuned   our Provisions was done   we wanted to Pay the man hear we was strangers in a strange land   the bullock driver must have his money   we both felt sick   we knew not what to do   i looked about me and knowing our chilldren must have somthing to eat   i saw a larg store that is for the place   i whent in and asked for a drink for i felt faint   i found they ware our own country peapol   i told them our case they caled my husband and told him to bring our things to his store and they wold advance the money till we heard from our friends and that we could have provisions   a mail was goin out on monday   we shold have returns by thursday   we very gladley accepted it

on the saturday night as we was returning [to camp] i picked a smale tin case up and i opened it   it was a prisoners tiket of leaf as they [are] caled but i did not understand them but we had not gon far when we saw a man and woman looking up and down   i asked if they had lost anny thing they said a tin case   it was moon light so i could not read the names   i shewed the one i had found   they seemed glad and asked ware we stoped we told them and went on our way to the camping place got our suppers

the next morning the man we gave the tin box came and brought us some cabbages and cucumbers and took ourer chilldren to thair garden and gave them some grapes   it was a treat

we passed sunday as best we cold and on monday came in to Yas and settled with the driver   with some difficulty we got a roome from 'jemey the flogger' as he was caled   he could not speak a dosen words without an oath   for anything els he was kind as far as i ever saw.

my husband soon got work, then his employer had to give his word for his tools   it was 3 weekes before we heard from our friends and then they was in a hurry to get us up so me and our 2 boys whent with the dray

my husband was to follow us in a short time and bring our yong Daughter aged 9 years   i had been told we had beeter stop as our friends was not a fit place for us   i looked on thair kindness as genuine   i thought if they was not good to others they had been kind to us and i considered we was in duty bound to go on els we could have soon returned the money our friends had advanced about six pounds on i think about the 1 of march

me and our two boys started to go to uncles as they was in glee to be thair

the first days journey i had to go into a creek as my youngest son was

thrown off the dray and nearley being drowned   i jumped in and got him
out   we stoped that night at a place caled Jugelong a publick house kept
by a mail contractor named Green   i soon changed my sons claus and my
own when we got thair & then had to go by another dray   transfered
again i was ready to turn back a distance of 20 miles but this other dray
was a man and his wife and chilld so i concluded to go with rather misgev-
ines   thair names was Cuningham   Poverty, wat pain it causes   we set
[out] with this dray and a spring cart, very comfortable for a day or two

the second day an aged genteel man came up to us leading a lame
horse   as i perfered walking as the roads was so rough we soon got in conversation, this gentleman and me   i soon saw thair was a kind of awe or
restrain manefest among our traveling company, i could not tell why   we
chatted away upon religion history and other things till we camped at
night at a farm house   i think thair name was Redman   the lame hors
was put in the stable and the gentleman was put in the best parlour   as
we had traveled togather all day i must go and have supper and my 2 little
boys wich i did very willingley but i was surprised to hear them call him
reverend   it was the reverend Terry   he traveled with us till mid day next
day   i was sorrey to part with his company as while [he] was with us thair
was peace

apperentley that night thair was quarreling   the man and his wife did
fight and made things very uncomfortable   no one seemed to like Mrs
Cunningham   wat ever habation we came near no one wold have her in
thair place neither publick nor private   i cold not think wat it was for
but it seems she got a man hanged some years before   i did not know that
till affter   they had the manegment of a station on the Billebong   affter
they had quarled the husband wold not lett either her or me sleepe in the
spring cart so i was a sufferer throu thair quarrels but if we came near
aney Dwelling i wold shelter if i could

one night they ware fighting she wold have throne her child in the fire if i
had not caught it and then she wold go and drown her self   that she wold
in the river for we ware camped on the banks of the murimbugee river   it
was dark   i had her child in my arms no one cared to stop her   i thought
as she knew the way thair she wold find her way back as i saw she wanted
a fus and she did find her way back in about two hours   her baby was
asleep and then she began to up braid me for not stoping her   i told her i
was minding her baby and did not wish to drown either it or myself as i
did not know the road to the river as i had not been thair before and it was

dark when we camped   as she knew the road thair she cold come back if she chose and if she had drowned her self her husband had the best right to see about it   she was sore pusled with my cooleness

the next night we camped near a publick house   thair was a blak smiths shop and a shepards hut   i asked the blaksmith if he could lett me have a room to sleep in as the night looked thretning and was very cold   he said he wold but i must not lett that woman in   if i did he wold turne me out   i thanked him and tooke my bed in   Mrs cuningham began to up braid me and said i was no good to go and sleep in a batchelors house   it was an inner roome so i put my little boys to bed under a cover and was making all snug for the night when the shepherd came in   he knew me as he came from the place i came from before i was maried   his wife came to see me in the morning and gave me some provisions for the road as cuningham was to find me and my 2 boys with food for the jorney but we shold have been very short but for kindness we met with on the road   one woman that was a stranger to me gave me 4 loves and some other things and the news whent before us how unkind they was to me and my two chilldren

the next night we came to kiamba, smiths place or station   he was noted for being very near to travelers but he had heard of thair bad conduct to me and as soon as we camped near his place he came down and took my two boys and gave them thair supper and got some of the men to go and sleep in a empty hut as he said it was not fit for me and i cold have. the [dormitory] as the night was likley to be stormey and so it was stormey thunder and lithning and heavey rain   Mrs cuningham wold not come in [from] the dray at first so she stopt out till the rain drove her in and then she wold have my dry bed but i wold not allow it   she scolded very hard about it but i was firm as she cold have come in at first but she wold not

the next night we reached thair station   my brother in law was waiting for us with a two hors cart   i felt glad to be away from that coupple   when she saw my brother waiting for us she turned and said she was sorry to part with me   o deaciet!   when we got to thair station on the Billebong our brother in Law was waiting for us as i said before so the next morning we started for the Ovens and got thaire in three days   i was very tired with the rough traviling and hoped to [be] happy among friends tho i had left my husband behind and my daughter i expected they wold soon be up with us

i had not been more [than] 3 weeks before i found i [was] in the wrong

On their farm at Porepunkah, near where the Buckland River falls into the Ovens, this mother and daughter pose in the midst of the family's achievements – a well-ordered farm with a healthy bullock team, a horse and plow, and plenty of properly stacked hay. Date unknown.

place and i [sent] a letter to my husband not to come as I wold returne to him as soon as i cold   i was near my confinement but he never got the letter as the Pos office was kept at [our relatives'] house   i expected a letter in return but none came

in about six weeks i was confined of a Daughter but about 2 days befor my confinement my husband came up to us but he left our daughter   i was sorley grieved at this but as his sister was goin down to Yas to get thair licence renewed she wold bring her up with her as she was taken a shay cart   i tryed to mak myself as content as possiabl   i was confined while she was away as she started the day my husband came to us

it was very wet in the beginning of May and was weat till August   i was very uneasey in account of the roads so maney creekes to cross and maney a prayer i put up for the safe return of my sister in law and my chilld   in about a month she did return but without my chilld   i was stund with surprise   i was sick at hart   i asked the reason   i got no proper answer but was told it was my own fault   i asked my husband what [the] reason [was]

he had been told [he] shold not like the [place]   so he told Mr & Mrs [_____] not to lett his sister [bring] her up without his written authority as they told him his sister was fond of drink for they knew her well   he thought he wold come and see us   if he found it so he wold work till he had paid them [the] outlay and then [return]   had he got my letter [he would] not have come but [would have] sent the money [for us]   boots and shoos was [the] artical [we needed] on the Ovens at that tim and as thair was a sale in Yas my husband laid all the money out in boost and shoes thinkin it wold Pay for what we had   he brought me a pair of boots but i never got them as he laid them in the store   they sold them for a pound   [what] they cold take from us [they] did   i had a preasant [sent] me of a robe for [the] new born babe and a dress Peice for my self   i did see them but did not even know they was sent for me till 2 years affter as i never got them   the doner asked me had i received them   i said no they was sold   i never knew [they was] for me   she said [she gave] them to my sister in law for me and i believe she did

when we had been about six months we begun to be very bare of cloes and both me and my husband worked as hard as we could   we did our duty   he put all the windows and doors and mad the house look tiddy in his [spare time]   he began to whant som things for him self but they told us we was in thair det still   i told them to make out thair bill as my husband had sent them a set of drawers and a pembroik tabl on pillar and

claw both worth about £12 and the boots sold for £12 at lest   our six months
labour for them [was worth something] and it was labour some times throu
drink day and night to watch the Mrs to keepe her from insult and from
being insultd and then caled fools because we wold not take advantage of
the drunkard and take all they offered when they did not know what they
was doing   we neither of us cold do it   i was disgusted with that way
of geting rich   the sister wold say 'you must throw a sprat to catch a
mackerel'   i did not understand that   [she] wold boast of her riches [and]
her cleaverness and tell i was no good and how well [we] might do if wee
wold do [as] she told us   she made me speak out to her one day for she
had told her husbands Mother had come out and brought a few hundred
Pounds and it helped them as the old woman but lived a few weeks   i told
her it mad a diffrence bein hellped   her father had been laid up for nearley
4 years and i had worked hard to mak him comfortable   it had cost us a
few hundreds that we might have laid by but that was nothing but it
lowered her dignity and i believe she hated me for telling her of it but it
was truth   i wished my self away from that place
    when they came to see us in sydney they called at a place on the road a
farm house old friends of thairs and asked to see the Master   the Mrs
made them wellcome but Master was not at home but some things transpired   the husband had been murdred about this time by his wife and
her paramer as it came out affter
    sister had to go to Berima nearley 300 three hundred miles as she had to
go throu Yas she wold bring our daughter   i did not wish her to do so as i
was determind not to stop the summer over on the Ovens   this was the
later end of July   i had never been well from my confinement but worked
as hard as i cold but i did not complain   i had got a sever cold in my left
brest   i fainted with the pain of it some times   she said it was because i
wanted brandy a thing i did not like but when she came bak from her
journey with out my daughter she did storm both at me and her brother
    it was saturday when she got bak   i spoke kindley to her   she stormed
and moked me   her husband hellped her   i thought this cannot last
long   on the sunday morning it was wors   thair was a publick house [on]
the other side of the river and the owners Mother had attended me in my
confinement [we] had great respect for her   news soon whent acros the
rivier that it was worse than it realey was and it was bad enough   we had
no money   i had a pound as i had [been] given at diffrent times but they
had borrowed it for change as they said but i had kept account as i saw

thair wold be a parting before long   wat thair motive was for treating us so badley i cannot tell to this day   we was with them six months

i began to be bad   i had a larg abses in my left brest   i was bad with it about 4 months but it was very bad a long time but i began that i could do my houswork and a little sewing   i could not do hard work such as washing or scrubbing

thair was but one publick house in Aulbury at this time and the mail was kept thair   it was kept by a Robert Brown   they was quit diffrent to our relations to us for if they was goin on a visit for a few days i must stop in the house and they paid me well and wished us to stop and i believe they gave my husband all the work [he could do] and got him work at other stations to do but he wold not turn his hand to rough carpentering els he migh have done beeter   joynering or cabinet work was all he wold do   at last he put up a bark hut for us to live in   i kept toiling on in hope of sumthing beeter   we had offers to go on stations but my husband wold not eacept them for thair was bad tales told of the settlers Licentiousness and we had sen a bit of that at our relations   i wished to either go back to Yas or go to melbourne

i was very much tryed for the first year that we was in Aulbury by men that wold pretend to want to befriend us under a disguise   they wold offer to mak me preasants but i had learnt what these was for i wold have non of them tho low in curcumstances   i had a honest hart and i looked to God for guidance and none never looked to him in vain   he sustained me

blessed his name for ever   if anney was sic i wold help them and read to them and make them as comfortable as i could but i could not join in thair drinkin bouts   they caled me proud   i was too proud to do wrong or encourage it   they was nearley all old convicts or convicts chilldren that lived in Aulbury at that time   i saw colonial life as the phrase is   you may be sure what a life it was   sunday was very little thought on but i could not forget it   they said if they had forgot what day it was they wold come to Davenports hut   we was put poor but we was respected

affter we had been thare some time my husband trusted a man with some money to bring our eldest daughter up six pounds much against my will for i had a bad opinion of the man tho i wanted my child bad enough

he was as i thought him   he did not sen her up and we neither saw him nor the money since   well my husband got an order for some furniture to be made of cedar   he entrusted his money again with a man to bring it up on his dray as he was goin down   we never saw him anny more neither money nor cedar

well our chimbley wanted reparing   we got some stones to mend it and we kept good fiers   the stones was full of mica   it looked much like goold   we washed some   having seen some goold dust in Liverpool we put some in a paper and it turned it red as gold leaf dose   well we thought we had made a grand discovey   we tryed it again   it was still the same but how to test it we did not know   we knew no one in mellbourne that we cold send it too and we did not wish anney one to laugh at us and we had been ronged by trusting money in what we thought [honest] carriers hands

this was in 1845   we had not yet got our oldest daughter with us yeat so my husband concluded to go to sydney and have it tryed and bring our daughter up with him   so it was setled   at that he took all the money we had and went on the mail   his fare was i believe about seven pounds   he took what he thought wold bring him bak and our daughter   i was quite pleased to think i shold see my child soon as he promised to be back in a month at the latest

he started at the begning of september   i shall never forget with wat anxityetie i counted the days and nights as i used to close the door of our bark hut and put the chilldren to bed   then i wold sit and sew for hours wondring if all was well with my absent ones and Praying for God to Protect them

he had been gon about 20 days   it had been raining a little but nothing to make me uneasey as the river had not rissen much   i put the fire togather and put a good back log on as i shold [want] a fire in the morning   when i awoke at day break i lifted my head to see how the fire was   i saw no fire   i wondred what was rong   i got out of bed to asertain   our bedstead was a bush beadstead rather high about 2 feet from the ground

i was 18 inches deep in water and the water rushing past the house a little distance   what a fright for the moment   a sheet of water all round me and the river about one hundred yards off   what was i to do   i must get out as quick as i cold   the nearest place was about 50 acres from me   i put a few close on and i tied my infant on my sholders and my two boys i tyed one on each side   if one was lost we shold all be lost for no one was stiring and i knew the water was rising   i thought it was the river but it was a creek that was over flowing its banks   however i led my chilldren across the water in safety i caled the firs neigbour up that i came [to] his name was hopgood   he was as suprised as i was and i think more frightned   he was   some time before he cold do annything and then he got his horse and dray to fetch some of our things   i caled annother man to help him and i made a fier to keep them warm till i cold geet them some dry cloas   the yongest was dry so i put her in bed   they brought our beds and bed cloaes and a box   the water rose and remaind for some weaks   the neigbours put me up a bark gunia and a bush temporary bedstead, that is tent fashion, instead of canvas it was bark, as none had a roome to spare and i perfered it   the river was bank high on the side we was on   it was the higher side   on the other side was two miles all covered with water

all trafik was stopped for about seven weeks   i got no work and wat i had done i cold not get paid for   our Provisions was done   thair was no weat on the township   we had a little rice and i got some milk from a neighbour but the chilldren was not satisfied   they wanted bread   i had no money and them that wold have given it to me i could not geet near them for the water   i began to be uneasey for it had got November and no word from my husband

a man came one day and asked me to give him a breakefast   i told him i had nothing to give him as all my provisions was done and the tears came in my eyes   he said 'i thought so   you gave it me when i was hear before and i whanted it then   your chilldren tooke a peice of bread from charley the punt man that he gave them so i thought i wold come and see'   he went but soon returned with some beef and a bag of vegatables tea and suggar but he cold not buy weat for money

the grog was all out at the publick house so thair was no drunkeness this was in November 1845   at last the river began to go down very slow

a dray started to go to Mr Dights station   as he had kindley promised to send me two bushells [of wheat] i was very thankfull   his wifes Mother was to have sent me six that was paid for but the flood coming prevented it for we had to grind our own weat for bread by hand as thair was no flower mils near at that time   the dray that started to go for the weat was seven days   it was seven miles to Mr Dights   the roads was so bad and [the wheat so heavy that they only made] two miles a day

thair was some cheuring when he came back with the weat and then the mill was bunged

thair had been no mail for some time as they was nothing to cross the river   the water was so high on the lower side for two miles   thair was a punt but it was oneley to cross the river   however a man whent a cross with a bark conow   he took the mail and brought the mellbourne mail he crossed 5 times in one day   as they was some drays had been waiting a long time to cross but culd not for the flood so he brought some suplyes and some grog   all seemed to be geeting over the tryals of the flood but i had no letter from the absent ones still   i was earning enough for my familey   we was not in want of provisions but we had lost all our boots and shose   thare was none to be had till they ware made

it was reported that my husband was drowned in the murimbege river but i did not hear of it till his return as they that brought the news was told to keep quiet and it must be told to me in a few week if he did not return   it was very kind of them   a settler came one day and asked me if i wold like to go on his station as my two boys was geeting big enough to mind a flock of sheep and we shold be on the home station   i looked at him in supprise and said i cold not go away till my husband came home

he said no more but it was soon known that he had made the offer for one or two asked about it and said it was a good offer as he was a man that bare a fair reputation   i said i tooke it very kindley but i shold not move till my husband came   [in] a few days he did come but with out our daughter as he had been robbed on his journy and he had been deturred by the floods

i felt sorry she had not come and glad he was returned safe

it was then that i was told why Mr Brown had made the proposal that i should go to his station   as soon as [my husband] had recovered from the fatigue of his journey he went to work for Mr Dight about 7 miles from where we lived

my husband had done some work for a settler but not got paid seven pounds   [the settler] had been away for months   he was at a publick house and a woman was scolding him for money   he was angry at her asking for it so i believe it was to vex her he said he wold pay me what he owed my husband if i wold sign my name for it   i wold willingly do that

a friend of ours the mail contractor was going to sydney and coming bak i asked him to bring our daughter up   i gave him also a written order for my daughter   in about fourteen days i had my long lost daughter restored to us   she was like a stranger for some time but we was all together once more

we now decided to go to mellbourne as soon as we could get a little money to pay expenses for we saw no way of bettering our conditions in the bush and we wanted schooling for our chilldren   i had taught them to read and spell but i could get neither slates nor copy books   i had sent several times by parties goin to mellbourne but he forgot to bring them we worked hard when we got anny thing to do and were very careful with wat we did get in August 1846 we started in a bullock dray for mellbourne we were sixteen days on the journey to mellbourne we took a small cottage we put our boys to school we soon got plenty of work i got washing and soon got things a little comfortable about us but where my husband worked they did not pay him his wages regularly he worked for five shillings per day sometimes he got ten shillings and sometimes he got nothing at all and this is at one of the head shops he worked about four months in that shop that was thwaites when he left they owed him twelve pounds he would not work for them anny more till they paid him then he went to work for a Mr Moody who asked him why he left thwaites he told him that he did not get paid his wages when he worked for them and that he would not work for anny man that wold not pay him

this shop was in Bourke St west he did piece work there and earned about two pounds five shillings a week he got his wages regularly

in March 1847 i had another little son my husband worked at the place for about fourteen months we got things pretty snug he made me a mangle i made fair money with it then he was taken with a sever illness in his head we had a little money in the bank it all went except five pounds for doctors and medical bills just as he was recovering and able to do a little work Mr Moody gave his cabinet shop for a publick house in Elizabeth st

[here a section of the diary is missing]

our money was nearley all gon but this time both of our sones was to go [to the goldfields with their father], one 15 and the other 13 they whent by the steamer to Geelong and walked from thare to Balarat carrying a tent that i had made of some bedticking and pick and spade and blankets billes and food so they was well loaded and so yong but they ware willing they got thair safe and got diggin for goold and got a very little as my husband had never been used to rough work his hands blistred and he began to swell very puffey he was

a man that i had been a friend to named tom had a spring cart he had been to Balarrat came down to take some pepol up he wanted a few more to make a load but i was not aware of this and thought he wold not come with a falshod to me he came and said if i wished to see my husband alive i must go at wonst it was sunday i did not know what to do for a little time he wanted three pounds to take me up i had not ten shillings i whent to a neighbour and asked her to lend me three pound she said if i wold wait till tuesday she might   now i had lent her more than that a few times   i knew she had it by her as she had drawn 30 pounds on the saturday   i said that wold not do for me as i shold go by the steamer to geelong and take the coach as thair was non i could get in mellbourne   all was bespoke   about half an hour affter she came to my house and brought annother woman with her and some half and half in a large jug and a bottle of brandy for me to take with me and the half and half was to drink in my house   i said 'i did not ask you for that, tak it away   when you asked me to lend you [some money] i did not insult but lent it to you   go' i said 'and learn beeter   you shall not come in my house with that stuff'   so i sent them away

we got our tea and my eldest daughter and Mary and Wille our two yongest   my eldest said 'mother how happy you look as happy as if you had the money in your poket to go to father'   i said 'some one will bring it me wat i want'   i did feel as calm and assured that som one wold bring me something   we read and sang some of the Psalms when a nock came to the dore and two weomun came in   the repport of my housband had reached them   they came and said one 'i know you cannot have much money   you have been kind to us and if 3 three pounds will do you anny good you are wellcome to it'   i said 'that was the sum i tryed to borrow of Mrs Leay' and i thanked them and i said i wold send it down as soon as i cold and i thank God for his goodness

well on the monday morning i whent on the steamer [to Geelong] at 6 o clock thinking i shold be in time to take the coach at half past twelve

the wind was against us   it was half past one wen we got in   i was too late for that day but i got booked for the next coach that started, paid my fare   i had about four shillings left

i did not know what to do   i whent to the hotel nearest to the coach office   i asked the lady of the house wat she wold charge me for a bed as i had not much money   i thought i wold pay for that   she looked at me and then went with me up stairs and shewed me a snugg bedroom   she said 'put your things in hear they will be safe and come down and get some dinner'   'i told you i have not much money   i must know what i have to pay' 'nothing wile you are hear so com, my husband whants to see you and have his dinner'   this was one that we had befriended and well they treated me as they had heard of our misfourtains by the fire

[the next 4-page section of the dairy describing her coach trip is missing]
we got to Balarrat by dinner time just as the digers was goin to thair

dinners   i soon found my husband and sons   they was pleased to see me
and yeat surprised till i told them wat tom had said   it was then it came
out he whanted to make sure of me for a passinger   affter our kindness
when he was in distress   i had but been a few days with them when my
husband seemed all right as i made things as comfortable as i could   thair
was a great deal of ruffans thair and they seemed to be the luckes but they
drank and fought each other   we ware not molested tho suronded by them

we was making about one ounce per day   before i went they was making about 2 ounces per week

word came one day that mount Alexander was the place   such a rush
tooke place   many a time in my quitate momeyts i think of that day when
the word cam   such paking up   all was bussel   a party that was camped
near us had cleared thair claim   thair [was] 5 of them   2 was rowdays 3
was what we may say stead men so they devided   the 2 went away and 3
stoped and was a party and very good neighbours   2 of the three whent to
looke for another clame   one stoped at the tent   a man that had done
well and wanted a spree came and offered his horse and cart for sail as he
was afraid it wold be taken if he got too drunk   he whanted sixty pounds
for it   the man that was left in the tent came and asked me if i could lend
him a few pounds to secure it and he wold take our things if we wanted to
go on the cart   on that understanding i lent him a few pounds and i looked
affter the hors myself for 3 days for my husband wanted to go [to Mount
Alexander] but he did not know how to get thair   such tales was told of
goold being got by the hundred weight and tru it was in some instances

he was quite pleased when i told him what i had done and baegan to
make preparations for the journey

these 3 men was what [was] caled 'vandamoinans'   som of thair old
aquaintances came and wished them to take thair things so one told my
husband he must get someone els to take us   it allmost made him mad   i
said   'make your self content if that hors and cart gose it must take our
things'   2 of the men began to bluster and wanted to frighten us   i said 'i
paid the money for that what is paid and our things must go if it gose'   the
party that wanted to go in our place was strong men   my husband was
quite nervous   they saw it and took advantage of it but when they was
loading i put some of our things [on] and they put them off   i looked at
them   'now' i said 'i bought the hors and if you do not tak my things i
will just brake one of his legs   i am a woman of my word   you cannot
hurt me   i bought it'   they looked at the receipet and found as i said so

 Above: this woman, with a veil on her hat to protect her from the insects, but no concessions to the obvious heat, is about to begin crossing the parched Nullabor Plain. Date unknown.
Below: women on a Western Australian goldfield, date unknown.

they put our things on   i should not have been so perseveary but my husband seemed so exiteted and i did not wish him to be disapointid

we had not travaled maney miles before one of the 3 men said he thanked
me for he did not want the other partys with them but he could not refuse
but throu wat i had done thair could be no ill will   they was old friends
and they [would] meet again but they was too fond of thair drink

we was four days traviling to Mount alaxander   at nights when we
camped one of us had to watch the horse all night for thair was plenty of
hors stealing as some of the partis that got drunk and neglected to take
that precaution found to thair los   we arived safe on November 5   we
looked for a quiet place to camp and put up our tents and got ready to dig
for goold   the next day they all soon began to get goold for it was plentiful   my husband and sons got a pach and was making about one ounce
a day   the 3 men was making two

we had not been thair maney days when me and another wife whent a
looking round the hills   we had each a knife and a tin plate to get goold in
if we shold find anny   i picked up a bit and shewed it to her   she [took it]
out of my hand [and dropped it]   i was not [able to find it] for the grass
was both thick and high but i soon picked up a peice about a quarter of an
ounce   my yongest son came for the dinner and said they wold make two
ounces or more 'tell father i will make three' for we had found a patch of
surface   we got a tub and pick and spade and washed one tub full   we
caried down to the creek to wash in a buket and washed it and finished in
a tin dish   [the] first tubful yealded about 3 ounces the next 4   we was in
high glee when both her husbands party and my husband and sons came
and to work they went and so we had to give in but we had made 7
ounces   it was fryday

on the sunday it was very wet raining heavy but some neither minded
the day nor the rain for goold was on the surface and it was very temting

we [stayed] insed our tent dores watching them   they laboured as if for
very life and death and i believed some got coulds that they never got over
but died throu that day for it had been very hot weather and it was very
cold after the rain   we started again on monday morning   i say 'we' for i
had to help   my sons was yong and my husbandwasbutweaksoto encourage
them i helped to wash the stuff for the goold

the troopers came one day and asked me to shew my licence   i looked
up at them for i was in the creek and they was on the bank of the creek
'have you got your licence?' i said 'my husband has got a licence and the

Parson made us one   he will be hear soon'   'you must have one'   i said
'the Parson made us one are you goin to devid us?' Mr Street was one of
them   he rode off lauging and the troopers folled him

we was making about 8 ounces per day   when we had got about seventy
70 ounces nothing wold do for my husband but he wold com down and
down he did come   i felt quite disapointed but was forced to comply   we
came down to mellbourne at the latter end of november   we sold our
goold for i belive two pounds sixteen shillings per ounce   we paid all dets
and bought a few things to make us comfortable wonce more and get reddy
to go up again affter christmas

we had some money to put buy besides our out fit to go again

one of our neighbours bought a house and about a quarter of an acre of
ground on collingwood flat   he had got some what near the same quanitys
of goold as we had but they must have finerey   when he wanted to go up
again he had no money so he tryed to sell his house again   now he had
suffered from poverty but when he got so much money they thought it wold
never be done till it was done   my husband offered him ten pounds more
for his house and ground than he had given for it   he sold it to my husband but as we was all goin up to the diggins in company he wold sign the
deeds when we came back   i objected to this but it was no use

the party he belonged and my husband had joined to buy a horse and
cart   i was grieved for i knew they was all too found of drink   we took
plenty of drink up with us as i thought to last for three months in a proper
use of it but alas it oneley lasted three weeks   no diggin in earnest whilst
the grog lasted   our party consisted of my husband and two sons and my
self   they was three strong men   they was to have the cart and horse one
part of the day and we the other part of the day but we was but a weak
party and surface suited us the best but whare we could do annything they
wold not stop ramble hear and thare   i began to grow weary but i went
and washed tailings whare thair was anney for i cold plainley see it wold
come to a rupture very soon   we had been 3 weeks   the grog was done
and i didnt think all the three men had five pounds among them   what we
had was what me and my sons had got   it was about 12 ounces and we
had sold 7 ounces   my husband was tired and saw his error in not having
had the deeds signed for the mans name was Walker   he boasted he
wold never sign them

my sons and husband whent to bendigo a prospecting and left me at
castlemain in the tent near these three men   they was away about 5

days   while they was away a man came up from mellbourne and brought
2 or three 15 gallon caskes of grog up to open a shanty   Walker was
aquainted with him   he came to me and asked me to lett the man put
them in our tent and represented what lots of money we shold make   we
must keep it in our tent and they wold retail it in their tent   i said no
firmley but quiteley   they bosted what injury they wold do if i wold not

i wold not nor i did not and then they asked me to lend them 5 pounds i
said i wold lend no money for grog   they thought i had non

as soon as my husband and sons returned and told them the news they
proposed to part company from us and we must either buy the cart and
horse   they made the proposal   'agreed' said my husband   'i will pay
you off'   they was surprised

Here in mid-adventure, the diary comes to a halt, its later pages lost.
Sarah Davenport is left on the goldfields battling her way towards the better
life promised by Australia but as yet unrealized. Not that she ever
expected as much as Penelope Selby, who dreamed of better times when
the work would not be as hard. Mrs Davenport assumed that life meant
hard work, and it certainly did with five children and a husband who was
inept, if not downright foolish. Sarah Davenport was concentrating on
survival.

And she did survive. She lived to be eighty-seven years old, and when
she died at Yarroweyah in 1896, the primitive 'bush' to which she had
come fifty years earlier, had been tamed into the more gentle and sedate
'country' where her children lived on farms. Sarah Davenport had not
similarly softened, however, this tough woman with the determined will.
Among her descendents there is a story of an old lady seated by the fire
smoking her clay-pipe. A squabble among her sons over the inheritance of
property belonging to their father's family in England enrages her. Instead
of dividing up the contested property, Sarah Davenport hurls the deeds
into the fire, saying that as she had worked hard all her life, her children
too could work for what they got.

Mrs Davenport did not expect life to shower gifts upon her. Neither did
Mary Jane MacGregor, although she was more fortunate in her choice of
spouse – and, indeed more fortunate all around. 'Little Janie,' as she was

called because of her size, had showed her spirited nature early on when at the age of seventeen she defied her father's ban, secretly married William MacGregor, and immediately left Ireland for Australia. Physically she might be tiny, but she was not to be intimidated. Her reminiscences, like Mrs Davenport's, are a celebration of her strength.

They are not *her* celebration, however; she never wrote them down. These reminiscences lived on as part of an oral tradition passed to her daughter who remembered them in such detail that she in turn could tell the story to her daughter and 'Little Janie' MacGregor's granddaughter could then write them down so precisely that she could convincingly adopt her grandmother's voice for the telling. This account is thus one step further removed from the events than memoirs usually are, and as such it testifies to the strength of memory and imaginative understanding which kept the bush experience alive through three generations of women in one family. With the words on paper at last, the experience opens up to anyone who will read, to anyone ready to think back into the period of initiation when the MacGregors, like the Davenports, felt strongly the sensation of being 'strangers in a strange land'.

Between forty and fifty years ago, I married and took a long wedding tour which lasted over four months. Finally my young husband and I landed in Port Phillip Harbour, being stuck inside the Heads on a sandbank for a long time and losing an anchor through the cable breaking. We at length got into Williamstown. After a few days, my husband went ashore and delivered his letters of introduction to the Reverend Mr Forbes and he at once obtained a situation as overseer on a sheep and cattle station then far up in the bush, (not 'up the country' as is said now but up 'the bush').

The day for starting for the bush arrived and my husband took a very hasty and slight breakfast – I may add an early one too – and started with the men and a mob of cattle that had been kept about the town for a time with little food and less water. I was to start immediately after. I went to where I was to start from. I found it with great trouble and a long, long walk. Having warm boots, warm clothes and the heat of the sun in the hot, dusty streets, I was in very low spirits when I arrived at the carriage and six that was to carry me and my belongings up the bush. Our young master was there helping to get all things ready to start. He showed me a shady tree to sit under for a rest. I sat down and had a weep.

When I heard the coach starting, oh, how the driver swore. I would not get on the coach, for with the swearing and such a long whip and the cracking I would not go near and kept as far off as possible. There were two men and the master. He stayed with me and led his horse and advised me not to be afraid, but to get up on the load for I would be so tired. (Indeed I was both sad and tired). I amused the master very much by asking him Would that man talk like that to the cattle all the way up the bush?

Night was coming on and no signs of my dear one. Whatever would I do? The master said, 'They will soon be here, but we cannot see them for the trees.' We stopped for the night and our master put a great piece of canvas over a large limb of a tree and a mattress under it and begged me to lie down and rest till my husband came up. I thought it very kind of him. And I did so. I heard one of the men (who had gone on ahead on his horse) say, 'They are lost', and I ran to the master and said, 'Oh, who is lost?' He told me it was something they had to light a fire with – tinder. I saw by his manner that it was something else, but he made a large fire and showed the man where everything was and brought me a pannikin of tea – no milk.

I drank it and was refreshed, but where, oh where was my husband? The man had gone away again and as it turned out, my husband, men and cattle were still at the Salt Water River. Some cattle on one side and some on the other, nothing to eat or drink but salt water, and they did drink it. It was the next morning when the men went with tea and food to them, but it was three days before I saw my husband and oh, how changed! His hat was lost, he had drunk the salt water, his eyes were bloodshot, his lips swollen and his face sunburnt, but he was well. I remarked that he was a-breaking in.

By midnight, a cooee was heard and a man answered and stirred the fire up. In a short time a gentleman with a lady on his arm came up to the fire. I was sitting watching out of my canvas house. They turned out to be Mr and Mrs L., who was a partner of our master. He at once asked for me and brought his wife to me. I was so very much pleased that she was to travel up the bush with me.

The next start, the day was far advanced and hot. Heat was no name for it, it was scorching. There was nothing for me then but to get up on the dray, for walk I could not – it was so hot and there was no bush, all plains. The driver knew I was frightened and he cracked the whip far more than was needed. He would bring it as near my head as he could without hitting me and crack it just like a pistol in my ear. About the middle of the afternoon, the driver called out to me, 'Look out "little 'un"', I am going to break the dray here and your neck!' I was sitting with my back to him. I looked round and there was an awfully deep gully and such a steep bank down to it. He drove on. I crawled to the back of the dray and leaped down – such a height! I could not get up for a moment or two.

Mr and Mrs L. were just a little way behind and came on quick. They generally kept pretty near all the time. When I told him why I had leapt down, he put me in the buggy with Mrs L. and warned us to stop there quietly. He ran down to see what had become of the dray and just as [the driver had] said, there was the dray on one side, broken. Everything was in the creek. Fortunately it was nearly dry, just a little water and great stones. There was nothing wet. Mr L. came up to us again and asked me, 'What did that fellow say to you?' I told him again. He said, 'You have saved your neck, but he has broken the dray.'

It was a sight to me when I saw the first damper made. A large fire was made and while it was burning down, a large tin dish full of flour, a handful of salt, a bucket of lukewarm water and then a hole made in the middle of the flour. The dish on the ground, the man on his knees on the ground also. Then he worked it all up into dough and kneaded it thoroughly. Then he spread it out and it resembled the small wheel of a buggy. Taking a long shovel, he opened out the fire, and made the bottom of the fire smooth with the back of the shovel. The damper was laid therein as if to be cremated. Rather cool ashes were laid on top first then the hot ashes over those and then left to bake. I watched it, and by and by the ashes rose up so high that I saw the edge of the damper. In about an hour, the ashes were swept off with the bough of a tree and then the bread was lifted up and beaten with the bag it was spread on. It really looked nice and had a nice crust on. No one would think it had been in the ashes. It was really good bread, but it took a great deal of kneading or it would be very heavy.

The next start we got to the Little River. All went smoothly but I had hurt my head and back, when I leapt off the dray, and the heat of the sun and cracking of that whip made me suffer very much, but I told no one. My husband was kept very busy with his charge. I had only to sit quietly.

The next camp was at Bate's Ford. There man and beast had a rest. As the [next] day advanced, my husband went to make things secure for the night by cutting some limbs off trees in a certain part of the camp. He took an axe and went up the glen a little way. I was sitting, watching him. I saw him standing at a tree for a long time. I went to him and found him in great distress. He had just found out that it was the sabbath day. I ran back to the camp and asked if it was so. They did not know. The cook laughed at me for crying and said there was no Sunday after we crossed the line. I went back to him, took the axe and put it away. We sat down under a tree. My husband was in great trouble. He said, 'After coming so many thousand miles, to work on the Lord's day.'

We knelt down and prayed to God to forgive us and to help us to do our duty as it was our first servitude and it seemed very hard to us both. It was only then I had courage to tell him that I had hurt myself by leaping off the dray, for I was told not to tell him for he would be very angry with me for doing such a mad thing. I at once felt sorry that I had told him, he was so distressed, but after that Mr and Mrs L. were always near and if there were steep places, I was helped down. I cannot remember how we got down the Clyde Hill but finally within seven weeks from leaving Melbourne we arrived at our destination, amongst the rough, rocky knolls.

Almost under one was the hut or house allotted to me. There was a hole in the wall with a wooden shutter on it, but a far bigger one in the chimney, for I could stand at the fire and look out on a nice green hill and when the wind blew, clouds of dirt would come down the chimney. After a time the cook left and there was no cook. I was asked if I would cook for all hands for a few weeks. I was better then and had had a good rest. I was quite willing, if they left me wood and water, for these articles had to be carried a long way. That was done for a short time. Then they gave me a nice big black boy to help.

I had to make a damper and I think it was the best I ever made for I paid great attention to the man on the journey up, but I found the table quite too high. I rolled a big log of wood inside and stood on it. There was not a creature about. After a little, the door darkened and such a yell of astonishment burst from about five or six black men, just as many as could get a peep in at me. Perched on my log – temporary platform – I could not move or speak for an instant. I had been told not to be afraid of them if they came about and not to let them see or think I was afraid. I just looked at them and went on making my damper and the black men did laugh and called out to others to come and see me.

More came. I saw they were women and children. The men moved inside to let them see me. I [went] to the fire and looked at them – they were still coming nearer. I took up a fire stick and said at the top of my voice, 'Be off!' and saw they were frightened, for the ones inside could not get out quick enough, but I threw the fire stick after them, knowing very well it would not hurt them, but I could hardly get my damper in the fire, I trembled so. Just when I had laid it in the ashes, one of the men sneaked back and said, 'You too much piccaninny Lubra' (too small a woman) 'you got a coolie?' (husband). Then more came and asked me the same questions and laughed and kept saying, 'You too much piccaninny lubra.' I found out after that they thought me quite too little a woman and they wanted to know if I had a husband.

There was a paddock of wheat and it was getting very ripe. On a Saturday night Mr L., the master, came and told my husband he must put the men on tomorrow (Sunday) and get it cut down. This was a trial to him to disobey, but he did. He would not go nor put the men on either. The master insisted, but no, and he used very bad language and left him, but in the night it came on such heavy rain and it rained all day on the sabbath. On Monday morning, master and my husband met. My husband said, 'Well sir, man proposes, but God disposes.'

When the wheat was reaped and cleaned, the men used to grind the flour at night for the damper tomorrow. I put a large white cloth on the table, put two long sticks along it and then a sieve, and sifted flour for my damper. It was hard work [with] the small room, the large fire and the heat of the sun, and added to that the bush fires which happened quite too often. Day after day passed in much the same way, only as time went on, work increased. The best of all was there was no time to be tired.

When the nice cool nights came, we were very thankful to lie down and rest, but I am sorry to say not to sleep sometimes, for we could hear the men playing cards in their room up to – I must not say a 'late' hour – but rather an 'early' hour. We were both tired and angry at this work and I was determined to try and find the cards.

Months passed; the coach driver and his team were sent to Corio and that day the station was quite clear of the men. I had not had a real sound sleep for many a night, but my husband had got the 'card players' to be quieter and it turned out they had been playing on an opossum rug, which drowned the noise. However, I started to try and find my enemies 'the cards' and I did so, in a black's 'beenack' (basket made of grass), but I was nearly caught for our young master came sauntering along [toward] my hut. I had a good fire. I ran in, took my fire shovel, opened up the fire and threw in the cards. I covered them up like a damper. He was at the door. He came in, walked up to the fireplace, turned his back to it and was chatting away to me, but in a very short time, 'pop' went one card right up the chimney. No notice was taken, but I was wishing him away, but in a second, another popped out. He started, but took no particular notice. I saw it just lying on the ashes, not burnt a bit. I was trying to get round to lift it when 'pop-pop-pop' went the whole lot and in an instant every card was out of the fire and just like a flock of birds through the room – dust and ashes. The master ran with such a swear, 'What is it? What the d – is it?' One hit him, he said, on the back of the head. He looked back (I was sorry to see) but when he saw the cards all lying about and very little the worse for their hot bed, he just screamed out laughing at me, for I was sorely bewildered. He put his head in at the door and said, 'Don't be afraid, I won't tell a word of it. I declare to my — I won't!' and he ran away yelling with laughter. Many a hearty laugh has he had since at me for it. He declared he thought he and the hut were blown up.

I gathered them up and made up the fire and burned them one by one. They soon burned, they were so dirty and greasy, but I waited and saw them all burned, and at night, the poor man that was away from them during the day was blamed for taking the cards. The master never told. He heard the poor driver getting blamed, but he kept quiet. There was peace for a long time after.

In the meantime, an old cook came. I often thought they did not want to get one. I thought aloud sometimes, about the matter and then they gave me another black boy to help. I sent him to bring in the milch cows one morning. There had come some of his family the evening before and they were camped near a large water hole in sight of our hut. Tommy did not come with the cows for hours. He lay down on the sunny side of a tree and just stayed until it pleased him to come. I was in a hurry and wanted to get them milked before breakfast, before the great heat of the day came on. When he did come, I scolded him and told him to be off for I would not have him any longer. He stood outside the yard and received all these orders quietly, but when he got away a little bit, he turned round. I had sat down on a round block to milk and he threw a stone and hit the cow in the bails on the head and made her kick. She broke the leg rope and kicked me back into the yard with the milk pail on the top of me. I lay an instant to get my breath for I was very much hurt, and when I crawled up, the cow was plunging in the bail. I did not know what was the matter. I heard the blow and was knocked over the same instant. I went to her and patted her for she was a quiet creature, and all at once I heard a wild yell and a laugh at the same time. I saw the big stone just at the cow's head and Tom standing grinning at me. I went out through the fence and he did not offer to run from me. I gave him a great slapping and told him to go away. I would not have him, for he was a bad boy.

I felt sick, but I managed to get through my milking. His people were watching all this. My husband and men were a long way off. It was very early in the month of January and the men worked early and late but rested in the middle of the day, but when I returned from the yard, there was Tom sitting with a foot on each hob of the fireplace, on a little block of wood that had been sawn off a middling-thick tree. That was one of our chairs. I did not speak, but just went behind him and caught him up in my arms and put him out of the door. I had just got to the fireplace when he had me in his arms and with my two arms pressed together. I could not move, he had me so tight. Off he went with me to the waterhole. The yells and cries of the blacks and a large dog that was kept chained up! The dog broke loose and when we were about half-way down, leapt on him and knocked us both down and held him by the shoulder. It was a mastiff. He held him down, and I rose and gathered myself together.

The master appeared and he could speak the blacks' language and he did so. Pluto (the dog) held on until the master ran in and brought out a gun and fired it off in the air, and then talked to the blacks. I ran in and was lighting the fire. When I heard the gun, I ran out. I really thought he had shot the boy, but Pluto still had the boy lying quietly and the other blacks were running off as fast as they could. The master had hard work to take the dog off the boy. He had never been off the chain since we arrived. I used to feed him and give him milk. We brought him up the country with us. When the master rescued the boy, he ordered him off, but he would not go and the chain being off the dog, he could hardly be held, nor until the boy saw the men come running would he go. He did run then, for the master told him my husband would shoot him. The men heard the gun and ran home. When they saw the blacks running they were much frightened. I did not know my danger. They told me the boy would have thrown me into the hole. It was a very large one with tall tea tree growing round it and the banks were steep and perpendicular, but they thought he intended his people to rescue me. If I had given the boy a good thrashing with a stick, he would have been subdued, for the blacks are frightened of their skins. That boy never came near again for some years after and I saw his grave, if grave you could call it. It was in the fork of a very large tree. He was sewed in a rug and lifted up there. After he had been in this place certain months they took him down and burned him at the foot of the tree.

Many years passed over and [the blacks] never did anything to bother me. They all liked me very much and would do anything for me they could. I was once alone and a great number came. The men came first, the women after, who always carry fire with them. There was a tree in those days that had a very thick bark and when once it is on fire, it will not die while there is any left. They lit a fire, not far from my hut, and by and by the women with their pack of dogs were crossing a paddock that my 'milk' cows were in and where I had a pet calf. It had rained a great deal for two days. A man with a horse had to go a long way up the river to get the cows home for it was running very high. There was a large tree which had fallen across the river and the blacks very soon came across on it. The wild, hungry dogs ran after the calves and caught my pet calf and had it down. The cries of the calf and the running of the cows was terrible. I ran to the river edge and called to the blacks to call their dogs off, but not one of them would stir or move a limb to get the dogs away. The cows saved it by making a ring round it.

When I saw [the dogs] at it and could not get across to save it, I said I would kill the first of them that came near my hut. The blacks just laughed and said, 'Merry jig (very good), you kill 'em,' and when the dogs tired themselves they ran to the women who had kept back in the bush for fear of the cows, for when cattle smell the blacks, they would run for their lives and they never approach cattle if they can help it. So the dogs went away and the cows went off with the lame calf. Then the women came. I did not see them cross the river, but cross it they did, dogs and all, and there was a great noise too amongst them for a short time.

I heard someone turning a grinding stone and went out to see whom it could be. It was two black men, one turning and the other sharpening his tomahawk. I turned to go in, for they were not doing any harm. Just at my door there was a dog and there was a great long stick a short distance from me. I took it up but let him run away. I threw it after him and in an instant the man that was sharpening his tomahawk came up to me and with his right hand gave me a most dreadful slap on the side of my head,

Standing confidently in the doorway of her pre-fabricated timber house, complete with pre-fabricated iron window frames, Mrs Simpson poses in her hoop skirt for her husband, the town chemist and early photographer of Queenscliff, Victoria. c. 1865.

and knocked me down with such force that I thought my head was split open. His hand was like a piece of wood it was so hard, but I got up as quickly as I could. I looked at him and he at me. He did not speak; I could not. He was the king of the tribe. It turned out it was his dog and he was between me and the door of my hut. I gave one glance round and saw the blacks, men and women standing round, and I saw a large bone. I picked it up and threw it at him, and hit him. He stood staring at me.

I thought – if I thought at all, or took time to think – that I was to be killed then indeed. I gave one terrible scream and called my husband and ran for my life to the crossing of the river where he and the men had crossed that morning. I was so frightened. I never was frightened of them after the first day till then. I was calling my husband as I ran, but he was far from me. I ran up the river to find a place to cross and to my horror an old black man ran between me and the river and caught me up in his arms and just ran back with me to the hut and set me down at the fire, oh, so gently, took a cloth off a peg, warmed it and put it to my face, then spoke not till then and said, 'No good, no good king William, no good your cooly (husband) big one cry you go in river and him kill everybody.' When the cloth was put on my face I knew I was safe, not till then. The cloth was to take away the pain where the king hit me on the head.

There was such a war amongst them outside. Some of the older men, and all the women, were so angry at their king, for they all were frightened of my husband and the young master. The king still stood where I left him. The old man asked me in such a beseeching manner, 'You no go to river any more?' I said, 'No'. He said, 'Merry jig, king kill him dog.' I went to the door and there was the king still standing. He called out something to the old man. It was that he wanted the old man to stay with me for fear I would go to the river again. I told him to tell him 'No, no, I would not,' so then he went to the camp, for they had been fixing their bark mimi or their house for the night. He gave orders to move away far into the bush, the king helping them. The old man sat down a little way from my door and never heeded them even when they were all going nor did he stir till he saw the young master coming across the river with the cows. Then he said, 'Me gego mago' (me go away now), so it turned out that the king told him to stay with me and watch me for fear I would go to the river, until my 'cooly' came in sight, and then to go quickly and indeed he did go quickly, for he heard the whips crack before he saw them. They saw him running and they galloped their horses up to the huts, for they thought there was something wrong when they saw the man running away. They were in a terrible state of mind about it, for the master said [the blacks] would rather anyone would hit themselves than their dogs, and they were so spiteful that there was no knowing what they would do when they would get a chance. My husband said he would go and give them such a talking to for they were always afraid of him, but the master would not let him.

Just as it was getting dark, all the black men came to the huts but no women. The king actually came to our door. I saw him and shut the door. They went to the master's hut and begged him to come and get my husband to beat the king and allgone sulky (all gone anger) but lubra had shut the door and by and by they were afraid my cooly would shoot the king, and he cried like a child. The master came out and talked to them all in their own language and warned them to keep away and they told him how I had hit the king in the head with a big bone, and indeed they showed it to the master and told him 'Missus merry jig for hitting him. Missus would not be angry any more but cooly long time angry.' I was all this time crying and begging my husband not to go out for I thought every minute they would come in and kill him. But no: it was quite the reverse. They told the master that the king was going to stand where I left him until my husband would come and beat him, but when the king saw the old man had caught me and I was safe he then killed the dog that caused all the mischief. They all went away that night quietly, but I could not rest for fear they would come back but the master assured me they would not, but oh, how he did beg me never to touch their dogs again, notwithstanding he was sorry to see the poor calf worried. I never saw king William again but once when passing through the paddock.

Many years after, we lived far in the west where the ground is very hollow and of volcanic formation. When riding along, the ground sounds as though the horses' feet would break through. There are a great many swamps and near one of the swamps there was a very large tree and when there was a bullock killed, the men used to draw it under this tree where there was a large strong limb and a pulley was fixed on it, and when skinned, the bullock was pulled up and left all night and this had often been done. But one afternoon, the men were pulling up a bullock and making just such a noise as the sailors do on board ship, when, all at once, the ground gave way and down went one man – but he held on to the rope and he was helped up. It was just close to a swamp or lagoon. The men stuck long boughs of trees in it, but it was very deep and more earth fell in than the men put in. It was well-marked for fear of horses or anything else getting in.

About a year after, I was left quite alone, with the exception of an old man named Jack who had to cart wood all day to an outstation and then bring a load home at night. His hut was not far from mine. My husband and all the men had gone about 30 miles off to a mustering of cattle and would not be home for days, perhaps a week or more. All the horses were taken except a few, a mare and foal. There was a large manger erected between two trees that sheltered it from the sun, and Jack kept it filled with hay and the horses would come galloping up to get their feed, and as I looked back on those times, how glad I was when I would see these creatures coming up, for I often felt very lonely.

One morning I missed the little foal and started off to look for it. We lived on an island about half a mile wide, surrounded by a lagoon except at one part, which was the only entrance to the island. The edges of it were boggy and I feared very much that the poor foal was stuck in the mud or drowned or that the wild dogs had killed it. I went all round the swamp with a long stick to guard against snakes in the long grass and shrubs, for you would see them wriggling out of your way. When I returned, the horses had gone away and I ran to see if the foal was with them, but no. I returned home again quite sorry, but could not think what had become of the foal, and all at once I remembered seeing a little old horse that had not been up with the rest when I started, standing near the hole where the earth fell in. Indeed I passed near him but was too intent on the one thing to heed him. I started off again just to satisfy myself.

The old horse had gone, the ground was all scratched, and when I went near the hole, I could see hair on the dry sticks that stood up out of the hole. I commenced and dragged them all up, but the boughs and small branches were broken. I had to lie down flat and reach as far down as I could and draw them up, but the dry mould broke away and fell to the bottom. I heard the little animal making a noise and tried hard to clear the hole. I got it cleared and lay down flat again and shaded my eyes, and just as I got my face down the foal neighed, quite loud, and I could see it. There was a tunnel leading out of the hole and all its body was down the tunnel, one foreleg was across the bottom of the hole and its head lying on its leg. I just saw its eye and was in a terrible state of mind as to how I would get it out of its living tomb.

Jack had not gone that morning. To my great joy, he was reaping some ripe oats not very far off. I ran and called him. He came very slowly indeed. I ran to the stockyard and got a rope for him and begged him to go down and tie it on the foal. He said he could not get down, although he could see it. He thought we could go up the tunnel for it was close to the swamp, but we found the water was far up the bank. What to do we did not know for were we to dig we would have smothered it. I could not get Jack to propose anything but he stood and looked at me. What I proposed doing was, namely, to tie Jack's two ankles together, put a noose on the end of the rope and hold the other end: for him then to go down, head foremost and put the noose on the foal's head and leg – I would hold his feet by the rope and pull him up again. Now, as I am writing this I can just imagine how poor Jack looked up at me and actually groaned out at my proposal, 'Oh mistress, I would never come up again.'

Just at this moment, the blacks came up and when I saw them I was very glad. There were a few piccaninnies with them. I took a little boy and told him I would give him something out of the store if he would go down and put the rope on the 'piccaninny yarraman' (the foal). He told his mother who came and looked down the hole, which was ten feet deep. When the young mother saw it, she picked up her little boy, flung him over her shoulder into the big bag that they carry on their backs, for she was afraid that I would persuade her 'cooly' (husband) to put the boy down. I was just distracted then, thinking the foal would have to die there and so many people looking at it. It neighed so pitifully when it saw any of us. I told them I would give them anything out of the store if they would bring it up alive. They held a consultation amongst themselves and told me to 'gego long way' and 'combe' (stand) behind a tree and not look at them and they would bring up the foal.

I went and stood out of their sight – such a long time it seemed to me. In about an hour, I heard such cheering that I thought the foal was up, but it was the man they had pulled up. I went back but in about a minute they set up such a cheering and a little boy ran to meet me saying, 'Missis, merri jig, yarraman up, yarraman up', and it was up, and not a bit the worse except that the hair was a little rubbed off its back through pulling it up out of the tunnel, it was so tightly jambed in. It galloped off with its mother, followed by the other horses and I was pleased indeed and so were the black men. I took them home and fulfilled my promise willingly. I made them a kettle of tea, gave them some bread and meat, but what I considered very thoughtful of them, they helped Jack to fill the hole before they left and they made it very secure.

Now I must try and tell you how they got the rope on the little foal. They cut down a long, straight limb off a tree with lots of branches on it, then chopped all the branches off, just leaving a short bit of each so as to put their foot on. That was their ladder. They stuck the straight end down so as not to touch the foal's head for they were afraid it would move and get out of sight down the tunnel. Then the man that was going down could not manage to get through as he was too big, so they then stripped a young lad, put the noose on his great toe and all the men and Jack held the top of the ladder and he went down, stepping on each little stump, taking the rope on his toe. When he could reach [the foal] with his foot he moved its leg and slipped the noose on leg and neck. Then those at the top pulled as he told them. It was by feeling with his foot he managed it all, for he could not see as he had to stand quite straight. Even then the earth was falling in – they held the rope and then he got up and they pulled it up very quickly. They thought the earth would have fallen in before they would get it up. They were anxious from the moment they saw it first. I certainly would never have got it up alive but for them.

Well, the blacks and I parted very good friends, indeed they always were very kind in their way to me, as they would cut wood and water when they would see me going to do so. I am sorry to add that all these fine strong men, some young, some middle-aged, were so soon cut off the land of the living after the diggings opened through drink, and the last of them I saw about twelve years ago, an old man, quite grey, who came to me in Geelong holding out his hand and saying, 'Oh little missis, how do you do? How is master?' Not 'cooly' now, as of old, but 'master'. I did not know him but he told me where he saw me and master last. Then I knew him. Afterwards his wife came up to us and a number of people were standing looking at the happy pair who had greeted me. He then said, 'Oh, give me sixpence for drop beer.' I said 'No, no, come and I will get you some buns,' and we walked up Moorabool Street to Mr McCallum's and I got them something to eat and we parted there for life. That man is not long dead; I think he died in Geelong.

But I must mention about the poor mother that had run off with her boy for fear I would put him down the hole. When I asked them, sitting and eating on a big log near the huts, where she was, 'Oh,' they said 'her combee along of big one grass, frightened of you missis.' I made them call her. She was lying in long grass having covered herself and boy in long grass so that no one could see them. She came when I told her I was not angry with her, and she said to me, 'When I see big one hole I was frightened you take my boy and he be killed.'

I spent many long hours in the bush when my husband was away after cattle and lost sheep, and drafting sheep that had got mixed, for between the California diggings and Ballarat diggings that opened soon afterwards, the men would not stay on the stations, nor would they be careful as they hoped to be discharged and then to go to the diggings. My plan was: when a message came for my husband from an outstation 'Sheep mixed' or 'Man bolted,' to have something nice and hot for him when he came in, but not tell him until he had something to eat. I was often blamed but I would never mind for he perhaps would be a whole day from early morning and nothing to eat and only a drink of (middling) clean water. I knew pretty well what was before him for another day and he was a very worried man.

Day by day brought its own little events. And I assure you that these first fourteen years of my young married life in this Colony were very happy ones, with no troubles to speak of in comparison with some sad events I have been called upon, in God's good Providence, to pass through since. But I am still spared in the land of the living and can see many changes in many ways. The climate is changed and I am changed. The climate is cooler and I have grown old and look at another generation growing up to take the old folks' places in their own good time and way.

I wish they may all spend their youth just as happily as did little Mistress Janey.

Goodbye.

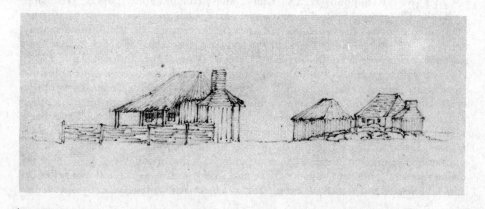

NOTES AND ACKNOWLEDGEMENTS

The Research Grants Committee of the School of Humanities at La Trobe University provided funds without which the research for this book would not have been possible. To the librarians who made available to me their expert knowledge of manuscript collections and who went out of their way to help me – especially to John Thompson and the staff at the National Library of Australia – my thanks are due. I owe a particular debt of gratitude to Mrs Oline Richards, in Western Australia, for her research initiative and perseverance.

Small changes have been made in the manuscripts in order to make them easier to read. I have introduced paragraph divisions, and have altered spelling and punctuation in places where the original meaning of words or the sense of things is obscured. Occasionally I have thought it necessary to add a word or words for the sake of clarity. When I have done this, the additions are indicated in brackets.

Every effort has been made to trace copyright holders but in a few cases this has proved impossible. I would appreciate advice on omissions.

FINDING THE WORDS FOR A BUSH LIFE: INTRODUCTION

Elizabeth Tierney. Diary, 1896–1909. MS 4935, National Library of Australia, Canberra. Bound typed carbon copy.

Agnes (Mrs Richmond) Henty. Diary, 1868. Henty Family papers, box 118/4, La Trobe Collection, State Library of Victoria. Original.

My attention was drawn to these diaries by the immensely useful bibliography which was to a large extent the guidebook for my research: *Women in Australia: an annotated guide to records*, edited by Kay Daniels, Mary Murnane and Anne Picot. This two-volume work, published in 1977 by the Australian Government Publishing Service, originated as a contribution to International Women's Year. It sets out to locate and describe material about women in Australia held by libraries and other institutions, organizations, and individuals. Naturally, some items have been missed, as they are bound to be in a first effort on such an ambitious scale, and by now a second revised edition is needed to incorporate the acquisitions of the intervening years, but meanwhile, the guide remains invaluable.

The information about voyages, here and in the section which follows, relies on Don Charlwood's *The Long Farewell: Settlers Under Sail* (Allen Lane, 1981).

THE LONG WATER VOYAGE HITHER

Anna M. Cook. Letters on board the *Scottish Hero*, 1883–4. MS 849, National Library of Australia, Canberra. Typed transcript.

Ellen Moger. Letter from Adelaide, 1840. MS 5919, National Library of Australia, Canberra. Typed transcript.

Mrs Eleanor J. Cross has given me permission to publish this letter, the original of which is in her possession, and through Mrs Cross I have learned that Ellen Moger came originally from Hull, where her father was a brewer. Mrs Moger's husband, Edward, followed the same trade and went into business as a malster and brewer when the family arrived in South Australia. The Mogers left Adelaide for the township of Mannum, where another daughter was born to them. Emily Moger, the one child who survived the dreadful voyage, did improve in health and grew into adulthood. She did not escape further pain, however. Charles Mends, the solicitor she married, died young and left her to look after two small daughters. She returned to her parents' home at Mannum where she opened a school.

FATIGUE AND BUSTLE AT AUSTRALIND

Louisa Clifton. Typed transcript of Diary 1840–41. MS 398A, Battye Library, Perth. Also, copy of typescript, MS 2801, National Library of Australia, Canberra. By courtesy Mrs Nancy M. Clifton and Dr Guy Henn. Copyright permission and material quoted below by courtesy Mr G. Keall.

Louisa Clifton's diary begins when the family is living in France. It covers the period in London while the final preparations were being made for the colony, and chronicles the voyage to Australia. The journal is very full, and cuts have been made to the section included here.

There seems to be no way of knowing whether Louisa Clifton stopped keeping the diary for some reason, or whether a subsequent section has been lost, but more than seventeen years later, she took up her pen again, writing in a sombre tone:

> Dec 19th – 1851 Bury Hill. Bunbury
> I have very frequently of late felt a strong inclination to renew the practise which for many years I have given up of keeping a diary or more properly speaking a journal. I think it would enable me to keep a closer watch over my secret thoughts & by scrutinizing the motives of my conduct, & examining my daily walk with a view to rigid truthfulness in judging of my inward self I may derive real benefit – whatever tends to introversion of the mind must I think help it forward in self government – great discouragement has been my experience at times & I often feel that if a share of the Christians rest is ever to be my blessed portion it can only be through the unutterable love of the Saviour whereby I shall be plucked as a brand from the burning box . . .

For information about the colony at Australind I have relied primarily on J. S. Battye's *Western Australia* (Clarendon Press, 1924), which includes in an appendix the prospectus of the Western Australian Company.

'DOING RUSTIC SO WELL': LETTERS TO HENRIETTA

Annie Maria Baxter. Sketchbook. MS 3276, National Library of Australia, Canberra. Original.

Annie Baxter copied these letters to Henrietta into a sketchbook while she was living at Yesabba. The sketches included in this chapter come from the same source. Some of the sketches were drawn at Yesabba and others at the next station established by the Baxters, Yambuck, in the Port Fairy District of Victoria.

'BUT WHAT, OH, WHAT CAN I DO?': JOURNAL AT YESABBA

Annie Maria (Baxter) Dawbin. Diaries 1834–68. Dixson Library Reference MSQ 181/2–3, Dixson Library, Sydney.

EXPECTATIONS SADLY BLIGHTED

Penelope Selby. Letters 1839–51. MS 9494, La Trobe Collection, State Library of Victoria. Photocopy of typed transcript.

On the top of the first page it says that the typescript was made in 1901 from letters then in the hands of Penelope Selby's son, Prideaux.

LADIES AND MUSHROOMS

Letter books of the Female Middle-Class Emigration Society, Fawcett Library, City of London Polytechnic, London. Microfilm copy in the National Library of Australia, Canberra.

I learned of these letters from Dr James A. Hammerton's *Emigrant Gentlewomen* (Australian National University Press, 1979) which looks at the women within the historical context of a larger social issue. The letter books were kept by the Emigration Society in their London office, where some neat hand was employed to copy out letters written by women sent to the British colonies, to America, and even to Russia.

TRAVELLING THROUGH A STRANGE LAND

Ann Williams. Diary, 1882. MS 2492, National Library of Australia, Canberra. Photocopy of the original. By courtesy Mrs Grace Brown.

Lucy Jones. Letter, 1883. MS 9167, La Trobe collection, State Library of Victoria. Photocopy of the original. By courtesy Mrs Judith Dowling.

'WE WAS COMING TO BETTER OURSELVES'

Sarah Davenport. Diary. MS 10541, La Trobe Collection, State Library of Victoria.

Some of the pages of Mrs Davenport's account have been torn along the edge, and I have had to guess at the missing words, sometimes going on a couple of letters and a sense of the space available. These words are added in brackets.

Mrs Davenport wrote on single sheets of paper, folded in half to make sections of four pages each. Some of these sections are lost (as I have indicated in the text), and in one place I have followed the transcript to cover a section now missing from the original.

There is no punctuation in the manuscript at all. I have divided sentences by using blank spaces, and occasionally have added commas or dashes for clarity, and inverted commas to indicate dialogue. The spelling is inconsistent. Mrs Davenport sometimes spelled the same word in two different ways on the same page, but she did seem to improve as she went along. Perhaps she showed the sketch to someone who told her about the 'u' in 'should', for example. I have tried to leave the spelling alone except when some phonetic confusion occurs, such as 'of' for 'off'. These minor corrections are not noted in the text.

Janie MacGregor. Report of an Australian Life: the life of Janie MacGregor as told to her daughter Mary Jane Brown. MS 8453, La Trobe Collection, State Library of Victoria. Typescript. By courtesy Mrs Rosemary Collins.

PICTURE SOURCES

YEAR ONE
John Tittensor

In June 1982, Jonathon and Emma Tittensor, aged nine and seven, were burnt to death in a house fire.

This is their father's description of the year that followed – an agonizing yet enlightening account of the process of grieving and survival.

'For me it is a way of being able to face what happened . . . and say: all is not lost.'

AN ABORIGINAL MOTHER
TELLS OF THE OLD AND THE NEW
Elsie Roughsey

Elsie Roughsey was born into the Lardil tribe on Mornington Island in 1923 soon after the first missionaries arrived. Raised in a dormitory mission and in the traditional life of her tribe, she writes about power, religion, love and marriage, childbirth, medicine, education, crime and punishment across both worlds.

This is a book of great charm – and a rare and significant portrait of an Aboriginal life during a period of acute and often traumatic change.